BUSINESS LEADERS PRAISE THE ART OF *CONCEPTUAL SELLING*!

"Our sales executives closed a previously stagnant account two and a half weeks after working on that account in the Miller Heiman program."
>—**Andy Alberts,** corporate sales training director, First Data Corporation

"With *Strategic Selling* and *Conceptual Selling*, we found it sticks with the best-of-the-best, and in our company that has driven revenue to a new level."
>—**Jim Farmer,** executive vice president, PDP, Inc.

"If you are going to use one book in sales, it should be *Conceptual Selling*. You can learn ideas that will make you more successful than you ever imagined."
>—**Dan Salbego,** senior account representative, Fort James

"*Conceptual Selling* helps set expectations of where the deal is and ties it to a realistic metric. This prevents pushing for commitment ahead of a client's ability to do so."
>—**Ed Valigursky,** director, sales development, Telecommunications Techniques Corporation

"*Conceptual Selling* is a new approach to an old target. A fresh and honest approach."
>—**Barbara Houghton,** manager, sales development, Citicorp Diners Club

"Many of our participants have said that Conceptual Selling is the best training program they've ever had and like the fact that they can immediately put the process to use."
>—**Mary Beth Rock,** sales training consultant, Ceridian Employer Services

THE
NEW
CONCEPTUAL
SELLING®

THE MOST EFFECTIVE AND PROVEN METHOD FOR FACE-TO-FACE SALES PLANNING

REVISED AND UPDATED

ROBERT B. MILLER AND STEPHEN E. HEIMAN

WITH TAD TULEJA

WARNER
BUSINESS
BOOKS™

NEW YORK   BOSTON

Warner Business Books
Hachette Book Group USA
237 Park Avenue
New York, NY 10169

Visit our Web site at www.HachetteBookGroupUSA.com.

Warner Business Books is an imprint of Warner Books, Inc.

Printed in the United States of America
First Edition: October 1987
Revised Edition: October 1999
Revised Edition with Preface: April 2005
10 9 8 7 6 5 4 3

Warner Business Books is a trademark of Time Warner Inc. or an affiliated company. Used under license by Hachette Book Group USA, which is not affiliated with Time Warner Inc.

Library of Congress Cataloging-in-Publication Data

Heiman, Stephen E.
    The new conceptual selling : the most effective and proven method for
face-to-face sales planning / Stephen E. Heiman, Diane
Sanchez wih Tad Tuleja.
        p. cm.
    Rev. ed. of: Conceptual selling / Robert B. Miller and Stephen E.
Heiman with Tad Tuleja. c1987.
    Includes index.
    ISBN 0-446-67449-4
    1. Selling. I. Sanchez, Diane. II. Tuleja, Tad, 1944– .
III. Miller. Robert B. (Robert Bruce), 1931– Conceptual selling.
IV. Title.
HF5438.25.H45 1999
658.85—DC21   99-26832
                                                   CIP

Book design and composition by L&G McRee

ISBN 0-446-69518-1 (prefaced edition)

CONTENTS

PREFACE

Most of the tactical face-to-face principles that you recognize as components of Conceptual Selling were originally part of the same seminar package, which was called "Sales Strategy & Tactics." But we soon learned that this was entirely too much content for one sit-down meal for most salespeople. So responding to the demands of our clients, we separated the principles of Product vs. Concept Sale, The Four Question Types, Golden Silence, Basic Issues, Joint Venture vs. Unilateral Selling, Valid Business Reason, Best/Minimum Action Commitment, and Credibility into its own package. Thus Conceptual Selling and Strategic Selling are really two halves of the same story. Conceptual Selling continues Strategic Selling, dealing with the tactical implementation of the sales strategy.

The relevance of Conceptual Selling today is not just an excellent step-by-step methodology for developing a sales plan. It is really much, much more, although you will have an excellent one if you follow the principles. Conceptual Selling is a tactical plan for developing vs. selling a *solution for your customer*, and doing so from the buyer's point of view, not the seller's. Most importantly, this is done in partnership with buyer and seller. The fundamental principle behind Conceptual Selling is that, as the seller, you do not know what you're selling until you know what your buyer is buying.

I can remember the dozens, if not hundreds, of times over the years when I could literally see the "light bulb" going off in people's heads in a seminar when they first realized that the *concept* we are talking about in Conceptual Selling is the *buyer's concept* and not the seller's. I have often times wondered how to get this small, but very profound, difference of focus more easily understood at the visceral level. It is what the Germans call a gestalt, a profound and integrated understanding. It is when you really comprehend at a gut level that excellence in selling today means making the venture customer-centric. It causes a total change in your selling approach. This is the goal of Conceptual Selling.

Conceptual Selling carries the philosophy of Win-Win forward from Strategic Selling, but it also assumes that you are searching together for a fit or match between the customer's problem and the solution your products and services bring. Since no product or service is a fit for everyone every single time, this also assumes that the seller will walk away if that fit does not exist. The implications of this are still anathema to many sales managers today who believe that any sale is a good sale. Not true. Every salesperson has made at least one sale he or she wishes they had never made. Every single one of us who sells for a living has made a sale where we promised more than we could deliver, the profit margin was so thin that we ended up losing money, the clients were so demanding that the hassle wasn't worth it, or the delivery and service requirements were so stringent they could not be fulfilled.

When the seller drives selling, it becomes a very one-sided venture. Because selling starts with the seller's sales objective, the focus is upon showing, telling, demonstrating, pushing, jamming all the features, functions and benefits of a particular product or service. It is by definition high-pressure and stressful, because you, the seller, are alone and you've "got to bear down and close this deal." When 'selling' becomes customer-focused and searches for a fit between the customer's need and your solution, it becomes a very different undertaking. This so-called joint venture approach is based upon asking, exploring, discussing, and testing whether or not the products and/or services match what the customer is looking for. This approach soon becomes a partnership mutually exploring options.

I remember well the first sales call upon which I tried this approach. I started off the discussion by letting my buyer know exactly how I would like to approach this interview: I remember saying something like, "I am really not trying to 'sell' you anything. Instead, because we are not for everyone, I would like us together to explore whether or not we have a match here. I know exactly where we fit and where we don't, so I am going to be asking you just as many questions as you have for me. Is this OK with you?" The buyer visibly relaxed and so did I. All the old garbage of yesterday went out the window and we had an excellent discussion. As we started winding down, he 'closed' for me by saying, "Well, how do we go about getting started? I think we are a great fit. What about you? Do you think we are a match?" It was a life-changing experience, because I literally threw out the window all of the traditional, manipulative myths and superstitions I had been taught about selling. I can remember specifically how exhilarated I felt and how I marveled at the ease of 'selling' this way. I have never looked back.

ROBERT B. MILLER
San Diego, California
September 2004

FOREWORD

At Schwab Institutional, our goal has always been to develop long-term relationships founded on trust and open communication. In pursuing this goal, we listen intently to our Investment Manager clients, and we develop our products and services based on what we learn from them. When I first read *Conceptual Selling* and *Strategic Selling,* I felt that I had "come home." The approach seemed a formalization of the intuitive methods we had developed at Schwab Institutional. So the adoption of Miller Heiman's Conceptual Selling process seemed very natural. Since 1994, when Schwab Institutional sent its first sales representatives and managers to a Conceptual Selling program—a program I personally attended—we have found repeatedly that this process enables us to serve our clients' needs better. In providing a sales process that is both consultative and ethical, Conceptual Selling supports Schwab Institutional's dedication to being our clients' most valuable ally. Rather than dazzling our clients with jazzy presentations, our focus is to listen and then tailor solutions that best fit the needs of these highly individualistic entrepreneurs. This is an approach that requires absolute respect for the individual client. To help ingrain this respect at Schwab Institutional, we require all of our new sales representatives to attend Conceptual Selling as part of their initial acculturation.

In addition to encouraging client focus, Conceptual Selling brings efficiency into the sales process—and into every sales meeting. By using the sales-call plans, our representatives are better prepared for every meeting. This shortens agendas, keeps each meeting focused on tangible benefits, and shows consideration for our clients' busy schedules. The efficiency also shows in our internal meetings, where we speak a common language in dealing with sales-related issues.

The customer commitment that is evident in Conceptual Selling has been heightened and made even more accessible in this revised edition of Miller Heiman's business classic. That is why we endorse *The New Conceptual Selling* and why its principles are fully integrated into the Schwab Institutional sales culture.

JOHN PHILIP COGHLAN
President
Schwab Institutional

TWO PEOPLE SPEAKING

What's the single most important characteristic of a successful salesperson?

Contrary to the conventional image of the sales professional as a charming, tireless ringmaster, it's not presentation skills or personality or even persistence. Those are surely significant assets in many selling situations, but they're secondary. The one characteristic that every seller must have—the one thing that can make or break you in today's competitive markets—is the ability to communicate effectively with individual customers, to establish a meaningful dialogue on each and every sales call.

Dialogue, which comes from the Greek, means "two people speaking." The definition is perfectly suited to the world of selling, for it reminds us of a reality that is often ignored: The most effective sales calls are not "show and tell" sessions but back-and-forth *conversations* between people who are trying to arrive at the same point together. In a great sales call, there's no mile-a-minute product pitching, no dumbfounded or embarrassed silences, no trial closes, and no overcoming of objections. The great sales call is neither an argument nor a debate nor an exercise in friendly persuasion. All of those scenarios imply one person speaking *at* another. In a great sales call, it's the two of you speaking *together*.

Two people speaking. It sounds ridiculously simple when you phrase it like this, but appreciating the fact that your sales calls should be conversations is actually a difficult lesson for many salespeople to accept. You may know intuitively that good sales calls are dialogues. You may even remember those exceptional calls of your own, where you didn't have to pitch the product because the "flow" was there and the order was the natural outcome of a great conversation. But even if you've been this fortunate, there's a lot of tradition against you.

For hundreds of years, salespeople have been told— and have been telling themselves—that a successful encounter with a customer is *not* a conversation. It's one person, the salesperson, doing all the talking—and the customer nodding in amazement and then signing an order. This idea is enshrined in a million sales training proverbs: "Keep talking"; "Don't let the customer get you off track"; "Stay in control." It gets reinforced, ironically, by your own comfort level, which tells you that you feel more secure when you're delivering a spiel and the customer doesn't have to say anything because all the speaking parts are yours.

And even if you reject this conventional thinking—as any sales professional should—that doesn't necessarily mean you have anything solid to replace it with. Even if you want to stop chattering and establish dialogue with your customers, the honest fact is that you may not know how. You may know, theoretically, that conversational flow is a great place to be but still not have a practical clue about how to get there.

At Miller Heiman, we know how to get there. We know how to get *you* there, too, if that's where you want to go. We've been doing it for almost twenty years through a unique, dialogue-oriented process called Conceptual Selling. The practical lessons of that process are outlined in this book. If you're frustrated by the limitations of product-pitch selling, if you understand the importance of establishing dialogue with your individual customers, and if you're looking for a hands-on guide that will help you dramatically increase the productivity of your individual sales calls, *The New Conceptual Selling* can change your professional life.

It may sound like an extravagant promise, but we

don't make it casually. Since the first edition of *Conceptual Selling* came out in 1987, we've received hundreds of accolades from readers and corporate clients, describing how the principles we explain here have brought clarity, precision, and efficiency to their sales calls. These rave reviews come from the top revenue producers in major corporations—including such respected firms as KLA Tencor, Fidelity Investments, SAS Institute, and Rockwell International. Time and time again, these leaders tell us that they have measurably increased their productivity by selling "conceptually."

When we analyze these accolades, two patterns stand out.

First, clients applaud our revolutionary insistence that all good selling begins in the customer's head, with the customer's "solution image," or what we call Concept. "When I started to sell with an understanding of the customer's Concept," one salesperson put it, "it was like I was suddenly selling with the blinders off. I couldn't believe I hadn't been doing this my entire life."

Second, our clients tell us that our listening-intensive approach to the sales call—highlighted by our unique questioning process—helps to dispel confusion about what their customers really want and makes it easier to identify those needs. "For the first time," another client puts it, "I've got a reliable handle on what I know, what I don't know, and what I still have to find out to make every meeting count. As a system for processing information, this is invaluable."

As pleased as we have always been to get such praise, we have also been eager to get feedback on how we could improve. Here, too, the reactions of our clients have been of prime importance. Recognizing that importance, we have put considerable energy over the past couple of years into updating and revising all of our programs, as well as the best-selling books that are based on those programs.

The first Miller Heiman book, *Strategic Selling* (1985), was also the first to be thoroughly revised; *The New Strategic Selling* came out in 1998. The book version of our tactical selling process, *Conceptual Selling* (1987), reappears now as *The New Conceptual Selling*. We'll be turning next to a revised edition of *Successful Large Account Management* (1991).

Like *The New Strategic Selling,* this book is new in content and not just in name. Although its fundamental principles are just as valid today as they were twelve years ago, we have thoroughly reworked the manuscript, page by page, to tighten the prose, clarify explanations, and provide up-to-date examples from Miller Heiman clients. One obvious change is the addition throughout of new graphics. But there are more substantive changes as well, in terms of both conceptualization and presentation.

As readers familiar with the original *Conceptual*

Selling will note, we have refined our understanding of Concept and product; the refinement is evident especially in Chapter 4. We have expanded our discussions of Question Types and provided clarifications of two concepts that often prove puzzling: Action Commitment and Valid Business Reason. We've also added a discussion in Chapter 5 on Single Sales Objective, a concept that was developed originally for Strategic Selling but that is now also a component of Conceptual Selling.

Most dramatically, we have revised the entire sequence of the Conceptual Selling "modules." This was in direct response to our program participants, who pointed out that the original arrangement was less linear than it could have been. In this new arrangement, we've aimed at presenting ideas in a natural, intuitive order. We begin with general concepts, then explain what you need to have in place before the sales call even begins, and finally discuss the three interlocking phases of the sales call—Getting Information, Giving Information, and Getting Commitment—as you would logically encounter them in a meeting with a customer.

Another new element is a question-and-answer epilogue where we address some of the interesting challenges that our clients have posed to us. This, we felt, was the most appropriate way to end *The New Conceptual Selling*, for the book's fundamental message is that you should listen, actively and deliberately, to what your customers or prospects are telling you *before* you try to "sell" them. In this final section of the book, we let you eavesdrop on *our* listening as we engage in some "two people speaking" with our own valued customers. We hope this will provide you with some insight into the exciting world of selling and that you will soon be profiting "conceptually" from your own sales encounters.

SPECIAL THANKS
FROM THE AUTHORS

Given what we've said about dialogue, it goes without saying that we are indebted to our clients and client companies. Since the first program in 1987, it has been our pleasure to run Conceptual Selling workshops for more than fifty thousand sales professionals. Space limitations prevent us from acknowledging them all personally, so as representatives of that honorable contingent, we'll name just the clients whose comments appear in this book.

Our thanks to Richard Brashier, vice president for sales at ATS, a Premiere Technologies Company; Jim Farmer, executive vice president of PDP, Inc.; Stephanie Kuhnel, program manager for Miller Heiman sales processes at SAS Institute; Bob Mayes, vice president of sales at Las Campanas; Dan Salbego, senior territory manager for Fort James Corporation; Kim Schneibolk, a senior account manager at TTC; and Margaret Shiver, assistant vice president for communications at National Medical Enterprises.

As for the many other Conceptual Selling program participants, here, with our deepest gratitude, we list the companies that they have represented:

Consumer Products and Manufacturers

3M Mexico
Applied Materials
Bell Helicopter
BASF
Black & Decker
Campbell Soup
Canon
Corporate Express
Eastman Kodak
Giddings & Lewis
Hallmark
Haworth
Herman Miller
Kimball International
Nabisco
Teknion
W.L.Gore & Associates

Financial

American Bankers Association
American Express Corporate Services

Charles Schwab
Citicorp Diners Club
Fidelity Investments
First Data
First National Motor Finance
Logica
Norwest Bank
Prudential Investments
Union Bank of California
Wells Fargo Bank

Hospitality

ARAMARK
Marriott
Promus
Omni Services

Industrial & Chemical

Allied Signal
Bently Nevada
Chevron Chemical
Dow Chemical
Electro Scientific Industries
Engelhard Corporation
Fisher Rosemont
Fort James Corporation
Griffith Laboratories
Hercules

PetroFina
Scott Specialty Gases
Siemens Building Technologies
Shell Services International
IT Corporation
The Trane Company
Zeon Chemicals

Professional Services

Adecco
ADP
Arthur D. Little
Brown & Caldwell
Ceridian
Dames & Moore
Deliotte & Touche
DMA
Experian
Heritage Environmental Services
Interim
PDS Technical Services
PricewaterhouseCoopers
Radian International, LLC

Technology

Applied Materials
CSC Computer Sciences Ltd.
EMC Corporation

Forrester Research
Giddings and Lewis
Hewlett Packard
IBM Global Services
JDA Software
J.D. Edwards
Lockheed Martin
MicroAge
Moore Process Automation
National Semi Conductor
Norstan
Origin International
PinkRoccade
Platinum Technology
Rockwell International
SAS Institute
Tektronix
Tivoli Systems, Inc.
Taiwan Semiconductor Manufacturing
Tokyo Electron

Communications

AT&T
Andrew Corporation
Cincinatti Bell Information Systems
Comcast Cable Communications
Ericsson Enterprise
Harris Telecommunications

Lucent Technologies
MCI WorldCom
Motorola
PageMart
Southwestern Bell
TALX Corporation
SkyTel

Utilities

Alliant Utilities
B.C. Hydro
Connecticut Natural Gas
Enron Energy Services
Oklahoma Gas & Electric
Siemens Power Corp. and Transmission

Insurance

American Phoenix
CAN
J&H Marsh and McLennan
MMI Companies
Protective Life
Wausau Insurance

Healthcare

Allegiance Healthcare
Becton Dickinson

Beckman Coulter, Inc.
Cigna Healthcare
Cole Managed Vision
Guidant
HBOC
Johnson & Johnson, Ethicon Endo-Surgery
Johnson & Johnson, Ortho-Clinical Diagnostics
Mayo Medical Clinic
PacifiCare
PCS Health
Pharmacia & Upjohn
Shared Medical Systems
Siemens Medical Systems

Other

Advanced Business Graphics
BAX Global
Compass Group
Corporate Express
Danka
Ducks Unlimited
Herman Miller
Kinko's
Mexicana Airlines
Ontario Store Fixtures
RHC Spacemaster
Stone & Webster
U.S. Army CERL
U.S. Naval Facilities Engineering Command

PART I

"NO SELL" SELLING

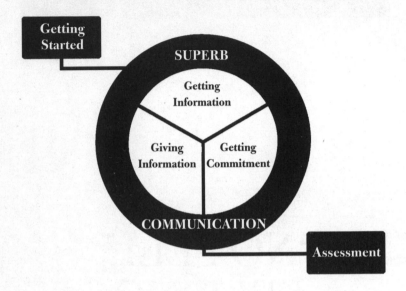

CHAPTER 1

WHY YOUR CUSTOMERS REALLY BUY

This is a book that shows you how to stop selling.

This may not strike you as exactly what you had in mind when you picked up a book with *selling* in its title. But if you're a sales professional, it's almost certainly what you need. Why? Because we are, right now, experiencing a shift in customer consciousness that is dramatically redefining everything we know about selling and fundamentally altering the rules of this ancient profession. To survive in sales today, you've got to junk the old rules and take a 180-degree turn on what you do when you "sell."

For centuries, sales success was an outgrowth of product knowledge. The great salesperson was someone who so thoroughly understood his product (or service) that he could persuade a person who didn't know anything about it—the ignorant buyer—that it could solve a problem the buyer didn't even know she had. In traditional selling, product knowledge was a magic elixir. Coupled with glibness—

allegedly the sales profession's unique contribution to human interaction—it could turn the most recalcitrant buyer into a willing victim by enabling the salesperson to "sell" her whether she wanted to buy or not. Hence the ultimate salesman cliché: "He could sell iceboxes to Eskimos."

When we say this book will show you how to stop selling, this is the kind of selling we have in mind. Call it "the art of persuasion" or "the snake oil method" or "hucksterism" or just plain "traditional selling." By any name, it's selling according to old rules—rules that are becoming as obsolete as snake oil itself. That's why the rules in this book are decidedly nontraditional.

If the old rules said you've got to "talk it up" until your prospect "bites," the new rules say you've got to start by *listening* to the prospect. This doesn't mean your product or service is unimportant. It means it is secondary to the customer's perception—not of you, or of your product, but of his own situation. We refer to that perception as the customer's Concept, and attending to the customer's Concept is the very foundation of a philosophy that might be referred to as No-Sell Selling.

For a quick fix on No-Sell Selling, consider this story.

No Dogs, No Ponies

A few years ago a major manufacturer was experiencing problems with the food service company that was managing its employee cafeterias and went shopping for a replacement. On orders from senior management, the vice president for operations invited the incumbent's four major competitors to the manufacturer's Chicago headquarters. Each candidate would have ninety minutes to present its case to a selection committee composed of finance, operations, and employee service managers. The presentation date was one: month away.

Because this multiple-site food service contract was worth several million dollars a year, all four of the invited companies expressed strong interest. Their sales managers designated top people to handle the new-account presentation and made it clear that their pitches had better be perfect. The four individuals who were chosen—all first-rate, experienced professionals—understood that this would be one of the most important sales calls they would ever make. So they spared no effort in preparing.

But they didn't all prepare in the same way.

Three of the four went the sales rep's time-honored route. They crammed their heads full of product and service specs and burned the midnight oil memorizing their companies' capabilities. They reviewed the presentation techniques that had worked for them over the years and prepared perfectly timed, brilliantly written pitches that made their service packages look like offers no sane person could refuse.

The pitches all had catchy openings (for establishing "rapport"), plenty of arguments and counterarguments (for deflecting the inevitable objections), and a copious supply of trial closes. Not to mention the usual supporting material: Among the three of them, these candidates had put together enough spreadsheets, statistical abstracts, overheads, diagrams, and colored slides to keep a congressional committee in session for a year. For the three of them, it was going to be the battle of the dog-and-pony shows.

The circus metaphor is appropriate because the idea behind such sales pitches is the same one behind big top performances. You are the ringmaster in charge of the show, and your job is to keep the action moving—to fend off boredom by engaging the spectators' attention at all times. Trot out enough dancing dogs and prancing ponies, and the customer will be so dazzled by your staging that the ink will dry on her check before she knows what hit her.

The rep sent in by the fourth candidate—we'll call him Gene—didn't buy this traditional wisdom. A few months before the manufacturer sent out its invitations, Gene had attended one of our two-day programs on Conceptual Selling. In those two days we had taught him a method for managing his face-to-face sales calls that reversed everything he had done in presentations before—and that went to the heart of the issue posed by the title of this chapter: why people really buy. We'll be talking throughout this book about why people buy and demonstrating how understanding your customers' decision-making process makes you a much more effective sales professional than even the most dazzling practitioners of the dog-and-pony method.

The first step in understanding that process is to remember a seemingly simple message we gave Gene:

People buy for their own reasons,
not for yours.

The message is crucial because until you know your customers' reasons for wanting—or not wanting—to buy, you're selling with blinders on. No matter how many reasons you may have for believing your product or service is a great buy, they will mean nothing unless each individual customer has solid reasons of his own for wanting to do business with you.

As difficult as it can be to discover those reasons, sales success depends on doing just that—and on staying in touch with each customer's reasons when they change (as they often do) from one sales call to another. In this era of accelerated change, when even your longtime customers face new problems every day that can radically alter the way they see your product or service, taking a customer's views for granted, even for a minute, can spell disaster for even the most "secure" account. That's just what had happened in the Chicago account: The incumbent was on the way out because he had failed to keep on top of the manufacturer's changing perception of their service needs.

Solid business begins and ends with the customer: with his or her needs, problems, and range of reasons for buying.

THE MOST OBVIOUS FACT IN THE WORLD

To anybody involved in selling, the fact that people buy for their own reasons ought to be the most obvious fact in the world. It isn't. To judge from the way most salespeople approach their customers, what's really obvious is that they've not only missed this truth, but also been encouraged, even trained, to ignore it. That was certainly evident in the way Gene's competitors prepared for the Chicago call. All of their statistics and slide shows and zippy phrases boiled down to a simple message: "Here are *my* reasons why you ought to buy from me."

Gene did things differently. In the month before the presentation, he kept the most obvious fact in the world firmly in mind. He prepared no dog-and-pony show, no list of objections to be overcome, no letter-perfect ninety-minute spiel. Instead, he focused on *the information he needed* to determine whether his company really could provide a solution for the manufacturer's problem. In searching for the customer's reasons for wanting to buy, he talked to people who had done business with the manufacturer before; he visited one of their plant sites to get a firsthand look at their current cafeteria operations; he tried to learn as much as he could about why they were dissatisfied with their current supplier.

He didn't get all the answers, of course; and so, as he had learned and practiced in our Conceptual Selling program, he started making a list—not of *statements* he would make to the committee, but of some very specific *questions* to ask at the outset. Those questions became the basis for Gene's presentation.

Did his maverick planning work? Did the question-intensive, client-centered preparation for this call turn out to be more effective than the traditional circus acts? After he had nailed down the contract and pocketed a six-figure commission, Gene explained just how well it had worked.

"It was almost too easy," he said. "I didn't have to say more than fifty words. I introduced myself, told them I understood they were having difficulties with their food service operation, and asked them to tell me what they were. For most of the next hour I could barely get a word in edgewise. They fell all over themselves helping me to pinpoint their problems. About every ten minutes there would be a lull. I would question them about an area where there was still a gap in my information, and the whole thing would start up again. Following your format for first getting the missing information, my job became to draw them out and take notes.

"When they finally wound down, I just scanned the notes and gave it back to them. 'It seems like you're having trouble in this area, and this, and this. Here's what we can fix, and here's how I think we can do it.' No pitch, no hard sell, no soft sell. Just a quick, no-bull rundown of how our company's strengths could address their problems. By that time we were in the sale together—we really had become partners in the process. I didn't even have to quote them a price; they begged me to get the contract work moving.

"As I was walking out," Gene finished, "and making mental notes for our lawyers, I passed the next rep coming in. He was lugging all these portfolios and projectors, and I had to hide a smile. The poor guy was dead in the water and he didn't even know it."

In the nearly twenty years that we have been introducing sales professionals to Conceptual Selling, we have heard stories like this hundreds of times. The storytellers always mention the same things: first, the near astonishment their customers feel in meeting a salesperson who keeps his mouth shut; and second, their eagerness to cooperate with a rep who spends more time listening to them than talking.

Dan Salbego, a senior territory manager for Fort James Corporation, has been practicing Conceptual Selling for several years. His experience with the "obvious fact"—which has earned him membership in his company's Hall of Fame—has been similar to Gene's. "I always start my sales calls with an open question," he says. "It might be 'What don't you like right now about the product you're using?' or 'In a perfect world, what would your service look like?' But whatever the question, I resist coming back with any answers until I understand why I'm there—until I'm clear about the specific customer problem I'm being asked to address.

"Almost invariably, this throws people," Dan says. "They just don't know what to make of you. Last month I had a customer ask me which of two of our products I personally preferred. I told him 'That doesn't matter. What we're trying to determine is which is the right one for you.' He just looked at me. I felt like I was the salesman from Mars. But we were able to clarify his problem and provide a solution."

In one way or another, all Conceptual Selling success stories are variations on this basic theme. Gene puts it well. "The Chicago call proved again what I've been discovering over and over since I started selling 'conceptually.' *I didn't have to sell these guys.* They already had a thousand reasons for wanting to buy. I just had to find out what they were and let them know there were specific ways I could help them with their specific needs and problems."

Unlike Gene and Dan, most salespeople never get to this revelation. Trained to think of their business as the art of persuasion, they try to stay in control of the sale at all times, pushing hot buttons and rattling off features and benefits until even the most reluctant prospect (so the theory goes) is talked into saying "OK, I give up, you can have the order." Increasingly, in these days of smarter and more exacting customers, this "method" leads nowhere.

In fact—as Gene's competitors found out in Chicago—it is often the salesperson's very desire to stay in control of the sale that sends the sale spinning wildly *out* of control. Far from being accidental, this is the inevitable outcome of the still widespread assumption that the expert salesperson is a take-charge ringmaster.

THE MYTHS OF TRADITIONAL SELLING

That erroneous assumption underlies most of the given wisdom of our profession. Consider four common beliefs that constitute a kind of mythology of traditional selling.

Myth 1: Push the Slinky Sphinx. In a television sitcom, a novice shoe salesperson, after fitting a customer for a pair of "Elite Petite" sandals, is called aside by the store manager. "I told you to move the Slinky Sphinx models, didn't I? Why are you showing her the Elite Petites?"

"She said she liked them."

"So what? You know we make four bucks a pair on the Elite Petites and five and a quarter on the Sphinx. Push the Slinky Sphinx!"

Allowing for comic hyperbole, this isn't an unreal situation. It happens every day, and not just in retailing: we see it constantly in corporate sales. The underlying assumption is that good selling is always "salesperson-driven." If, for any one of a thousand reasons, you (or your boss) want the Slinky Sphinx pushed, your job is to take charge, stay in charge, and convince each and every customer that the Slinky Sphinx is what she wants too.

The idea that this "product push" is good selling is the oldest, the most durable, and probably the most harmful of selling myths. It goes hand in hand with the old idea that selling has to be a numbers game: that is, the more money you pocket each time out, the better off you will be. According to the numbers game philosophy, the customer's needs or wants become important only if they don't happen to tie in with what you're pushing. When that's the case, given the fact that your first consideration is always volume, your job is to change the customer's mind. How? Push the Slinky Sphinx.

Myth 2: Use anything that works. If your major concern isn't to satisfy your customers but to get as much of their money as you can in your pocket, you're probably not going to worry too much about how you accomplish that. You're allowed to do anything—including lie, plead, cajole, intimidate, and embarrass the customer—as long as you get his or her agreement to buy. Since all dollars are alike, any sale is worth making.

At its worst, this attitude leads to the pernicious game of Beat the Buyer, popular with snake oil salesmen and the less scrupulous door-to-door drummers. But you don't have to have it in for your customers to fall for the "anything that works" myth. Plenty of ethical salespeople walk into their calls with nothing but a bag of selling "techniques," and so, just like the hit-and-run artists, they are forced to keep on pushing buttons blindly in the hope that, sooner or later, something will work. Even when they succeed in making a sale, because they have no idea *what* has worked they have no method for repeating their success. With this trial-and-error approach, you start every new sales call at square one. So, honest or dishonest, you're always a novice.

Myth 3: Keep things on track. In the pseudo-methodology called "track selling," the salesperson memorizes a script (usually designed by her company's "buyer psychology" experts) and delivers it orally, verbatim, to every customer she meets. Typically the track selling script begins with a "grabber," proceeds through a maze of "If . . . then" objection-killers, and ends with a hodgepodge of trial closes. According to track selling theory, the salesperson should stick to this game plan, whatever the individual prospect says, because at the end of the script is the signed dotted line. Hence the term *track selling*: Just like an engineer keeps his locomotive on the main line, the track seller is supposed to steer the customer away from any sidings and drive the sale straight to the close.

The problem with this script technique is that it assumes your customers are stupid and/or infinitely malleable. It assumes they'll *let* you take charge because they've been to the same sales training program you have. But the chances of that are slim to none. In fact, track selling, which promises you so much control, really fosters a kind of tunnel vision that can easily alienate the customer and kill the sale. Often the gung-ho track seller, putting on steam so he can get to the light at the end of the tunnel, finds out it's the headlight of an oncoming train.

Myth 4: Do more legwork. If you've bought in to Myths 1, 2, and 3, you know that no matter what your monthly numbers are right now, your ultimate success is spelled out in one word: *more*. So if you're pulling out all the stops on every call and you're still not meeting your quota, what do you do? If you subscribe to the traditional wisdom, you don't try to analyze what you might be doing wrong. You continue to assume that your techniques are fine. The problem must be that you're not working them hard enough.

Because you've been told over and over that selling is only a numbers game, you have to reason by the numbers. You know a certain percentage of your prospects will never buy your product, no matter how great your floor show. But a certain percentage will. So the answer is simple. Even though your "hit ratio" may stay exactly where it is, if you make more sales calls you're going to pull in more money. Simple logic, right?

It's simple, all right, but it's not logic. Nothing illustrates this point better than a story Tom Peters and Bob Waterman tell in their classic business book *In Search of Excellence*. They quote a sales executive who stayed "close to the customer" one year and came in at 195 percent of quota—tops in his division.

> A fellow at corporate called me and said, "Good job, to be sure, but you average 1.2 sales calls a day and the company averages 4.6. Just think of what you could sell if you could get your average up to par."
>
> You can guess my response, after I came down off the ceiling; I said, "Just think what the rest could sell if they could get their calls *down to* 1.2."

The point isn't that you should make fewer (or more) sales calls than you're making now. What's essential to sales success isn't numbers at all. It's having a system for ensuring that however many calls you make, every one is managed as effectively and predictably as possible. It's knowing that you won't be derailed by "You've got thirty minutes."

You achieve that kind of confidence only by stepping beyond the hit-ratio metaphor and focusing on the many different reasons your many different customers may have for wanting to buy. The sales executive quoted here understood that. He knew that success has everything to do with getting to know the individual customer and almost nothing to do with how many doorbells you ring.

Myth 5: You gotta believe! You're committed to pushing the Slinky Sphinx, you're pulling out every trick you know to get the order, you're doing it a hundred times a week, and you're still not Salesperson of the Year. You know what your problem is? You don't have the right attitude. You don't make those sales because you don't *believe* you can make them. What you need is Positive Thinking. Learn to feel good about yourself, and the commissions will follow.

Wrong again. A positive attitude is what a logician would call a "necessary but insufficient" condition for sales success. Sure, it's helpful to be confident. All of us in sales need the conviction that we can go that extra mile or put in that extra effort for the once-in-a-lifetime presentation. But if positive thinking alone could make the difference, racetracks would be churning out millionaires faster than a Pentium computer chip.

The rah-rah, motivational approach to selling leads nowhere in today's frenzied, competitive economy because it lacks the same thing the other myths of selling lack: a solid, verifiable *system* for going beyond trial and error. In the end, you need something to be confident *about*. And the first thing to be confident about is your sales-call *process*—the systematic, repeatable way you interact with your customers.

FOCUSING ON THE CUSTOMER'S DECISION-MAKING PROCESS

We provide that method of interaction by shifting the focus away from the tricks you're supposed to perform—that is, away from false promises of control—and toward the driving force behind every sale: the individual customer's decision-making process. *The New Conceptual Selling* is a road map to that process.

When we say "the process," we don't mean there's a set, formulaic pattern for all people. Customers make buying decisions in hundreds of ways, and seeking to understand each one individually is central to the successful management of any sales call. But there is a model—a general form of decision-making that individuals apply to their unique circumstances. As a preview of what you'll learn about this general form, here are the main principles we'll be developing:

1. Buying is a special case of decision-making.
2. Every time one of your customers makes a buying decision, she does so in a series of predictable and logical steps.
3. The steps of the person's decision-making process take place in an equally predictable and logical sequence that can be identified and tracked by the seller.

4. By systematically following this sequence and helping your customer to follow it, you discover one of two things. Either (a) there is a solid fit between his needs and the solution you can offer, which can lead to a quality sale; or (b) there is no such fit, and you shouldn't be doing business together in this particular situation.

5. By ignoring or working against the customer's decision-making process, you ensure confusion, resentment, and—sooner or later—lost sales.

Obviously, our focus on the decision-making process makes Conceptual Selling a "customer-driven," not a "seller-driven," system. We realize this may make you apprehensive. Many of our corporate clients initially express the fear that allowing the customer decision-making process to direct the course of the sale will take things out of their hands—will cause them to lose control. They soon find out that exactly the opposite happens. When you start to work with your customers—when you act as a facilitator of the decision process—you always end up with more control, both in the individual sales call and in terms of future business, than you had when you relied on trial-and-error "techniques."

There's a good reason for this. When you help someone to do what he already wanted to do—make a wise buying decision—he knows he has actively bought in to your solution and not been passively sold it by force-feeding or manipulation. Someone who knows that is buying much more than your current product or service; he is buying in to a partnership with you that is the linchpin of predictable, long-term sales success.

Tactical Planning: The Three Phases of the Sales Call

To manage each one of your sales calls so that your customers know that doing business with you is a partnering experience, you need to do tactical planning—that is, consciously thinking through in advance, and writing down as part of a Sales Call Plan how you are going to handle the *three key phases* of the sales call: Getting Information, Giving Information, and Getting Commitment.

Phase One—Getting Information—involves learning what you need to know about your customer's business so you can effectively understand her situation. In other words, it's finding out the customer's reasons for possibly being interested in doing business with you. Contrary to the conventional wisdom, this is where every good sales call begins.

Phase Two—Giving Information—involves describing and demonstrating your product or service, but only in relationship to the needs of the individual customer. It means giving him the information he needs to make a sound buying decision. We show you how to give information that goes beyond the "features and benefits" of your product, and that effectively differentiates you from other information givers (including your competitors).

Phase Three—Getting Commitment—means resolving any uncertainties that might prevent your potential customer from buying, even though the fit between her needs and your solution is a good one. We don't mean "overcoming the customer's objections." We mean working with her so that the two of you share commitment to the buy/sell process.

One caution: Don't think of these three phases like the phases of the moon, coming in the same invariable sequence every time. There is no set order to these phases; we number them merely to make the distinction between them clear. Every sales call is a dynamic interaction between buyer and seller, and that means you must be able to move freely from one phase to another at any time, not in response to some hypothetical, ideal sequence but in response to what's actually happening in the sales call.

Tactical planning enables you to do that. When you use this three-phase framework, you always know three things with precision. At any given moment in the call, you understand exactly where *you* are, exactly where *your customer* is, and exactly *what still needs to be done* to move the sale toward a Win-Win conclusion.

In the two-day Conceptual Selling programs we deliver to corporate clients, participants plan their actual sales calls in a series of hands-on workshops. Because we intend to make *The New Conceptual Selling* as immediately useful to you as our programs are to them, you'll do the same thing here, in a series of specially designed Personal Workshops based on the live program format. You'll need to get some pencils and a notebook and to choose three or four upcoming sales calls, with specific customers, to serve as the models for your tactical planning.

You'll be planning face-to-face tactics for these calls in all of your Personal Workshops, and because we want that planning to pay off as well as possible, we recommend that you choose not necessarily "typical" customers in "typical" encounters but calls that are significant to you, for whatever reason, and about which, again for whatever reason, you are uneasy or uncertain. Planning tactics for meetings with difficult customers, or those who are hard to figure, is the best and fastest way we know of for understanding the buying process and bringing predictability into your most significant selling encounters.

In our live programs, participants do intensive planning for sales calls they know they will make very soon—usually a day or two after the programs end. Since you'll probably be spending more than two days on *The New Conceptual Selling,* it's not practical for you to do quite the same thing. We suggest you choose sales calls that are scheduled a few days, a week, or even a month or so from today. This will give you time to learn and practice all the Conceptual Selling principles before implementing them face to face.

If you're one of the thousands of sales professionals who work behind a counter, on a selling floor, or in another situation where customers come to you, you can't pick specific upcoming encounters; you'll have to choose "typical" encounters. We recommend you select some recent situations with "tough sell" customers—situations where perhaps you didn't make the sale or where making it was a fight all the way. For you no less than for our corporate clients, our tactical selling system can help to move such difficult sales forward. Once you turn the final page of *The New Conceptual Selling,* of course, you will be able to apply our principles to encounters with all your prospects and in every face-to-face situation. The tactical planning you'll do here, on your chosen selling encounters, will provide the live, working model for all your future planning efforts.

Fundamental to an understanding of No-Sell Selling is an understanding of *how* your customers arrive at their buying decisions. In the best of all possible selling worlds—the world you want to work in—they do so by following the "predictable and logical steps" that we mentioned earlier in this chapter. In the next chapter, we describe these logical steps.

CHAPTER 2

HOW YOUR CUSTOMERS MAKE BUYING DECISIONS

Every time you begin a sales call, you make a conscious or unconscious choice between two basic methods of selling. In the traditional method, you assume that your prospect has a need for whatever you're selling, and you try to manage the call so that he or she comes to acknowledge that need. In the less common method, you don't assume this need but instead search for a fit between what the customer may need and the solution your company can offer.

We call this second, less well-recognized approach Joint Venture Selling. We'll describe it in some detail in Chapter 13. Here we'll introduce the basic rationale for adopting it, which is that, unlike traditional, "create a need" selling, Joint Venture Selling follows the customer's *natural thought process.* That process is composed of three types of thinking that people put into operation every time they grapple with a decision.

THREE TYPES OF THINKING

These three types of thinking were differentiated some thirty years ago by psychologist J. P. Guilford in his book *The Nature of Human Intelligence.* Guilford's clinical research showed that human decision-making involves three distinct but interrelated thinking processes, which serve the decision-maker much like computer subprograms. These subprograms do not function haphazardly. In any decision-making process, even though the subprograms are different from and independent of each other they almost always appear in the same order or sequence. It's possible to subvert or ignore this sequence, but in any logical and coherent decision-making process, you will always encounter this same natural order:

1. *Cognition* thinking allows the decision-maker to understand the situation he or she is facing.
2. *Divergent* thinking helps the person to explore options and solutions.
3. *Convergent* thinking enables the person to select the best solution.

The three types of thinking are represented in the diagram on page 38. Let's see how they work.

COGNITION THINKING

Whenever you're faced with a situation in which you will take some action, you begin by attempting to acquire a clear understanding of the situation. When a decision for action is required, all of your senses come into play, bringing raw information into your brain. Cognition is the process by which

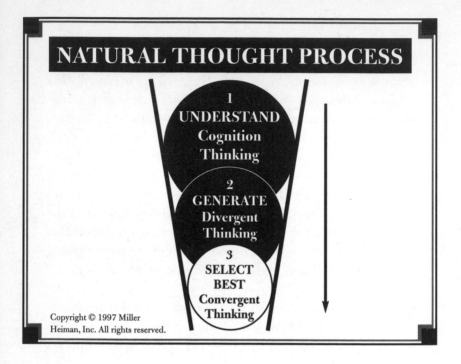

that raw information is given sense and structure; it's what provides you with a mental picture of what you're facing. If you could record this internal process, cognition would sound like this: "What . . . ? How much . . . ? Where . . . ? When . . . ? Why . . . ?"

Until you go through a cognition process to clarify your understanding of a situation, you are like a person locked in a dark room, fumbling and stumbling into furniture. Cognition thinking is turning the light on: It won't solve any problem by itself, any more than turning on an electric light will unlock a door. But it will perform the essential first step of *letting you see where you are*. Without good cognition, it is only by pure, blind accident that anyone ever reaches a sound decision. The probability of that is very low.

Cognition thinking is critical in selling because unless both you and the customer fully understand the parameters of your mutual situation, there's no way short of blind chance you're going to reach a mutually satisfactory conclusion: The customer won't know what he really needs, and neither will you. The result will be a poor fit and a poor solution, or one that isn't based on mutual ownership.

We see the results of bad cognition all the time in selling. Frequently, the sales rep who has an incomplete cognition of a client's situation will end up frustrated after pitching a product that has no relevance to the customer's needs. Or the salesperson may get an order for 20 units of Product A and miss a potential order for 100 units of Product B because the customer's cognition of the seller's product line was incomplete. In good selling, both the potential buyer and the seller have good, complete cognition, and they are able to build on that cognition to generate real matches and real solutions.

Sound selling always begins with what's in the customer's mind. It proceeds as you come to share that understanding—as you begin to appreciate the customer's mental picture. This doesn't mean you and the customer have to see everything exactly the same way. It means that an effective sales process must begin with questioning that helps you make sense of your customer's cognition.

DIVERGENT THINKING

The second stage of the decision-making process is called divergent thinking. It is *necessarily* the second stage because you cannot do good divergent thinking until you first have clear cognition. In divergent thinking, the decision-maker considers a variety of solutions that might address his particular needs. Divergent thinking sounds like this: "How about ...? We could ... What if...? Let's consider ... "

This creative and often freewheeling process is designed to generate options or choices. In everyday language, it's often called "brainstorming"—except that, since it follows cognition, it's a focused and precise form of brainstorming.

As anyone who has ever conducted a brainstorming session knows, divergent thinking works best when there are no constraints put on the people who are looking for solutions. Say you're the moderator of a study group that's trying to solve an inventory control problem. If you open an initial meeting by demanding nothing but solid, well-thought-out suggestions, you're going to get few suggestions, if any. If you want a brainstorming exercise to be truly productive, you've got to consider all suggestions, no matter how offbeat or unconventional. You'll get a lot of junk ideas, sure, but you'll also get far more good ideas than you would ever be able to get if you limited the discussion.

The point of divergent thinking is to explore possibilities, not to exclude them. This is as important in an interaction with a potential customer as it is in any brainstorming session. Once your customer understands the basic situation through cognition thinking, she then has to be able to spend a reasonable amount of time sifting through all the possibilities. Not just the "obvious" solutions, or the "most reasonable" ones— and not just the solutions *you* can offer her. For the three-step decision-making process to work properly, you have to let your prospect's divergent thinking subprogram run its natural course. If you don't do that, you're inevitably going to generate confusion, resentment, and, very likely, a No-Win outcome to the sale.

CONVERGENT THINKING

Once the decision-maker has had the opportunity to consider all available options, the final step is to select the best one for her particular situation. She does this via convergent thinking, so called because when we converge on a solution, we are narrowing and focusing our viewpoint; we are zeroing in on the answer. Thus, convergent thinking might sound like this: "We should . . . The logical choice . . . It's obvious."

This step is what people are usually referring to when they say "She made the decision." But that's inaccurate. "Making" the decision is a more elaborate process than just pointing your finger at a solution and saying "That's it." Convergence is decisive, but it's only the final step in the decision process.

Convergent thinking entails an interesting paradox. You might think that coming up with "the answer" would be the hardest and most tedious aspect of the decision-making process: Since you don't want to choose wrong, it might be expected that you would spend inordinate amounts of time to make sure your final selection is the right one.

Actually, in a good decision-making process, this doesn't happen. If you're agonizing over the final-selection phase of a decision, that's proof you haven't spent enough time working through the previous two subprograms. If you spend enough time developing a sound cognition of the problem and considering the available options with divergent thinking, then converging on the final answer often becomes a quick and almost automatic operation.

To understand why this is so, notice three things about the diagram on page 38.

First, notice that the circles indicating the three thinking subprograms are not drawn the same size. The size of the three circles corresponds to the amount of time a decision-maker ideally should spend on each of the three thinking steps. This follows the way our minds work. We have found over and over again, in a variety of selling situations, that the more time you give potential customers to do cognition thinking, the easier it becomes for them to do the divergent thinking that must follow. And the more time you allow them to generate possible solutions with divergent thinking, the less time will ultimately be required to zero in on the best solution.

Second, notice that the three circles overlap. This indicates that the three thinking processes are interrelated, just as the subprograms of a computer program are interrelated. The interrelationship is important because if any of the subprograms is faulty or incomplete—that is, if you don't allow the decision-maker to "run the program out" at her own pace—then it becomes difficult, if not impossible, to proceed logically to the next phase of the process.

Finally, notice that there is a specified direction to the decision-making process. That direction is indicated by the arrow to the right of the diagram. In every sound decision, cognition comes first, divergent thinking comes next, and convergent thinking comes last. Since buying is a form of decision-making, this means selling ought to follow the same sequence. The seller ought to perform cognition thinking with the prospect first; help her to perform divergent thinking next as a survey of possible solutions; and encourage the prospect to perform convergent thinking only after the first two steps have been adequately performed.

But that's not always what happens.

Traditional vs. Joint Venture Selling

Instead, what salespeople often do—because it's what they've traditionally been trained to do—is to turn the customer's decision-making process on its head, as indicated in the diagram below.

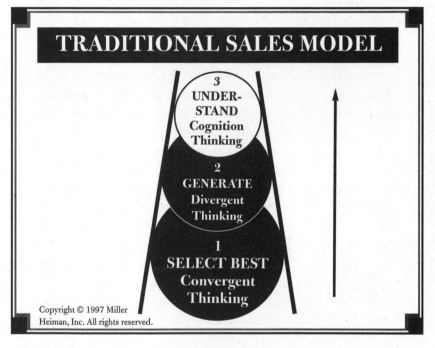

TRADITIONAL SALES MODEL

3 UNDER-STAND Cognition Thinking

2 GENERATE Divergent Thinking

1 SELECT BEST Convergent Thinking

Sellers have typically been told that their job is to make the customer think he needs whatever they have to sell. They've been told that the whole point of selling is to get him to see *you* as the answer—in other words, to make the final, convergent-thinking selection in your favor in spite of the fact that he hasn't been through the two earlier subprograms of the decision-making process. Much sales training, in fact, tries to obliterate those earlier subprograms entirely because they "get in the way" of pushing the product and securing the order—in short, of "selling him."

As the diagram indicates, this means the traditional salesperson is actually *fighting* the natural order of the customer's thinking by asking the person to first select, without ever thinking about alternative options, and later come to an understanding of why he's bought. What this says to the customer is: "I've got the best possible product out of the few (or no) others that you've looked at, for a situation neither you nor I understand."

Sounds crazy, doesn't it? And yet it's done all the time, by salespeople who come away without an order, wondering why the "stupid" customer wasn't persuaded by their once-in-a-lifetime presentation.

Why would any seller approach a customer in this illogical—actually antilogical—manner? The answer, aside from its traditionality, is that it *looks* easier and safer. People who sell this way commonly assume that the quicker you get the order, the better. And the quickest way to get the order is to maintain control by putting on a great floor show, slipping the pen in the customer's hand while she's smiling, and then dancing out the door to the next room of suckers. This time-honored pattern, sleazy as it is, still feels more straightforward and efficient than walking your customer through all that cognition and convergence.

It's not, though. This type of upside-down selling, while it may work on some customers some of the time, is increasingly becoming a professional liability. "Slam-dunking" the client into convergent thinking before he fully understands what he's getting into is a classic case of playing Win-Lose, and in today's markets, where customers are savvier than ever, that's bound to backfire, usually sooner rather than later.

In addition, and again contrary to popular opinion, asking

your customer to perform convergent thinking first is not nearly as "quick and easy" as it looks. In fact, this kind of selling is actually much slower and less efficient than following the customer's natural thinking process. Why? Because if you force a customer into a decision before she is mentally ready for it, one of two things is going to happen: (1) She'll balk, throwing up roadblocks and objections until you're entirely on the defensive, and losing; or (2) She'll cave in, sign the order, and then, after thinking about it, have a severe attack of Buyer's Remorse. If, on the other hand, you prepare the way by enabling her to understand what you're doing, there's a far greater chance you will create mutual ownership and a solid solution.

It all comes back, again, to No-Sell Selling. People love to buy, but they hate to feel they've been "sold." When you practice upside-down selling, you're usually going to be seen as the typical pushy hustler, trying to manipulate a mark into signing away his money. As a result, very often you'll be left out in the cold, doing your great floor show for nobody but yourself.

Because the upside-down method of pushing product often leaves you talking to yourself, we sometimes call it "unilateral" selling. Unilateral means one-sided, and that's exactly the situation you put yourself in when you adopt this traditional though misguided method. All the pressure for "making" the sale rests on you; you get no help from the customer because you don't ask for it. So you're left alone, trying to cram round pegs into square holes and seeing the customer as the opposition. Whenever you ignore the client's cognition process (and your own) and try to force the sale, you set yourself up to be isolated in this way.

At the same time, you often surrender to the customer the one thing you *should* be in charge of: explaining the logical connection (if any) between your product or service and his understanding of what needs to get done. When you practice upside-down selling, you confine yourself to pitching product—and you rely on customers themselves to connect the product with their needs and experiences. That dramatically limits the percentage of potential customers who will decide to buy from you, because it's just not logical to assume that all people have a real need for your product or that even if someone does have a need, he will necessarily be able to understand it.

Traditional selling, therefore, involves two false assumptions. It assumes, first, that *all* potential buyers can use your product and, second, that if you only "show and tell" them about it, they'll appreciate the "obvious" benefits and rush to buy from you. These assumptions violate a central principle of business interaction, the one we pointed out in the opening chapter: *People buy for their own reasons, not for yours.* Traditional, product-focused selling ignores that fact.

Joint Venture Selling, on the other hand, acknowledges it as central. As the name implies, in Joint Venture Selling the burden of "making" the sale rests on both buyer and seller. It's up to both the buyer and the seller to move the process forward by mutually encouraging positive information flow. There's no assumption that the customer already has a need for the seller's product. On the contrary, the entire questioning process, and the entire cognition phase of the sales call, is geared to determining, up front, whether or not there really is a need. Thus Joint Venture Selling follows the natural order of decision-making, by beginning with cognition, moving next to divergent thinking, and ending with convergent thinking.

The immediate benefit of this approach is that—contrary to conventional wisdom—it gives the salesperson greater control and more flexibility by making him or her a facilitator of the customer's natural thinking. In the longer term, establishing a dialogue with the customer in this way brings even greater benefits. To show why, we'll return to the concept of No-Sell Selling and explain the basic philosophy behind the dialogue approach. In that philosophy, the desired outcome is a Win-Win sale.

CHAPTER 3

WHAT WE'RE STRIVING FOR: WIN-WIN

Underlying everything at Miller Heiman is a commitment to a Win-Win selling philosophy. In Win-Win selling, both the buyer and the seller come out of the sale understanding that their respective best interests have been served—in other words, that they've both won. It is our firm conviction, based on thousands of selling situations, that over the long run the only sellers who can count on remaining successful are the ones who are committed to this Win-Win philosophy.

The reason isn't just philosophical. In this era of intense competition and sophisticated customers, the successful sales professional cannot rely, practically speaking, on "taking the order and running like hell." We doubt if it was ever enough simply to "win" the order and leave, but certainly it's not enough today. Today, to ensure that your success will last from customer to customer and from sales call to sales call, *getting the individual order is never enough.* You also need:

- satisfied customers
- long-term business relationships
- solid, repeat business with your "regular" customers
- enthusiastic referrals to new prospects

If you don't consistently and predictably get these four things out of your sales calls, sooner or later your business will be nothing but a series of one-night stands. You may be writing orders at a record pace, but in today's markets that pace will not last. That's a major paradox of modern selling. The salesperson who takes the money and runs eventually finds himself running in place; the salesperson who knows that getting the order is only the beginning finds not only that he's writing *more* orders than the competition but that those orders are *solid.* They are linking him up to an ever expanding network of future business.

The reason is implicit in the nature of selling itself. In selling, two parties—a buyer and a seller—have to come to an agreement. This means every sales transaction involves *mutual dependence.* Our philosophy of Win-Win selling recognizes that mutual dependence and gives you a reliable method for building on it, long term.

THE WIN-WIN MATRIX

It's one thing to say that both the buyer and the seller should win in each sales transaction. It's another to bring that about in the real world. What looks simple and basic on paper isn't always easy to carry off in an actual selling situation—especially when the competition is breathing down your neck, the sales manager is demanding that you meet quota or else, and you're not even sure that your prospect *wants* to play

Win-Win. It's sad but true. All sales professionals confront situations where they try to get to Win-Win, but just can't make it come out.

The first step in getting the Win-Win philosophy to work for you is to recognize that a Win-Win outcome is only one of four possible outcomes of any sale. We're not talking about the "close but no cigar" situations where you got aced out at the last minute by the competition. We're talking about sales where you've already ostensibly "won" because you got the order and the commission. Since there are always at least two parties involved in these sales—you and your customer—there are a total of four scenarios or outcomes that can exist after you have the money in your pocket:

- Win-Win: Both you and the customer feel satisfied with the deal and you both feel satisfied with your business relationship.
- Win-Lose: You feel good about the sale but the customer feels that, for whatever reason, she has gotten the short end of the stick.
- Lose-Win: Your customer is satisfied but in some way you've had to "buy the business"—so you feel you've gotten the short end.
- Lose-Lose: In spite of the fact that you've closed the deal, you both wish you'd never done business together—and you are probably determined never to do it again.

We represent these four possible scenarios in a diagram we call the Win-Win Matrix (page 52). The upper, or Win-Win, quadrant is highlighted to indicate that quadrant is where everybody—at least everybody in his right mind—wants to be all the time. It's the goal of all intelligent sales call manage-

ment to put you and each of your customers in this quadrant
and keep you there.

WIN-WIN: WHY IT'S ATTRACTIVE

People find the Win-Win quadrant attractive for two basic
reasons.

First, it's more *profitable* than any other quadrant. As
we've already pointed out, a Win-Win outcome generates not
just one order, but an expanding network of future business.
So salespeople in the Win-Win quadrant make more money.

Second, being in the Win-Win quadrant is more *comfortable* than being in the other quadrants. When you manage a
sale so that both you and your customer feel well served, then
you both look forward to doing business together again, and
neither of you feels either guilt or resentment. And as any
freshman psychology student will tell you, you've gone a long
way toward a sense of well-being when you've gotten rid of
guilt and resentment.

The Win-Win outcome, in short, is the only outcome to a
sale, or to a sales call, that will lead to enduring success. No
wonder sales professionals who know where their bread is
buttered want to end up there all the time.

WIN-LOSE: THE "BACKLASH" QUADRANT

When Win-Win doesn't happen, it's frequently because the
salesperson has not made a conscious enough effort to ensure
that it does happen. Most commonly, she assumes (a) her win
is all that really matters, (b) it's more important than the customer's win, or (c) the customer will win automatically

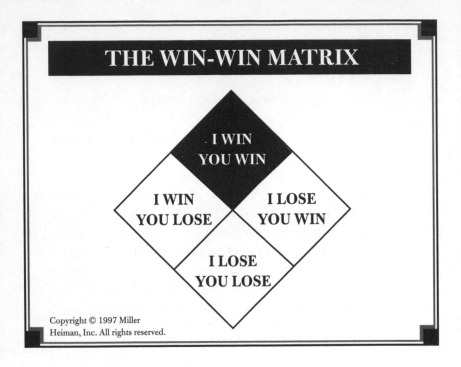

THE WIN-WIN MATRIX

I WIN
YOU WIN

I WIN
YOU LOSE

I LOSE
YOU WIN

I LOSE
YOU LOSE

because he's gotten a "great buy." In other cases, salespeople don't even think about this at all. In all these cases, they end up with Win-Lose.

Sellers find themselves in Win-Lose scenarios for a variety of reasons, but probably the most common one is thought-lessness. Here's an everyday example. You make a reservation at a fancy restaurant for a special occasion, and you fully expect the establishment to live up to its reputation. You're going to shell out good money for the meal, and you expect it to be worth it. But the evening turns out to be a disaster. The restaurant has severely overbooked, so you're kept waiting an hour for your reserved table. The food is late and overdone, the orders are scrambled, and you end up paying a premium price for service you could have gotten at Sloppy Joe's. The restaurant, with its eye on short-term profits, comes out of the evening with a win, but you, and all the other customers that evening, come out of it feeling abused. That's a classic seller wins–buyer loses scenario.

Now, in this scenario it's probably safe to assume that the restaurant management didn't actively set out to win at the customers' expense. This brings up an important point about Win-Lose. Win-Lose selling can be either conscious or unconscious. You don't have to *want* to burn your customers in order to give them that impression. In many cases, in fact, customers will feel they've lost even when you believe they've won.

It's crucial to remember that when such a situation occurs, the "facts" of the case don't really matter. What matters is what the customer *perceives* to have happened. This is one of those cases in which the old saw about the customer always being right really does apply. If a customer sincerely believes that you've been playing a Win-Lose game, then that is the reality you have to confront, even if the customer is "objectively" mistaken.

You may not have to confront it immediately. Whether the Win-Lose scenario is conscious or unconscious, sometimes it takes a while before the customer's Lose perception sets in. It may take weeks or months, for example, in cases where an industrial parts salesperson sells a factory the wrong equipment or exaggerates her company's service capabilities. But whether the buyer finds out immediately or later, the eventual result is the same: backlash. Backlash is an inevitable consequence of allowing a sale to end on Win-Lose. It usually comes in two stages.

Stage One: Buyer's Remorse. In this stage, the customer who feels burned recognizes what has happened and takes the guilt and resentment on himself. He realizes that the software you've sold him is obsolete, or that he's paid too much for the car, or that the service policy is not what he thought it was—and he starts kicking himself for being taken. "How could I have been so stupid?" he asks himself.

Stage Two: Buyer's Revenge. In this stage, he gets the answer to his question. He feels he's been sold a bill of goods by a sharpie who didn't give a damn if he lost or won. Once he feels that he's been "sold," the burned customer's resentment miraculously shifts off himself and onto the seller. He's got somebody other than himself to blame. If that somebody is you, look out because somebody who feels you have tricked him into buying (whether it is true or not) will inevitably be looking for revenge.

Buyer's Revenge can take many forms, and none of them is good for the seller. The very least a resentful buyer will do is decline future business; that is, he'll simply *get out.* That's bad enough. But a more dangerous, and more common, scenario is for the wronged party to *get even.* If you make a Win-Lose sale with a client, bet on having made an enemy for a long time. Bet on him making sure that if he can foul up your business anywhere, not just in his own company, he will do it. With a smile.

A study conducted for the White House Office of Consumer Affairs in 1985 makes the point well. It produced the following sobering statistics:

- 96 percent of unhappy customers never complain directly to the salesperson about their dissatisfaction, but

91 percent of those dissatisfied customers will not buy again from that salesperson.

- The average unhappy customer will talk to at least nine people about how he or she got burned.
- 13 percent of those unhappy customers will tell over *twenty* other people what happened.

The lesson for the professional salesperson is brutally clear. Trying for Win-Lose with a customer—or allowing a Win-Lose to happen—doesn't just ensure that your professional reputation will be damaged. Because of that "noncomplaining" 96 percent, Win-Lose almost guarantees that your resentful customer will be getting back at you even when you don't know it's happening. Buyer's Revenge is nothing if not insidious.

We've said that Win-Win is a stable quadrant, relatively speaking. That cannot be said of Win-Lose. Eventually this kind of selling works against you as well as against the customer. Win-Lose is highly unstable: It almost always deteriorates into Lose-Lose.

LOSE-WIN: BUYING THE BUSINESS

This instability is even more dramatic in the Lose-Win scenario, where you make a conscious sacrifice for your customer as a way of "buying the business." In a "seller loses–buyer wins" scenario, you get the order by giving something away—by allowing yourself and your company to lose in the hope that you'll make it back in future sales. Maybe you offer the customer a ridiculously low introductory price, or a special volume discount, or service commitments that are out of this world. Whatever it is—time, terms, price, training, financing—you're essentially saying to the customer, "I'm letting you win at my expense because I value your business."

There's nothing fundamentally wrong with a "loss leader" or "investment" strategy; retail stores use it all the time, often with good results. The problem arises because Lose-Win is by its very nature a temporary expedient. It cannot possibly be offered, to any customer, every time—and yet that's exactly the way many of its recipients read it.

You offer a customer an extraordinary payment schedule on an initial contract as a way of attracting her business. You know it's only a one-time, special arrangement, but she doesn't get that message. She thinks the extraordinary schedule is typical. Therefore, when contract renewal time comes up and you tell her, "We'll have to return to our normal payment schedule for this contract," she acts like you've just stolen her car. "What do you mean, 'normal'? I thought we had a deal!" You did have a deal, but your customer has failed to appreciate its temporary nature. And she's fallen victim to the curse of Lose-Win: false expectations.

Think of the ridiculously low introductory finance rates that credit card companies offer to lure new customers. The rates are attractive, without question—sometimes as low as 2 or 3 percent. But after the introductory period (usually three to six months), customers suddenly find themselves paying the usual usurious rates—18 or 20 percent—and many of them then transfer their balances to another loss-leader offer. This kind of "card hopping" is an irritating game for everybody concerned, and it provides no long-term stability for the credit card companies. Nonetheless, it's a predictable response because Lose-Win is a natural invitation to customer disappointment.

When you employ a Lose-Win strategy, therefore, you can anticipate one of two problems. Your customers will suspect there's a trick involved (since we all know you don't get something for nothing) and back out of the room with their hands on their wallets. Or they will buy in to the Lose-Win option expecting it to go on forever.

We've said that when the customer feels you've taken advantage of him, the situation eventually deteriorates into Lose-Lose. The same thing happens in Lose-Win, when you let the buyer, in effect, take advantage of you. But you get to Lose-Lose in this case by an indirect route. We've pictured that route in the diagram below. You can see that it's a kind of dogleg.

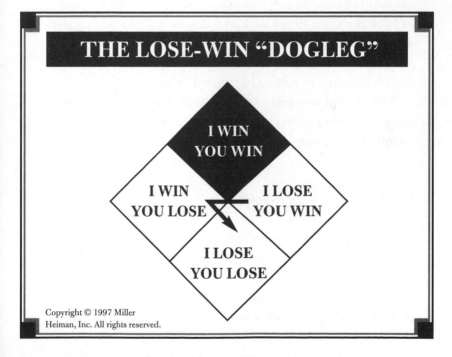

THE LOSE-WIN "DOGLEG"

I WIN
YOU WIN

I WIN
YOU LOSE

I LOSE
YOU WIN

I LOSE
YOU LOSE

The first part of the leg depicts what happens when you tell the "favored" customer that things are now about to return to normal. He doesn't see it that way; he thinks you're trying to cheat him, and his perception becomes that he's losing. Thus, without trying to, you become the villain of a Win-Lose scenario.

In the second part of the leg, the inevitable happens: The buyer who thinks he's losing gets out, gets even, or does both. And you both end up in the doghouse, at Lose-Lose.

It's not always the seller who sets up the false expectations. Many customers *ask* for Lose-Win because they believe (mistakenly) that it's to their long-term advantage. A client will demand a better credit structure or a more favorable price than she, or anyone else, has ever gotten in the past—because she knows you want her business so badly that you're willing to hock the store to get it. The interesting thing here is that such a customer, far from stealing a march on the "sucker" salesperson, is usually just setting up her own false expectations and therefore setting herself up to lose.

The bottom-line lesson is the same. No matter who initiates the idea of Lose-Win, it's almost always, in the long run, a double-fault game.

When It's Worth the Gamble

"Almost always" suggests there may be situations where the calculated risk is worth taking. You may want to consider Lose-Win in situations where the potential return is so good and where the prospects for long-term business are so promising that you'd feel like a fool just walking away. Obviously there are no rules we can give you for determining which accounts and which situations these are because nobody knows your business like you do. But we can give you a story that makes the point.

A friend of ours runs a plant-care service in Manhattan, supplying and supervising the care of decorative houseplants for corporations and large retail outlets. Some time ago, she was offered the opportunity to supply the foliage for one of the largest banks in the city—a company with dozens of locations that could have doubled her income overnight. Because she was so eager to get in the door, she agreed to supply and tend plants for a midtown location for six months at approximately half her usual rate. At that kind of introductory discount, she made nothing at all on the deal. In fact, she lost money. But she considered it worth the gamble because of the expected return.

Our friend explains how she presented that gamble to the bank: "What I do, I do extremely well—but there was no way the bank would have ever found that out if I had gone head to head with the competition. They would have priced me out of the business from the start. So I told the bank that I was willing to prove to them how good I was by taking a bath on the trial period. I spelled it out very clearly. I was giving away the store up front, and I told them so, in writing. And I made it perfectly clear that, if they wanted my service to continue, it would be at my usual rates. I've now got a ten-site contract for two years, and I never had even a hint that they thought I was 'upping' my prices."

That illustrates perfectly not only the single exception we're pointing out—that is, *when* it's all right to operate in a Lose-Win fashion—but also *how* to do so. The reason Lose-Win so often degenerates into Win-Lose and then into Lose-Lose is that *the salesperson fails to point out that the client is getting a special deal.* So if you find yourself in a situation where Lose-Win seems a reasonable gamble, go for it. But be up front with your clients. Tell them what you're doing. Admit this is difficult for you and your company. Tell them why you think their business is worth it. And—most important of all—tell them exactly when, and under what "new" conditions, reality is going to be reintroduced into your relationship.

LOSE-LOSE: THE "MAGNET" QUADRANT

Win-Win selling is never the result of accident or luck or good intentions. It's always the result of a conscious decision on the part of the seller to work actively toward mutual satisfaction. We believe that as a salesperson today, you have two basic responsibilities:

1. You have a responsibility to help your customers win.
2. You have a responsibility to help yourself and your company win.

These two responsibilities are equally important, and in Win-Win selling, they are inextricably connected. When you fail to fulfill either of them, there is one inevitable result: The selling process degenerates into Lose-Lose.

The Lose-Lose quadrant, in fact, seems to exert a kind of magnetic influence on sales. Whether it's because of inertia, or laziness, or neglect, or a combination of factors, all potentially good buy/sell interactions have a natural tendency to move toward disarray—toward the chaotic state that physicists call entropy. The only way to prevent that from happening is to consciously and actively manage every one of your sales calls in the direction of Win-Win.

It's not easy. What's easy, in most cases, is to consciously or unconsciously manipulate the customer into buying (Win-Lose) or to give away the store to get the business (Lose-Win). Staying Win-Win can be hard work. We're not minimizing the difficulty—only saying that it's worth the effort because it's the only thing that can keep you both from losing.

CHALLENGES TO STAYING WIN-WIN

Let's address some specific difficulties. When we tell our clients "Always try to remain Win-Win," we frequently encounter objections, and in this section we'll discuss the four problems that they most commonly bring up. We don't have surefire solutions to these problems, and those who say they do haven't been selling very long. But we can give you some guidelines.

Problem One: "There's no fit." What if the product or service you're selling doesn't clearly fit the customer's current business or personal needs? Is it possible to have customers win when you sell them something that does not clearly, and uniquely, provide them with answers? The simple answer is No. So you should walk away from that business. The more complicated answer is Maybe—if you can bring them and/or their companies something nobody else can provide.

If the piece of machinery you're selling the XYZ Corporation is only 90 percent as efficient as the machinery your competitor is prepared to offer, you might still make the sale come out Win-Win if you have a solid-gold support system, if your service policy is extraordinary, or if you're willing to run out the payments for twenty months longer than the competition. Nobody today simply sells product. So you might be able to construct a good fit from follow-up or other intangibles.

Just be sure, if you're selling in this kind of situation, that you make it very clear to the client, up front, exactly what you're offering and where the critical difference lies. There's no point in giving anyone a great deal on service and then trying to make him believe that you've sold state-of-the-art technology. Or vice versa. The point is to level with your customers. If you do that, you can sometimes make a fit that isn't obvious. If you don't do it, no matter what kind of a fit you make happen, sooner or later it will blow up in your face.

The same advice applies in those problematic situations where the customer in effect asks to be abused by demanding something that you realize is a poor fit—for example, a high-end solution for a very simple problem. Customers fool themselves like this all the time, and shortsighted salespeople compound the problem by going along with the customer's misperception and assuring themselves, "That's what he said he wanted." That may get you a quick commission, but it's not Win-Win selling, and it's just as likely to bring you trouble down the line as consciously setting out to mislead the customer.

Problem Two: "I've got to meet quota." It's a fact of corporate selling that sales and marketing management—the people you would most expect to be on your side in developing Win-Win scenarios—often feel like your worst enemies. We're not talking about all sales and marketing managers. Just those number-crunching whiz kids who tell you three months before you've ever gone into the field exactly what you're going to bring back when you get there. The fortune-tellers who check out the Dow Jones and your company's market share and their own astrological signs and then pronounce, with no hint of humor, "We've calculated your quota this quarter at six zillion units."

We have nothing against marketing projections per se. But to anybody in sales it's obvious that the figures you're given each quarter—whether they come from a branch manager or corporate HQ—may bear only a marginal relationship to what's happening, day to day, in the field. That's why you, as the person who's closest to the sale, have a responsibility to *educate your management:* to explain, just as we've explained it here, that you will all reap bigger benefits in the long run by working *with* your customers rather than against them.

It's very common for sales representatives to get mixed signals from sales management. On the one hand it's the old bromide "We're out to meet the needs of our customers." On the other hand it's "Make him need what we have. Make quota, however you do it." We hope what we've been saying here is ample evidence that such mixed signals are counterproductive. Sometimes meeting quota in a given quarter actually goes *against* your long-term best interests.

Problem Three: "My competition is undercutting me." We've already hinted at this problem: It's the dilemma of trying to decide whether or not you should play Lose-Win when your competition, on the surface, is offering your potential customer a better deal. In this kind of situation, when matching the competition's offer would clearly be a Lose for you, you have three choices. You can (a) stay

Lose-Win for now, in the expectation of future returns—and we've already pointed out the hazards of that approach. You can (b) sell your product or service on a "value added" basis by showing the client that in spite of your competition's better price (or delivery schedule, or whatever), you can offer better value for her money. Or, if neither of these options works, you can (c) let this particular piece of business go.

Sometimes this last option, although it looks unattractive, is the best one, long term, because it acknowledges one simple fact: *If you're committed to Win-Win selling, you cannot sell everybody, every time.* Many salespeople, clinging to the "volume first" philosophy, would probably prefer the first option: going with Lose-Win as an "investment." We don't say that's always wrong. But if you decide to do this in order to nail down future business, make sure the temporary sacrifice is likely to be worth it—and make sure your customer understands that the arrangement *is* temporary.

Problem Four: "My customer won't let things stay Win-Win." Face it. No matter how hard you try to work it out with each individual client, there are always going to be people who like to see you—and everybody else—lose. You can give these charming characters everything they want, and they're still going to be hanging around, hovering like vultures, until they see an opening and they can feast on your misfortune. Luckily they are rare (maybe the bulk of them have been done in by ulcers). But you're bound to meet one now and then.

When you do, our advice is very simple. After you've sized up the situation and determined that the person does not care if you lose, get up, explain, "Sorry, we can't make that come out"—and back quietly out the door. Not exactly your basic

Selling 101 advice, we realize, but it's good advice nonetheless. You cannot stay Win-Win with everybody, and you sure can't stay there alone. Therefore, if you're truly committed to Win-Win, you have to be able to size up those situations that are inherently No-Win. And be willing to walk.

GETTING OFF THE DEAD HORSE

Walk? Do we really mean that you should turn down business?

In certain situations, that's exactly what you should do. We'll explain this in more detail in Part 5, when we talk about the need for mutual commitment. Here let's just say that if you're not willing to turn down business when things go sour, you're going to be doing the equivalent of riding a dead horse.

According to an email we received recently from one of our more whimsical colleagues, Dakota Indian wisdom says that when you find yourself riding a dead horse, you should dismount—but that business people often adopt less sensible strategies. Some of these strategies (along with their translated equivalents) are to:

- buy a bigger whip (flogging the sale until it cries uncle)
- run a training session to increase your riding ability (your selling skills)
- harness several dead horses together for increased speed (ten No-Win customers must be better than one)
- declare that "no horse is too dead to beat" (or that "no sale is so far gone that positive thinking can't rescue it")
- provide additional budget to increase the horse's performance (by throwing good resources after bad at an unresponsive customer)

The whimsy aside, you get the basic point. Your goal as a selling professional should be to increase not just any and all business, but good business. And good business is, by definition, Win-Win business. Either you try for Win-Win, or you try to sell everybody, every time. You cannot have it both ways.

BASIC GOALS

We'll end this chapter with a summary of the basic goals you should keep in mind every time you go out on a sales call.

- Don't oversell on expectations. Don't overpromise so that you're forced to underdeliver. Be straight with your customer from the start. This is in your own best interest as well as the customer's because if you oversell at the beginning, both of you will be undersold by the end.
- Don't get suckered into a giveaway. Don't be so eager to get a particular piece of business that you forget what you're in business for: to satisfy your customers and yourself. One without the other won't do.
- Hear the customer out. Don't assume you know what she is thinking about you and what you're trying to do for her company. Let your customer talk. That's the only way you can be sure of getting the information you need to facilitate her natural thought process and manage the sale into the Win-Win quadrant.
- Be willing to walk. Be willing to let a piece of business go if it's clear you can get it only with somebody losing. If you're not willing to walk sometimes, then face it: You're only playing lip service to Win-Win, and you'll always

end up at either Win-Lose or Lose-Win, both of which eventually deteriorate into Lose-Lose.

Personal Workshop #1: Win-Win

With these objectives in mind, you can now make the concept of Win-Win real to yourself by applying it to your own situations. In your notebook write down the heading "Win-Win." Then set aside about fifteen minutes for this first Personal Workshop.

Step 1: Define your past sales. Think back over the sales you've made—that is, over the orders you've actually gotten—in the past couple of months. Below the heading "Win-Win," list six or seven of these sales on the left-hand side of the page. Identify them simply: "The 3100 deal with Macro," "service renewal with the Comram Group." Just be sure you understand, for each individual sale that you list, exactly what account you are talking about, exactly what you sold them, and when.

Now, for each sale that you've listed, write down a brief description of how you and the customer both felt at the end of the sale. We emphasize the *end* of the sale—and by that we really mean how you both felt *a month or two after* the customer had the opportunity to understand what the sale meant to him. You will have to make an educated guess as to how your customer felt; just do the best you can, briefly describing, how you and the person you sold to probably felt several weeks down the line.

Look over the comments you've made, and *compare* how you felt about these sales with the way your customers probably felt. If your sales have a high percentage of "I felt great–customer felt lousy" comments, then the chances are pretty good you've been—perhaps unconsciously—playing Win-Lose. If you have a preponderance of comments like "He got a great deal; I got burned," then the chances are equally good you've been playing Lose-Win.

There are no right or wrong answers here. We urge you to review the history of your own recent sales in order to make you aware of the Win-Win possibilities—and of the various ways those possibilities are often thwarted. You will probably find that the sales where you have actively and vigorously served your customer's interests as well as your own have been the sales where you came out feeling good; and the sales where you have actively (or inadvertently) thwarted those interests have been those where you have also thwarted your own.

Step 2: Assess your current Win-Win position. Now apply the Win-Win way of thinking to your current accounts. Pick two or three of the upcoming sales calls you're using as models in this book. For each of those upcoming calls with specific individuals, ask yourself the following questions:

- Am I firmly committed to finding a fit between my product or service and what this customer actually needs? In other words, do I want her to win?
- Does this person fully understand that I want her to win? What evidence do I have that she believes this?
- Is this person clearly committed to having me win as well, or is she aiming for a good deal at my expense?
- Have I made it clear to the customer that she must share the responsibility for making the sale come out Win-Win?

We urge you to ask these questions so that you can get a preliminary fix on your current position with each of your customers or prospects. If it helps you to write down brief notes about each customer, do so. Anything that makes your position more *visible* to you works to your long-term advantage in maintaining a Win-Win relationship.

Step 3: List actions to get you to Win-Win. Win-Win doesn't simply "happen" to lucky salespeople. Getting to Win-Win is a conscious and active choice, and on any individual sales call you can make a decision as to what quadrant you want to be in. That decision won't guarantee that you'll end up there, but failing to make the decision will almost certainly propel you toward the "magnet" quadrant of Lose-Lose.

In this step, therefore, think about specific *actions* you can take on the next sales call with this customer to manage the selling process toward Win-Win. We suggest you ask yourself one question, but stressed three different ways:

- What *can* I do to assure Win-Win?
- What can *I* do to assure Win-Win?
- What can I *do* to assure Win-Win?

You'll notice that the first form of the question stresses *reality:* in listing actions you can take, you have to start with the immediately possible. Say you're meeting Harrison at the end of next week, and she has been playing an obvious Lose-Win game with you by demanding that you cut your price to an impossible level. Your company simply won't allow that kind of discount, so there's no point in listing an action like "Agree to the rock-bottom suggestion." You might list a more realistic compromise like "Counteroffer at 10 percent above their figure" or "Explain to Harrison how her suggestion will set us both up to lose."

In the second form of the question, you focus on your *personal responsibility*. If credit terms in your company are governed by an unchanging formula over which you personally have no control, don't bother listing "Try to rearrange the credit terms." What *you* can do personally with Harrison might be to "explain our credit options more fully" or "arrange a meeting with our credit manager."

Finally, in the third form of the question, you focus on what is *actionable and concrete*. You need to identify actions that relate directly to what the client thinks she needs from the sale and that still allow you to win. The actions you list should be specific and should be designed not just to keep the ball rolling, but to move the selling process forward. And they should be actions that you can perform, face to face, with the customer on the upcoming sales call.

The term *action* here might be misleading. We don't mean only physical actions like "Take her to lunch" or "Deliver the new spec sheet by Friday." Those kinds of actions may be fine, but remember that *questioning* is also a type of action, and it's a type you can definitely perform in that upcoming sales call. If you're not in the Win-Win quadrant with a client, or if you're not sure where you are, the actions of choice should always include drafting questions that are designed to improve your understanding.

This exercise won't give you all the answers. But it should give you a handle on which of the four quadrants your sale is in at the present time. With that preliminary fix in mind, you're ready to start planning your next sales call. The planning process follows naturally from an understanding of why your customers buy and of how they arrive at their buying decisions. To apply that double understanding to specific selling scenarios and specific sales calls, you begin with what we call the customer's Concept. We turn to that seminal notion in the next chapter.

CHAPTER 4

LIFE BEYOND THE PRODUCT PITCH

Why did the chicken cross the road?

The conventional answer to this old chestnut is "To get to the other side." But that answer, while accurate enough, doesn't tell us very much. It defines why chickens in general might cross roads in general, but it says nothing about why a particular chicken might decide to cross, say, the main drag of Reno, Nevada, at 4 o'clock on a given October afternoon. If you wanted to understand the decision-making process of that particular chicken, you'd need to find out more about the situation.

Maybe the Reno chicken was motivated by thirst, and it was crossing the road in a search for water. Maybe it was getting sunstroke, and it was trying to reach what it saw as the shadier side. Maybe it was being chased by an ornery dog or a chef who saw it as potential soup. It might have crossed the road for any number of reasons, and if you were even marginally interested in poultry psychology, you'd seek the specifics of that chicken, that road, that afternoon.

The principle of seeking specifics is equally relevant to understanding the decision-making process of the higher primates. Every time a customer makes a purchasing decision, he or she crosses a conceptual "road." But the reasons he embarks on this or that crossing are both (a) highly personal and (b) likely to change from one crossing to the next. You cannot simply assume, as the traditional product-pushing salesperson often assumes, that "buyer psychology" is the same for all buyers, everywhere. In fact, buyers make decisions for the same range of reasons that chickens cross roads. But, because they're human beings and not birds, the reasons themselves are more ambiguous and more complicated.

Therefore, to succeed in Conceptual Selling you must begin with the recognition that every decision begins with an *individual perception*. Failing to appreciate that fact is like saying customers, no less than chickens, are indistinguishable.

We said in Chapter 1 that people buy for their own reasons, not for yours. A corollary to this observation is that in developing Win-Win scenarios with your customers, you must begin with their interest in crossing the road, rather than luring them to the other side with your product's "irresistible" features and benefits. No matter what your product or service, you start by zeroing in on each individual's reasons for wanting, or not wanting, to buy. Which means you have to get beyond the old product pitch.

The reason can be stated in the form of a seemingly crazy proposition: Nobody has ever bought a product.

NOBODY BUYS A PRODUCT PER SE

It's not as crazy as it might sound. Think about the last time you bought something. Whether it was something as minor and disposable as a newspaper or as major and durable as a car, what you paid money for was not really the physical, tangible object itself, but the expectation of *what it would do for you.* In a sense, all buyers are futures traders: When we buy, we anticipate the satisfaction of certain needs from the purchase, and it's really the idea of "X need satisfied" that we're paying for.

If we've just put down fifty cents for a paper, for example, we expect to be informed about the day's events. If we shell out several thousand dollars for a car, we expect a certain level of performance, prestige, or convenience. We never buy an "it," but what "it" will bring us. In the words of a Conceptual Selling adage:

> *No one buys a product per se.*
> *What is bought is what the customer thinks the*
> *product or service will do for him or her.*

This idea—this notion of what the prospective customer thinks the product or service will be able to do—is what we call Concept. A customer's Concept is her "mindset" or her "solution image" of what she wants to get done. Today, more than ever before, selling to the customer's Concept is the beginning of all good selling.

AN INDIVIDUAL MATTER

Here, and throughout this book, when we say "customer" we mean the individual human being you're hoping to sell to— the single, unique person you're calling on. It could be a customer as that word is usually defined, that is, a person to whom you've already sold something and with whom you already have a business relationship. It could be a new prospect you're calling on for the first time. As a shorthand in Conceptual Selling, we use "customer" to indicate any individual who could have an impact on your sales—past, present, or future—whether or not that person has an official purchasing or decision-making responsibility.

It's important to focus on these many individuals *as* individuals because the Concept is subjective and different for every customer or prospect you deal with. No two people ever buy (or refuse to buy) a given product or service for precisely the same reason. That's why we insist that it's never the product or service that makes or breaks the sale, but the individual customer's subjective view of what the product or service can do for him.

Your customer's Concept, furthermore, is linked to his individual values and attitudes. We'll be talking more about values and attitudes later in the book. The basic point is to broaden the traditional salesperson's emphasis on "product specs" and to note again that people buy for their own reasons. Those reasons are always subjective and internal. Hence another Conceptual Selling adage:

Companies don't have Concepts.
Individuals do.

Which means that if you're selling to a company with multiple decision-makers—the individuals we usually refer to as Buying Influences—you've got to address a multiplicity of customer Concepts. Even if you think you're selling the four people on a purchasing committee the exact same product, your actual challenge is to understand four different Concepts.

It gets even more challenging, too, because customers' Concepts are *dynamic* as well as individual. They change, by definition, as a customer's perception changes. Therefore, you've got to be prepared to start almost from scratch every time you walk into a customer's office. And you've got to be willing to listen rather than speak.

Unless you're a mind reader, there's no way you're going to be able to understand even your oldest, most "reliable" customer's *current* Concept at the beginning of a given sales encounter, unless you are ready to do more asking than telling. Therefore, you should follow a simple rule. Whenever you sit down with someone, whether you've known her for five minutes or five years, make no assumptions about what she's thinking. *Treat every sales call as if it were your first call on this customer.* No matter how long you've been doing business with "good old Jill," the fact is that her Concept can always change between one call and the next in response to factors about which you may be ignorant and over which you have no control. The customer's Concept, therefore, is something you have to identify, and reidentify, on every call.

The reason you should do this has less to do with "rapport" than with cognition—both yours and the customer's. If sales begin with the customer's solution image, they proceed by your visualization of that mental picture. This means that a solid sale involves meshed cognitions and that it cannot begin until you've explored what the customer is thinking— today. A colleague of ours in the high-tech field puts it radically but accurately when she says, "Until you know what the customer is buying, you don't know what you're selling." That has to be determined anew on every call.

IDENTIFYING THE CONCEPT

Before we say anything more about Concept, we should clear up a confusion that we often encounter when we introduce this idea to our corporate clients. It's common for people who have spent time developing and "pre-selling" a product to say something like "I'm really glad you're focusing on this. We've been trying to get our customers to understand the concepts behind our products for years, and we haven't had much luck in getting it across."

No, we say, and you probably never will. Because what a salesperson or selling organization usually means by "the concept behind the product" may have nothing to do with the customer's Concept. To people in sales, "concept" often signifies a kind of preproduction blueprint—the theory underneath the product that the marketing and R&D people had in mind before the product became a reality. To some prospective accounts, of course, that "concept" will be significant, but it's a fallacy to assume it will be equally significant to all potential buyers—or that it's ever going to be as significant to the customer as his own ideas.

Here's an example. You've seen the free-glass promotions put on by fast food restaurant chains, where the customer who purchases a certain soft drink gets to keep the container. Typically the free glasses are donated by the soft drink supplier, which initiates the promotion as a way of boosting fountain sales; the restaurants are happy to participate because their own sales also go up. In most cases, then, these promotions provide an ideal fit between the beverage supplier's promotional "concept" and the restaurant's Concept. But there is one major fast food chain that has never accepted these promotions. We once asked one of their divisional managers why. His answer illustrates very well that there is no necessary similarity between the seller's and the customer's "concept."

"Sure, we'd sell more soda," he acknowledged. "But I'd have a mutiny on my hands in half my restaurants. You've seen our floor space. We pride ourselves on space efficiency, but that's because we have to be efficient: We've got half as much space in a typical unit as our competitors. So we always say no to the promotions. When a salesman tries to hand me giveaway glasses, you know what I see? A twelve-cubic-foot box of kitchen stock that's going to get in everybody's way."

This customer's Concept, in other words, was a mental picture of potential clutter. No matter how great the seller's "concept," there was no way it was going to mesh well with the customer's claustrophobia. Trying to sell your company's "concept" of a product, therefore, is ultimately going to be no easier—and in many cases may actually be harder—than trying to sell the product itself. Selling your concept of the product is really only a sophisticated form of product cramming, and it very seldom gets you good results. It may, in fact, lead to negative results because it can tend to distract you from the one thing that is going to make the sale work or not work: what your customer is thinking.

Since every sale and every potential buyer is different, we obviously cannot tell you for an individual selling situation what your customer is likely to be thinking. This book, however, will show you how to find that out every time you sit down face to face. Right now we'll confine ourselves to a few guidelines or general clues to look for when you're scoping out your customer's Concept.

Focus on Results: Three Clues

We've said the Concept is the potential buyer's expectation of what you and/or your product will be able to do for him or her. Another way of saying that is to point out that customers, like everyone in business, are always looking for results. Only if they think you can provide them with the results they need will they want to hear about your product. To be more specific, the Conceptual results a customer expects always relate to one or more of three basic areas:

1. Discrepancy. By discrepancy we mean a perceived gap in the prospect's mind (not your mind) between where she is right now and where she wants to be. Unless someone perceives such a gap between the current situation and an ideal—and unless she believes you can help her bridge that gap—you can pretty much forget about making a sale. You know the old joke about how hard it is to buy something for the guy who has everything. It's ten times as hard to sell that guy something.

This ties in with the relationship between Concept and desired results. If your potential customer is perfectly content with his current situation, there's no way he'll expect you to deliver results that can improve it. In short: no discrepancy, no sale.

For example, say I'm currently driving a five-year-old car with 90,000 miles on it. It has most of the options I want—except for a decent tape player—and it looks fairly good for its age. If I'm completely satisfied with it as is, there's no discrepancy and therefore no point in your trying to sell me a new car. But if the neighbors' stares are getting me down, or if the rust on the left rear fender is beginning to embarrass me, there is an obvious gap between where I am and where I would like to be. Discrepancy has changed my Concept of "new car" so that I am more open to a possible sale.

2. Importance. In addressing the customer's Concept, you always need to be alert to the level of importance he or she assigns to a given task to be accomplished. Take the car-minus-tape player scenario. If I'm just vaguely dissatisfied with the lack of a tape deck—I'd like some music as I drive but it isn't a necessity—then the discrepancy is low, the importance is low, and there's not much chance of a sale. But say I'm on the road twenty or thirty hours a week, I've got to review taped material frequently, and I want to optimize the use of my driving time. Then the importance level may rise, and a salesperson who addresses my Concept about a tape player— that is, my expectation that it will improve my road time—will have a good chance of selling me one or of selling me a car with one in it.

3. Solving a problem. We've mentioned that a synonym for Concept is "solution image." If your customer has an urgent problem, the discrepancy level is by definition going to be great. If you can provide something that dovetails with the ideal solution he has in mind, your chances of making the sale are very good. That's obvious enough. What's not so obvious is that even if your customer's problem is not staring him in the face at the moment, you might still be able to sell to his solution image by demonstrating that your solution can help him avoid a problem in the future.

Take the car with the 90,000 miles. Let's face it—at that mileage the maintenance and repair bills are probably going to be running me a couple of hundred dollars a month in the near future, so I may be faced with the classic "trouble avoidance" option of "Pay me now or pay me later." If my Concept about a new car is that it will free me from the anxiety over the old one breaking down, then your chances of selling me one will be good—if you pick up on my Concept and focus on your maintenance-free models.

To sum it up: Picking up on the customer's Concept is not incidental to good selling. It's the basis on which all long-term success is built because it's the only thing that ties in directly to what the individual customer wants to get done.

"CUSTOMERIZED" SELLING

What we're talking about here can be described as customized or, more accurately, "customerized" selling. In a highly competitive environment, where buyers have a vast array of choices, customerizing the sale is the only way the seller can survive, long-term. We can illustrate this with two examples.

First, an example of how *not* to customerize a sale. A friend of ours once drove his road-worn sports car up to a car showroom, got out, and was met at the curb by an eager young floor salesman. Since our friend had arrived in a sports car, the salesman made the ostensibly reasonable assumption that he probably wanted a replacement. So, once inside, the youngster fell all over himself pointing out the compression ratios and zero-to-sixty speeds of the sports models they had on display. But his assumption was unreasonable—and fatal.

In fact, our friend and his wife had just had their second child and had reluctantly decided that it was time to trade in the sports car of his wild-oats youth for a more practical model. His Concept of "new car," in other words, was built around his need for more room—not for an Indy 500 ride. Because the young salesman didn't find this out up front, he wasted our friend's time, and his own, and eventually assumed himself right out of a commission.

The second example. Another friend of ours entered a men's clothing store intending to buy a blazer. He asked the sales clerk for assistance, and instead of giving him the usual "Size 39's over there, sir," he said, "Why don't we sit down for a couple of minutes, and you can tell me about your wardrobe." For ten minutes they talked about the colors he liked, the styles he preferred, the kind of functions he attended. "It was amazing," our friend told us later. "He actually took notes about color schemes. I walked out of there with two jackets, two pairs of slacks, a sweater, and three ties." *That* is customerized selling.

When we published the first edition of *Conceptual Selling* back in 1987, customerization struck many people as somewhat radical—not to mention extremely difficult to achieve. Today, as "mass customization" becomes accepted practice for so many manufacturers and marketing teams, it sounds more like an idea whose time has come. As business consultant Joe Pine puts it in his classic study *Mass Customization,* we have now entered a world of intensely fragmented markets, where sales superiority comes to the company that "better satisfies its customers' individual wants and needs" by providing "tailored" versions of its products and services.

That's the macro view, but customerization works at the micro (or tactical) level too, where it's the logical counterpart to No-Sell Selling. It's the only kind of selling that makes no assumptions; that begins not with the product but with the customer's individualized interests and values and needs; and that demonstrates once again the basic truth that an effective dialogue with your customers always starts with their Concept.

TWO ESSENTIAL SELLING TASKS

Haven't we forgotten about the product? Aren't we focusing so much on intangibles like values and expectations that we've made the product (or service) itself seem irrelevant? Not at all. We're not saying that all you have to do is to understand the Concept. And we're not saying that product information is unimportant. Knowing your product or service intimately has always been essential to good selling, and that's no less true today. But we're now living in a world where competition is more intense than ever, where customers have become extremely sophisticated, and where the choices they are being offered are wider than ever before in history. In that world, concentrating on product alone is a way of digging yourself into a hole.

Yes, you have to sell the product. But that's only one of your tasks. Every time you sit down with a customer today, you need to perform two distinct but interrelated selling tasks: first, *understand,* and then *connect.* Understanding we've already discussed. It's the process of identifying what your customer thinks your product or service can do for her. By connecting, we mean that you then relate your product or service to the identified Concept—just as the men's store clerk related his particular product line to our friend's Concept about "clothing." In connecting, you provide the nuts-and-bolts information that most salespeople are so eager to give out. You provide, for example, product specifications, implementation details, price schedules, and so forth. Other examples are given in the chart on page 84.

TWO ESSENTIAL TASKS

You have two tasks to perform in a sale:

First, *understand* the customer's Concept: what this individual feels is important to accomplish, fix, or avoid.

Second, *connect* your product/service by relating

Cost/Price	Descriptions
Specifications	Demonstrations
Packaging	Technologies
Capabilities	Proven results

You'll notice in the chart that what you provide in the connection phase is essentially the features and benefits of your product. In spite of what we've said about getting to the Concept first, there's nothing wrong with emphasizing those—in fact, it's one of your two essential tasks. The reason we have been playing down F&Bs up to this point is that they are so often overplayed. In traditional sales training, the salesperson is asked to unscrew the top of his head, stuff his skull full of terms and pictures and figures, and then go out and throw all this stuff in the customer's lap. One obvious problem that's created by this kind of data dump is a loss of feature and benefit *specificity*.

Salespeople love their products and services—that's a principal reason they sell them. The problem is, they know so much about them, they're likely, with the best of intentions, to overload their customers with product data that they neither need, nor want, nor in many cases even understand. Especially today, when so many products are highly technical and complicated, your own broad knowledge can become a liability if you fail to distinguish between relevant and merely interesting information. Without a filtering mechanism to make this essential distinction, you're inevitably going to give your customers more than they want to know.

The filtering mechanism you need is the customer's Concept. That's what helps you decide what you say today and what stays in your F&B grab bag until a more appropriate time. Unfortunately, many product-infatuated reps never install this filter and proceed with the data dump in one of two versions:

- They forget about the customer's Concept entirely and try to make a unilateral "product sale."
- They attempt to talk about the customer's Concept, but only *after* they have trotted out the bells and whistles.

The bad effects of the first mistake we've already pointed out in the sports-car scenario. But it can be just as deadly to put the Concept on hold so that you can launch into the more familiar and comfortable work of describing what your product can do. In fact, trying to make a "product sale" first is probably the single most common mistake in traditional selling.

The Traditional Salesperson's Most Common Mistake

This mistake follows from the old view of selling as product-pushing; it is perpetuated by the ease with which most sales-people tell rather than ask; and it is aggravated by the common "track" style of presentation technique, in which you're supposed to begin your spiel with a grabber about the product: "This car can do 130 miles per hour," for example, or "Watch me slice through this steak like it's butter."

Such product-oriented teasers work fine if you happen to be talking to the right person. But what if you give the 130 mph pitch to someone who thinks 55 is too fast? What if you're putting on the steak-slicing show for somebody who turns out to be a vegetarian? Your bells and whistles are going to blow up in your face. There's a kind of boomerang effect that operates in a lot of product selling, where the seller with superior product knowledge tells the customer more than he ever wanted to know about the product and ends up sub-merging him—and the sale—in useless data. Sure, knowing your product inside out can help you make certain sales to certain people. But you can also kill a potentially good sale with product specs if you lay them out in front of a customer who cannot relate to them.

We see this happen all the time in high-tech selling, where many of the reps are engineers who have been sent into the field precisely because they know the products so well. It's a common error for such "field engineers" to try to sell the vice president or general manager of a major corporation as if he were also an engineer. That almost never works—as a field engineer from one of the major computer companies once explained to us.

"In my first major corporate sale," he said, "the customer

was a big textile firm that had been having inventory problems. Their information systems people, who had asked us for a presentation, ate up everything I told them. But then I had to make a pitch to the general manager, a crusty old guy who had to approve the deal because it was going to top five hundred grand. I was giving him the whole nine yards—all the ROM and RAM, bit and byte stuff the IS people had loved—when he cut me off in mid-sentence. 'Son,' he said, 'the only bites I give a damn about are the ones I take at dinner. Can this son of a bitch keep track of 400,000 yards of sixteen different fabrics every month and tell me exactly where they are, or can't it?'

"I just gulped and said 'Yes sir, it sure can.'

" 'Good,' he said. 'Now why don't you show me how.' "

The rep ended up making the sale, but only after putting the bit and byte fandango behind him and concentrating on this individual customer's very specific and personal understanding of what the new computer system might do for him and his organization.

Notice that the two things the manager asked of the salesperson link up directly to the two essential selling tasks.

- First, he wanted to know whether or not the new computer system could solve his problem—could match his solution image. Addressing that concern first was part of *understanding* this individual's Concept.
- Then, once the manager was assured that the sales rep was interested in solving his problem, he wanted to know how the rep proposed to do it; he wanted him to *connect* the product to the desired solution.

The lesson is that both selling tasks are important, but that a cognition of the Concept must always come first.

Beyond the Jell-O Fling

Our client associate Jim Farmer gives another illuminating example of the distinction between product-driven and Concept-driven selling. Jim is executive vice president at PDP, which provides sophisticated behavioral profiling for Fortune 500 employers. On one joint call to a prospect's review committee, Jim saw a possible contract almost lost forever because the sales representative presented a lengthy "product dump."

"There were five people on the committee," Jim recalls, "and instead of finding out something about their individual Concepts ahead of time, the rep went in with the conventional twenty pounds of material and the idea that he should lay it all out in gruesome detail. It was a painful experience. He must have spent an hour running down the R&D background, another hour on implementation options, half an hour or more doing a demo—yakking on and on, with no sense of how anything related to the people in the room. It was like flinging Jell-O at a wall, hoping something would stick.

"When we left—after three hours of nonstop talking—we were in a hole and we both knew it. We also knew that if these people were willing to give us another chance, it was going to be our last.

"They did give us that chance, and we used the opportunity to plan a call that was a hundred eighty degrees away from the first one. Well before the second meeting, I made sure that the rep did some pretty intensive digging to research the individual committee members and to find out what *they* were looking for. We used our other inside sources to inquire about the members' individual solution images, and then we called the individuals themselves to verify what we had learned.

"Of course, their Concepts varied a lot, but we did find some common threads. What most of the committee members wanted in an employee profiling solution was that it be fast, reliable, and easy to understand. So on the second call, that's what the rep concentrated on: the three points that mattered most to these individuals. With so much less to talk about, the entire second presentation took thirty minutes.

"Here's the best part. On this second call, the rep didn't even have to phrase a closing question. After he explained what our fast, reliable, and easy-to-understand profiling system could do for each of the committee members, a vice president spoke up and said, 'What are the steps we need to take for implementation?' Once we related our services to their concerns, there was almost no selling involved. By focusing on individual Concepts, we ensured a done deal."

FURTHER ADVANTAGES

Avoiding the dangers of the product dump is only the most obvious advantage of understanding the Concept first. There are many others. When we follow up on the salespeople who have been through our Conceptual Selling program, we ask them to tell us what benefits they have noticed in their own businesses from starting each face-to-face encounter at the Concept. Here's what they tell us:

• Focusing on the Concept first allows you to *learn more* about your customer than you could possibly learn if you started off by pitching a product. Even the most product-oriented seller will acknowledge that the more you know about your individual customers, the better your chances of keeping them for the long term. Starting with the Concept is preeminently a "close to the customer" approach.

- By drawing out the customer's current interests and concerns, you can *focus on results* that she really wants to get accomplished—not just the results you think your product can or should deliver. This in turn makes it possible for you to highlight the specific objectives you can address and to tailor your presentations accordingly.
- Because focusing on Concept first is so rare in today's environment, you *differentiate yourself* from the competition. As we illustrated with the story of the food-service presentation in Chapter 1, the very novelty of the "question first" style gives the questioning salesperson a unique advantage over all those competitors who concentrate mostly on telling.
- Starting at the Concept minimizes the importance of *price competition.* It lets the customer know that you are interested in delivering value—value that he specifically needs—and it therefore puts you several steps ahead of those competitors who are merely playing low-bid games.
- In the majority of corporate sales, although several or many Yesses are necessary for the sale to go through, there is always one person's Yes that counts as final approval. Focusing on Concept first is an ideal way to *position yourself with the person who makes the final decision.* As we pointed out in the anecdote about the general manager who didn't care to hear about bits and bytes, such final-approval decision-makers are typically less interested in nuts and bolts than they are in what you can do for their organizations. With such people, focusing on Concept is critical.
- Finally, focusing on Concept first enables you to spot, early in the selling cycle, those customers or situations where you cannot come out Win-Win. Let's face it—not

everybody in the business world wants to play Win-Win. Some people are constitutionally unable or unwilling to let you win—they thrive on making others lose. By focusing on Concept first, you not only scope out good opportunities, but you also identify, early in the selling cycle, sales you should not pursue.

Many novice salespeople are still being taught that you should go for every piece of business every time and that there's no such thing as a bad sale. If you've been selling for any length of time, you know that's not true. Every sales professional has written business that turned out to cost him more than it was worth. We'll be showing you throughout this book how focusing on your customer's Concept can keep you clear of that kind of No-Win business.

Personal Workshop #2: Concept

In this Personal Workshop, you'll have the opportunity to apply our idea of customer Concept to your own real-life situations. Write the heading "Concept" at the top of a notebook page, and set aside about thirty minutes to go through the following two-part exercise.

PART A: WHEN YOU'RE THE CUSTOMER

Step 1: Select a significant purchase. To clarify the notion of customer Concept, begin by thinking about a situation where you yourself were the customer. Select a recent significant purchase you have made—not an impulse buy, but a major product or service purchase, where the buying decision had to be well thought out. Examples might be a new car, a business suit, or an extended vacation. Choose one such purchase that was important to you, personally, and write down the item in your notebook.

Step 2: Record your pre-purchase thoughts. Now, thinking back to just before you made this purchase, list in your notebook the expectations and considerations that went into your decision-making process. We've said that the pre-purchase Concept in any customer's mind relates to:

(a) a feeling of discrepancy between where the customer is and where she wants to be;
(b) the desire to accomplish something of importance; and/or
(c) the need to solve a more or less urgent problem—or to head off a problem before it arises.

Using those three criteria as guidelines, write down what you felt the selected purchase was likely to accomplish for you.

Remember that the same item can be bought for any number of reasons. What we want you to write down here are the pre-purchase considerations that were important to *you,* personally. These considerations—these personal reasons for looking around for a car, a suit, or a vacation package in the first place—make up your mental picture or Concept of the purchase.

Step 3: Identify your reasons for the specific purchase. No matter what your general Concept was before buying, you had to make a very specific decision when you laid the money down. You had to have a reason or reasons to buy this particular vacation from this particular agent at this particular time. Write down here the reasons you made that specific choice. Then, looking at the pre-purchase thoughts you just wrote down, notice the relationship between your original mental picture of the purchase and attributes of the specific product or service you selected. In other words, identify how well or how poorly the product you purchased connected with your pre-purchase Concept.

Step 4. What was the salesperson's effect on your decision? To gain perspective on your own selling efforts, reflect on your feelings when you were the one being sold to. When you made this significant purchase, what influence, positive or negative, did the salesperson's style have on your decision? If he made it easy to buy, why was that? What type of dialogue did the person establish that made you feel comfortable with the decision? How did he demonstrate that he understood— or was making an attempt to understand—your pre-purchase Concept? If the salesperson made it difficult, why was that? What manipulative or pushy tactics were in evidence? Were you the unwilling victim of a product dump? And what factors overrode your dissatisfaction and made you buy anyway?

Step 5: Record your after-purchase thoughts. Finally, write down a brief description of how you felt after making the purchase and after you had used the product or service for a while. Specifically, record how you felt with regard to:

- Utility: How well did the product work?
- Value: Was its performance worth the price you paid?
- Satisfaction: How happy were you with the purchase?

Once you've written down these after-purchase thoughts, you should have a pretty good idea of how well the specific product or service you bought satisfied the requirements established by your original solution image. In other words, you'll know more clearly how well the product tied in with the Concept.

PART B: WHEN YOU'RE THE SALESPERSON

Now that you've examined the idea of customer Concept as it relates to your own buying decisions, perform the same excercise with the shoe on the other foot. We asked you earlier to select a few sales calls that you could use as working models in these exercises. In this and in all subsequent Personal Workshops, we will be giving you directions to plan tactics for one of those selected model calls at a time. We encourage you, however, to perform the Personal Workshop exercises for two or three of your upcoming calls so that the applicability of the Conceptual Selling format becomes all the more immediate and vivid.

Begin by choosing your most important upcoming call, and write down the following information:

- the name of the account
- the name of the person you'll be calling on
- your Single Sales Objective for this account

We'll explain Single Sales Objective in the following chapter. For now, take it to mean "whatever you're trying to accomplish in this account that isn't happening right now." A good Single Sales Objective is a specific description of *what* you want to sell to the account, *how much* of it you expect to sell, and *when* you want to accomplish this objective. For example: "Sell the Xanadu Corporation one dozen Alpha model relays by June 1."

Once you've identified your sales objective, and you know whom you're going to be speaking to, put yourself in that person's place and then, as if with her mindset, focus on her thoughts about the sale.

Step 6: Is this purchase significant? Imagining yourself to be your customer, ask yourself whether the Single Sales Objective described above is significant to you or not. Do you, as an officer (or purchasing agent, or line operator, or whatever) of the Xanadu Corporation, really want or need the Alpha models? Can they make an impact on your operation, on your profit picture, or on your level of personal satisfaction? If you don't know the answer that your prospect would give to these questions, write down simply, "Don't know."

Step 7: Record your customer's pre-purchase thoughts. We're asking you in this step to write down what your customer may be thinking with regard to the Alpha model sale. What expectations and considerations are entering into her mental picture? Is the Alpha sale likely to:

(a) overcome a feeling of discrepancy between where she is and where she wants to get to?
(b) accomplish something of importance to her?
(c) help her to solve an urgent problem?

If the answer to any of these questions is Yes, specify. Write down which discrepancy, what importance, which problem. If the answer is No, write that down. What you're trying to get here is an understanding of what your customer thinks your product or service can do for her. You're trying to pin down your potential buyer's Concept.

We realize this isn't likely to be easy, and in fact that's one of the principal reasons we're asking you to perform this exercise. When we have our program participants do the same exercise and then ask them as a group what they've learned, invariably someone shakes his head and says, "I've learned that it's a hell of a lot easier to understand your own Concept for buying something than it is to understand somebody else's." To which we respond: "Terrific. That's exactly what we hoped it would show you."

If this exercise does nothing more than make you aware that your customer's mental picture is fuzzy or even hidden from you, that's great. Since good selling always begins with the customer's Concept, it's extremely valuable to realize, early in the selling cycle, that often you don't understand what he's thinking. The entire Conceptual Selling sales call process is designed to help you pin down the areas where you're missing information about Concept—and then to help you get that information in the most efficient manner possible.

That completes the Personal Workshop exercise, and we realize you may be asking yourself why we asked you in Part B to repeat only the first two steps of Part A. The answer reinforces what we just said about understanding your customer's Concept first.

The third step of Part A showed you how the specific product or service you purchased tied in with your pre-purchase Concept. You can't perform that exercise for your customer yet because until you understand his Concept more fully, you don't know whether your particular product or service—the one you're trying to sell him—ties in with his Concept at all. And you can't gauge your customer's level of satisfaction with the sale, as you did for yourself in Step 4, because you haven't made the sale yet. We'll be showing you later in the book how to relate your specific product or service to the prospective buyer's Concept and how to determine his level of satisfaction.

"Developing" the Customer's Concept

Your customer's Concept isn't static. Like everything else in selling, it evolves in response to new experiences and new information—including the information you bring him or her. In fact, no matter how you as a salesperson handle the sale, the Concept is inevitably going to change over time. There are three ways this can happen:

- The Concept can evolve internally in response to the customer's own personal perceptions and expectations.
- It can evolve in response to information the customer gets from your competition.
- It can evolve with you, as you work with your customer to refine and shape the Concept to your mutual advantage.

It's obvious which is the best-case scenario here. It's always preferable for you to manage the evolution of a customer's Concept with her, rather than allow it to be shaped by her alone or, worse yet, by her with your competition.

Because you can strongly influence the way someone thinks about doing business with you, we speak of the customer's Concept not so much as something you have to *discover* as something you can help *develop*. Bob Mayes, a Miller Heiman client who is vice president of sales for the Santa Fe real estate company Las Campanas, emphasizes the importance of this nuance. At Las Campanas, he says, "We co-create a communication process that helps someone decide. We help them process information, show them alternatives, and provide them with a better way to verbalize what they're seeking but may have only been internalizing." Bob's goal is to be a "facilitator" of the buying decision.

Another example comes from Richard Brashier, vice present of sales for ATS, a Premiere Techologies Company. A global group communications provider, ATS offers its corporate clients conferencing solutions for a wide range of venues, from three-person team meetings to international events that may involve thousands of participants. Obviously these conferences can't all be treated alike. Each one has to be managed according to the client's specific needs, and this often means helping the customer to develop the Concept.

"We dealt recently with a high-tech equipment manufacturer," says Brashier, "which was experiencing difficulty in getting software upgrade information out to its many different distribution channels. We helped them set up product and user seminars, but it was obvious that this particular customer needed much more than that, so we had to sit down with them and design a very specific solution, uniquely configured to this manufacturer's distribution network. We ended up providing them not just the standard conference calls that many companies could provide, but a suite of marketing and educational services that were specific to their needs. We ran the telephone-based seminars, assisted with the registration process, distributed materials, and provided follow-up feedback and coaching. Their underlying issue, we discovered, was trying to drive down the cost per contact with their distributors. We were able to address that issue with full event management."

Not that ATS will deliver only high-end solutions. "We can certainly provide a lower-end solution, if that's what's required," says Brashier, "and in fact a certain portion of our business entails just that: technologically straightforward dial-ups for small weekly meetings. But you've got to offer a range of options. And the level is always determined by what the customer wants. We recognize that business operates on multiple levels, so we have to customize our solutions to the specific situation. This often means working with the customer to develop the Concept."

Successful salespeople like Mayes and Brashier think of their work as a process of continuous refinement. They approach each individual sales call with the understanding that the call begins, but never ends, with the preconceived Concept. Gradually, building on a series of sales calls, they evolve a Concept of mutual success with every person they contact. But it all begins with the initial Concept, that cluster of impressions and past experiences—successes and aggravations, satisfactions and gripes—your customer has in his mind when you first enter his office.

Understanding that cluster is always easier if you *prepare* for each sales call before you walk in. In the following section, we'll begin to show you how.

PART II

GETTING STARTED: FOUR QUESTIONS TO ASK YOURSELF *BEFORE* YOU MAKE THE CALL

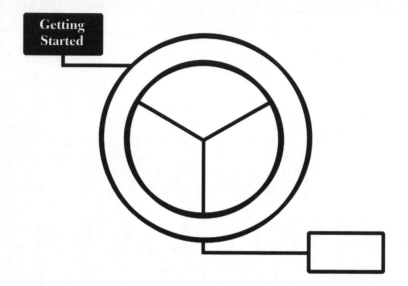

Getting
Started

CHAPTER 5

WHY AM I HERE?

Salespeople call on customers for dozens of reasons. Many calls are related to getting a speciffc order and are therefore, conventionally and legitimately, spoken of as sales calls. But other calls on customers and prospects are not really sales calls—at least not directly and immediately—because they are not aimed at securing a specific piece of business. On these calls, your objective in being there is the general one of developing, building, or sustaining a relationship. You may meet that objective by providing information, learning about the individual and her company, or working to further projects that, somewhere down the line, you believe may generate revenue for your company. But both you and the prospective customer know you're not there to close business.

There's nothing wrong with making calls like this. In fact, they're essential to your long-term success and that of your company. But they are quite distinct in intention from true sales calls, and it's a distinction that we highlight with a particular terminology. The distinguishing characteristic of a sales call is that you go into it with a Single Sales Objective.

SINGLE SALES OBJECTIVE DEFINED

By Single Sales Objective we mean the specific revenue objective, or piece of potential business that you anticipate you will secure by calling on this person. The achievement of that objective, that is, the close, may be just around the corner or months away. But every time you go into a true sales call, it's this Single Sales Objective that defines *why you're there.*

Because you prosper, eventually, by closing business, your life in selling is really composed of a series of Single Sales Objectives that you've defined and closed on. Whatever your long-term relationship with a company or a prospect, and however healthy or erratic your revenue profile, your professional success is a composite of your achieved objectives; it's a picture of the accumulated sales you have made over time. A Single Sales Objective is therefore both the unit of your progress and its measure. If you don't have (or close) Single Sales Objectives on a regular basis, you're by definition going nowhere.

This may seem almost too obvious to warrant our mentioning it, but in fact the identification of Single Sales Objectives is, for most of the sales profession, anything but obvious. When we ask salespeople to tell us why they called on a particular customer or prospect at a particular time, we routinely get answers that indicate the reason for the call wasn't single, had nothing directly to do with sales, and strictly speaking wasn't even an objective. Here are some examples:

- "We're target marketing this quarter to major firms in his industry."
- "I hadn't seen her for six months and it was time to reestablish contact."
- "He asked me to drop off some literature on our new product line."
- "I was checking on the implementation of our last solution."

All of these may be valid reasons, even great reasons, for calling on a customer or prospect, but none of them is a Single Sales Objective. Should you pursue "objectives" like these? Sure. But when you make a call to "reestablish contact" or "check on implementation," don't fool yourself that you're making a sales call. A sales call is much more focused, and what it's focused on is action.

The process we're outlining in this book is a guide to the sales call. It therefore focuses only on those calls to your customers where you have and can identify a Single Sales Objective. Doing this is the first preliminary to actually making the call. Doing it effectively means observing certain criteria.

FIVE CRITERIA

A Single Sales Objective is an anticipated result. We often say that it provides an answer to the question "What am I trying to make happen in this account that isn't happening right now?" In other words, when I achieve my objective, what will be different? Whatever the "different" is, it has to be measurable in very precise terms.

SINGLE SALES OBJECTIVE CRITERIA

- **Product/service related**
- **Specific, clear, concise**
- **Definable and measurable**
- **Tied to a timeline**
- **Usually not connected by *and***

A true Single Sales Objective defines the who, what, when, and how much of the sale. In order to be sure your sales call objectives actually do that, we provide a checklist of five essential criteria. Every real Single Sales Objective is:

Product/service related. It tells you exactly which product or service you intend to sell, and how much of it. Not your entire product line or service capabilities, but something much more specific. The Model 42X, the January promotion, a specific service agreement.

Specific, clear, and concise. There is no ambiguity in a Single Sales Objective. If it's defined properly, you should be able to read the definition to a colleague or customer and have that person know exactly what you're talking about. If she says "How many of the 42X?" or "Which January promotion?" you haven't defined your objective precisely enough.

Definable and measurable. A Single Sales Objective is so clearly defined that when it's achieved, you can measure the accomplishment. The contract is signed, the shipment is in your customer's warehouse, the commission is in your pocket. If you can't document that it's been done, it's not a Single Sales Objective.

Tied to a timeline. This is a further refinement of the "measurable" criterion. A Single Sales Objective has a deadline, or at least a likely time frame for its achievement. A true Single Sales Objective is achieved "this quarter" or "by March 15," not "sometime in the near future."

Not connected by *and*. Poorly defined objectives are often dual or multiple. "I'll sell twenty of these *and* secure that service commitment." A Single Sales Objective is just that: single. If you intend to sell a given company five separate items, fine—but they should be defined as separate Single Sales Objectives.

PERSONAL WORKSHOP #3: SINGLE SALES OBJECTIVE

Having a clearly defined Single Sales Objective is the first step in a process that you'll be practicing throughout this book: the detailed advance *planning* of your individual sales calls. As we emphasized throughout the first part of the book, communicating with your customers is the most important thing you do.

Therefore, planning those communications is critical to maintaining effectiveness. One important place to start is to ask yourself why you are calling on this person at this time. In other words, what Single Sales Objective do you have for this call?

We recommend that you ask that question now and that you write the answer down in a very specific format. On a new notebook page, write the heading "Single Sales Objectives." Divide the page into five columns, and write headings for them as we've indicated in the sample on page 109.

Step 1: Identify your current Single Sales Objectives. Now, pick six or eight of your upcoming sales calls and for each one, fill in the relevant information on the chart in your notebook. For each Single Sales Objective you are identifying, you ought to be able to define it in the following format: "In calling on [customer], I am trying to sell [amount] of [product or service] to [company] by [date]." If for a given upcoming call you can't do that, you may not have a true Single Sales Objective for that call—and it therefore may not be a true sales call. No doubt you'll still want to make it, for your own good reasons. But it's not among the calls you should be working on in this book.

Step 2: Select one or two model calls. Looking over the various calls you've identified, with their corresponding Single Sales Objectives, select one or two that can serve as models in this book. Eventually, we trust, you will be applying the lessons of Conceptual Selling to all your sales calls, all the time. But begin here by choosing one or two calls as the initial cases to apply the material to. You'll be working with these calls in all the subsequent Personal Workshops in this book. So pick calls that you care about, for whatever reason; that have clearly defined Single Sales Objectives; and that you will be making in the near future.

SINGLE SALES OBJECTIVES

Customer (individual)	Company	Product/ Service	Amount (in dollars or other units)	Close Date

Step 3: Test against the five criteria. To be sure you've selected the appropriate type of calls, test their corresponding Single Sales Objectives against the five criteria we've given you above. For each Single Sales Objective that you've identified, ask:

- Is it related to a specific product or service?
- Does it define the who, what, when, and how much of the sale?
- Will I be able to measure it when it's accomplished?
- Does it say exactly when it is to be accomplished?
- Is it truly a *Single* Sales Objective?

Step 4: Test against your customer's mental picture.
Finally, ask yourself how well the Single Sales Objectives that
you've identified fit with the Concepts of the customers
you're about to call on. Review the information you identified
in the Personal Workshop on Concept in the preceding
chapter, and use it as an acid test of your Single Sales Objectives. A Single Sales Objective has to be realistic, and this
means realistic from your customer's point of view, not yours
alone. So, given the solution image in your customer's mind,
ask whether your Single Sales Objective is a match or a mis-
match. If your Single Sales Objective isn't something that
your customer could agree to—maybe not now, but eventually—then it fails the test of realism and ought to be revised.

The purpose of this Personal Workshop is to give you a
clearer understanding of the eventual goal you're reaching for
with an individual customer. But between your current position and that "eventual" may be many steps and many sales
calls. To ensure that each one pays off, you need near-term
objectives, and you need to secure those objectives by
near-term commitments. We turn to the near term, and those
commitments, in the next chapter.

CHAPTER 6

WHAT DO I WANT THE CUSTOMER TO DO?

Having a clear Single Sales Objective allows you to visualize what you expect to achieve with a customer or an account in a specific time frame. But the only way you get to that objective is to secure incremental achievements along the way—to make sure you come out of each and every sales call closer to that objective than when you went in. To achieve that, you need to set near-term accomplishments for each call. We call these near-term accomplishments Action Commitments.

Let's head off a potential misunderstanding right at the outset. In Conceptual Selling, we use the term Action Commitment in a precise but somewhat unusual manner. It's not something that *you* will do or commit to. An Action Commitment is a *customer's* promise to do something concrete for the buy/sell process.

Because such a commitment obviously meets a selling

objective (it moves things forward), and because often your involvement has made it possible, it's tempting to think of the promise as your accomplishment. That's fine, as long as you remember that the fulfillment of that promise is your customer's responsibility. If she doesn't meet it, it doesn't matter how "committed" *you* are. When you're truly Getting Commitment, you and the customer are walking together toward Win-Win. In this sense, every sales call has the same goal: to get commitment from your partner in the process to *do* something.

It may seem obvious to you that a seller ought to have a goal in mind before she enters a sales call. Salespeople are results-oriented. Working with marketing departments and sales managers, most professional salespeople constantly have their eye on *some* goal. They're constantly setting levels of achievement for themselves that will make them the top producer for this quarter or the branch commission leader or Salesperson of the Year. But our research shows that in spite of this results-oriented attitude, most salespeople do not set clear and realistic goals for themselves from one sales call to another. Even among highly experienced sellers, annual objectives and career goals may be defined clearly enough, but Tuesday afternoon's accomplishment remains uncertain.

TRADITIONAL SALES CALL GOALS

When we introduce the Action Commitment concept in our programs, we ask the participants to identify and describe success measurements that they had set for themselves at the outset of several recent sales calls. These are highly experienced professionals. Yet we find over and over that even they have difficulty pinning down specifically what they were after when they made those calls. Typically, we find three related problems. Their anticipated achievements are too general, they are unrealistic, and they are almost always salesperson-driven rather than customer-driven.

Too general. Unless an accomplishment is specific, tangible, and measurable, it's very easy for the seller to leave the call not knowing whether or not it has been achieved. A good Action Commitment is a benchmark, and if that benchmark is something as vague as "moving the process forward," you may be uncertain about how far, or in what direction, you've come when the call is over. Good sales call management tells you exactly where you are in the call and what still needs to be done—by you *and* the customer—to move the selling process toward Win-Win. The more precisely stated your goal, the better you can perform that management. With a specific goal, you can see the bull's-eye every time, and you can revisit it after the call to see whether it's been hit. With a nonspecific goal—one that accepts any motion at all as "progress"— you're just shooting into the wind.

Unrealistic. Ask any ten salespeople what they want to get out of the next sales call they're going to make, and nine will say "the order." In certain types of selling, of course, such as retail floor selling or selling where the typical sticker price is low, that's not always unreasonable. But in most kinds of selling it is. In most corporate selling, for example, where the typical selling cycle may involve five or ten calls on several different customers, "getting the order" is a realistic sales call accomplishment only on the last call of the cycle. Yet in an impatient world, where the glamour of an end result often obscures the process that it took us to achieve it, "getting the order" remains a commonly stated sales call goal—even though a very small percentage of sales calls are ever managed to this happy outcome.

Having a clear sales call goal brings reality into this situation. Clearly defined goals can lend a sense of direction to your selling that no wishful thinking or "supersales" techniques ever can. They can help you avoid the misery of those rudderless calls that wander aimlessly from one point to another and never seem to get you anywhere. Every seller we know has experienced "sales drift" of this sort. So think of the "sales goal" concept as a navigational tool by which you can spot and correct that drift as you go—before you hit the rock.

Salesperson-driven. When our program participants state their sales call goals, most of them focus exclusively on what *they* will do rather than on what the potential customer must do. This is natural because most sales professionals are still being told that they should stay constantly in control of the sale and never let it fall into the enemy's (that is, the customer's) hands. So they set "goals" like "Lay out all the packaging specs" or "Highlight our great service record." These are subsets of the vague aspiration "I'm going to give a brilliant floor show," and while there's nothing inherently wrong with brilliant floor shows, they're *really* brilliant only if they deliver results. And the way you deliver results is to start with the customer.

To reiterate the most basic principle of Conceptual Selling, all good sales are necessarily customer-driven, not salesperson-driven. Since everything begins with what's in the customer's mind, you cannot manage a sales call properly if you focus exclusively on what *you* are thinking and doing. In addition, when your sales call goal involves you alone, it's easy to let yourself be fooled by two common misconceptions. In one, you convince yourself that you achieved the goal when you weren't even close by taking your customer's "good vibrations" as a sign of solid interest. In the other, you leave the meeting empty-handed but let yourself off the hook saying, "I did my job. I tap-danced like crazy. It's not my fault the call went nowhere."

So "Start with the customer" is a basic lesson of all sound selling. A second lesson is that all good sales depend not just on mutual satisfaction, but on mutual *commitment*. A good sales goal by definition involves the customer in commitment.

COMMITMENT TO ACTION

You should never end a sales call without getting from the customer a specific kind of promise we call an Action Commitment. The reason is directly related to the fundamental premises we outlined in Chapters 2 and 3. By committing to action, and *only* by committing to action, your customers demonstrate their belief in Win-Win and Joint Venture.

It's the fundamental conviction underlying both Win-Win and Joint Venture that the only truly sound business relationships, long term, are those in which the parties are mutually committed to each other's satisfaction. That's why every sales call must conclude with a specific commitment by the customer to take action. That commitment lets you, the sales professional, know that you aren't selling alone but working *with* the customer.

This seems eminently logical once you spell it out, but it's amazing how rarely it is put into practice. As PDP executive vice president Jim Farmer observes, it's just not something that comes very naturally to salespeople. "You see this," he says, "when you go over quarterly sales projections. In our forecasting reports, we have a 'next steps' line, where the rep indicates what's going to happen before the next call to move that piece of business closer to an agreement. In any given quarter, I may review thirty or forty reports on business that's supposed to close within ninety days. Before we got involved in Conceptual Selling, I could usually count on the fingers of one hand the reports that indicated something the *customer* was supposed to do. Yet without that customer commitment, you're going nowhere."

To be sure you're always heading in a positive direction, you've got to adopt what another colleague of ours calls a "cordial ruthlessness." If you allow your customers to "commit" to something vague or imprecise—or if you don't hold them to their word once they've made the commitment—you're inevitably going to be playing a Lose-Win game, even if neither of you might define it in this way. That's why "commitments" like "I promise to think about what you've said" or "We'll get back to you real soon" are in a certain way worse than no commitment at all.

Stephanie Kuhnel, a Miller Heiman client associate at SAS Institute Inc., the data warehousing and decision support software solution market leader, draws a useful distinction between passive and active commitment. "Salespeople are so used to doing all the work themselves," she says, "that they sometimes confuse a customer's mere willingness to see them again as a commitment. Maybe that's a commitment at the very first stages of a selling cycle, but if you've been working on an order for three or four months, it doesn't show much ownership on the customer's part. So when somebody tells you the customer's commitment is to agree to another meeting, you've got to point out how passive that is: All the customer has to do is to block out thirty minutes in a day-book, and that's not enough investment to be a commitment to action."

Commitment isn't free. Real commitment, for the customer as for you, involves an opportunity cost. It means the customer—again, just like you—is willing to *give up some of his or her time to do something concrete for the sale*. And that something has to be action, not just words.

Let's get more specific. In Conceptual Selling, we speak of two levels of commitment that you can ask for on a given sales call. Together they define the parameters of commitment possibility between, on the one hand, the most that you should realistically hope for and, on the other, the least you should accept. Let's look first at the more desirable of these two commitment levels. We call it Best Action Commitment.

BEST ACTION COMMITMENT

As the name implies, the Best Action Commitment is the high end of the commitment scale. It's the best level of commitment you can realistically expect your customer to make as a result of this particular sales call. The ultimate Best Action Commitment would be a signed order, but as we've already emphasized, that's seldom a realistic goal. For most sales calls—and for all but the last call in a lengthy, multi-call process—you'll have to aim for something less than the order. What you want throughout the selling cycle is incremental commitment. "Get her to set the date for giving me the final review committee report" might be a reasonable Best Action toward the end of a complex selling cycle; toward the beginning of that same cycle, it could be highly unrealistic. The idea in setting Best Action targets is to be sure that the action you want is appropriate for *where you are in the selling process,* that it builds on the client's past Action Commitments, and that it looks toward firmer, future commitments.

Suppose you're trying to sell a large manufacturer a solution that will increase its production capabilities. You have a sales call coming up with Jack Jeffries, the vice president of operations, and he's already committed to your proposal. You're in a comfortable Win-Win situation with him, but you know he cannot give final approval for this deal. And you don't know who can. Your Best Action Commitment for the upcoming sales call might be: "Get Jack to agree to identify and introduce me before the Cincinnati meeting to the person with final approval authority." That would build on your already good relationship by continuing to involve him in the selling process, and it would look forward by putting you in touch with another crucial decision maker. That's incremental commitment.

There are any number of other Best Action Commitments you might set in this scenario. There's no single, "ideal" Best Action for a given call, only a range of good actions from which you, the "managing" seller, have to select your best. Because you know each of the sales you're working on much better than anyone else does, we can't define what would be best for you. But we can give you some guidelines to be sure you are focusing on actions that really do tie in with commitment. In selecting a Best Action Commitment for a given sales call, we suggest you ask yourself the following questions:

Is this Action Commitment *specific?* Does it define the who, what, where, and when of the action? In asking customers for commitment, you have to be attentive to specifics, and especially to the specific *timing,* because the "when" of a commitment is often the most diffficult aspect of it to pin down—and if it's not pinned down, you'll soon be spinning your wheels. It's great for Jeffries to agree to introduce you to the division manager, but if he won't give you a time frame for that commitment, you may be waiting around for six months on the basis of a promise. That's why, in this scenario, we suggest "before the Cincinnati meeting." You should use whatever time frame is realistic in terms of your business.

Does it focus on *what the customer will do?* If you're not getting effort in exchange for *your* effort, you're wasting your time. So be sure your Best Action Commitment puts the burden on the customer to expend some energy for your mutual benefit. And be aware of one potential problem. You've got to be sure that the action Jeffries is committing to is not only something he wants to do, but something he *can* do. Many sales reps make the mistake of getting Mack to agree to do something that involves Janice as well, in situations where Mack does not have the authority to get Janice involved. In our scenario, it's reasonable to assume that Jeffries, as VP of operations, can get you in to see the division general manager; but if Jeffries were a line operator or dispatcher, that probably wouldn't be a reasonable assumption. Sensitivity to your individual customers' responsibilities and authority, as well as their business needs, can go a long way toward helping you define what they can and can't do.

Is the statement of Best Action *measurable?* We mean measurable by you, the sales representative. In other words, once Jeffries performs the Best Action you're asking of him, how will you know it? People don't always say what they do or do what they say. When you ask for Action Commitment, therefore, don't be afraid to ask for the *evidence* later.

If the commitment is an appointment with the division manager, the evidence might be a confirmation phone call from his assistant. If the Best Action Commitment was to send your report to a review committee, the evidence might be the committee's response. We don't mean you should be sneaking around checking up on your buyers. But you're expending your time, and you have a right to know what commitment you're getting in return. Commitment means something will be done. If in fact it *was* done, then your customer should not hesitate about providing you with the documentation. If he does hesitate, then you ought to ask yourself: Is this really Win-Win?

Does this Best Action Commitment *move the sale forward*? No matter what concrete steps your customer is willing to take, and no matter how exquisitely those steps demonstrate her commitment, the two of you are in this thing, ultimately, to do business together, not to demonstrate that you're happy in each other's company. So ask about any prospective action, what it does for the sale—and, more broadly, what it does for your Win-Win relationship. Incremental commitment should track incremental progress. So ask yourself, at the very least: When the customer performs what she has promised to perform, will I be closer to my Single Sales Objective than I was before this call?

Is this Best Action Commitment *realistic*? This is always the final test, and it's really a summary of the other four. A realistic Best Action Commitment is specific, it focuses on what the customer can and will do, it can be measured by you when it's done, and it moves the sale forward. If Jeffries's meeting between you and the division general manager is set at some vague point in the future, if you're not sure he even knows the manager, and/or if there's no way for you to check that the meeting will actually come off—then by definition your Best Action Commitment is not realistic.

Realism is the basis of getting any solid commitment, but you wouldn't know that from the way many sales trainers talk. With their emphasis on "positive thinking" and the "Go get 'em!" attitude, they often seem to be saying that the facts of the situation are less important than the way you look at them: "There are no problems, only opportunities." We questioned this simpleminded, "mind over matter" view of selling back in Chapter 1, and we reiterate our criticism here. Always start with reality. Not pessimism or negative thinking, but reality. If you sell with your eyes open, you know what reality is. You know what Jeffries can reasonably be expected to do for you and what he cannot. So set Best Action Commitments that start, every time, from that baseline.

If you really don't know what's realistic in a given situation, you have one sound way of finding out. Ask. On this call, and the next, and on every call in the future, ask questions to help you clarify your view of Jeffries's reality so that you do know what he can and can't do, as well as what he will or won't do. In Part 3 we'll speak more about the questioning process and show how it can help you understand what's realistic and what's not.

As realistic as you try to be, however, you're not going to get your Best Action Commitment every time. In some cases this will be because you've misinterpreted the possibilities. Sometimes it will be because the situation has changed since your last meeting. Or it may be that, for any one of a thousand reasons, the customer just doesn't see the situation the way you hoped he would see it. That is why, when you're setting a sales call target for an individual call, you should define a low end of the scale as well.

We call this low end the Minimum Acceptable Action. Before we describe it, we should make it clear that it isn't the only alternative to the "best" that we've just discussed: It's the low end of a *range* of Action Commitments that you might secure on any given call.

SAS's Stephanie Kuhnel emphasizes this point in her Conceptual Selling workshops to warn against the tendency to see things in black-and-white terms. "There can be some distance between Best Action Commitment and Minimum Acceptable Action," she says, "and salespeople need to understand that it's not either-or. If you don't get a Best Action Commitment, there are any number of other Action Commitments that you might want to aim for before resigning yourself to accepting the minimum. Minimum Acceptable Action is only what it says: the least you're willing to accept as a proof of customer ownership."

MINIMUM ACCEPTABLE ACTION

By "ownership," Stephanie means investment in carrying the sale forward. That's a critical point. The Minimum Acceptable Action is the least you will settle for because it's the least the customer can do to make it clear to you that there's still a mutual interest in producing a Win-Win outcome.

Current analyses suggest that the average high-level sales call today may cost a company upwards of $1,000. That's a

ACTION COMMITMENTS

BEST ACTION COMMITMENT

What is the best commitment to action I can expect this customer to make as a result of this sales call?

MINIMUM ACCEPTABLE ACTION

What is the minimum I can accept from the customer and continue to invest in this sale?

major commitment from the seller's side of the table. Minimum Acceptable Action defines the lowest exchange you will be willing to accept from your customer for major investment of your time and energy. If you don't get that level, you are at the very least going to be discussing with your manager the wisdom of investing more time here.

In defining a Minimum Acceptable Action, you should remember the same guidelines that we laid out with regard to Best Action. Each Minimum Acceptable Action—even though it's at the low end of the scale—should still be specific; it should still focus on what the customer will (and can) do; the outcome of the action should still be measurable by you, the seller; it should still move the sale forward; and it should still be realistic.

But even though the Best Action Commitment and the Minimum Acceptable Action must fulfill the same criteria, they shouldn't be seen as merely a "larger" and a "smaller" version of the same thing. Avoid the temptation to make the Minimum Acceptable Action simply a scaled-down version of the Best Action. You should watch out for this especially if you're intending to "get the order" on this sales call. For example, if your Best Action on a call is "Have the customer sign an order for 80,000 units," it's tempting to say that your Minimum Acceptable should be something like "Have her sign for 40,000 units." Tempting, but not necessarily designed to move the sale forward, because the customer may not be ready for an order of any size.

Rather than supposing that "the order" is always the Best Action, therefore, we urge you to think about *where you are in the selling process* so that you can define Best Action Commitments and Minimum Acceptable Actions that are realistic reflections not only of your position, but of your customer's readiness to expend effort on your behalf—in other words, that are realistic from both your perspective and hers. A good minimum commitment is not a consolation prize. It's a smaller than hoped for increment toward mutual satisfaction.

WHAT IF YOU CAN'T GET THE MINIMUM?

We're asked this question all the time. Sales professionals seem to have little difficulty understanding the concept of Best Action Commitment, but the idea of having a "floor" under which you won't go seems unrealistic to some and threatening to others. "If I walked away every time I failed to get the least I wanted," we sometimes hear, "I'd be out of business tomorrow. It puts too much pressure on everybody to demand an outcome like this. Sometimes you just have to settle for nothing and come back to fight another day."

That argument is superficially convincing—it sounds both realistic and flexible—but it can easily serve as a cop-out: an excuse for letting both you and your customer off the hook. It can be a veiled way of saying, "I haven't done my homework and I'm afraid I'm going to be turned down, so let's let it slide and hope she feels better next time." This is wishful thinking that seldom gets results because unless a customer absolutely cannot live without your product, when you shirk your responsibilities for moving the sale forward the customer's natural tendency is to follow suit. And soon you're at the default position of drift.

Sticking to your minimum expectations is a hard but crucial lesson. If you're really going for long-term business relationships in which you get the best possible results from every sales call, then when those results aren't happening, you *must* be willing to say "This isn't Win-Win" and consider the possibility of bowing out, or at least of reevaluating the Single Sales Objective you're pursuing. The value of the Minimum Acceptable Action concept is that it gives you a handle on where progress is being made in the sale, and where it isn't. If your customer is unwilling to meet even your lowest expectations for the sales call, there's something seriously wrong with the selling process, and you need to find out—before spending another $1,000—what it is.

Whenever a customer won't help you move things forward, you need to ask yourself first of all whether or not there's real potential here for a match between his Concept and your product or service. If there is a potential match and you can't get even Minimum Acceptable Action on a call, you really have only three choices. You can (1) ask questions to uncover why the customer is resisting. You can (2) revise your Minimum Acceptable Action downward in response to what's happening (or not happening) in the sale. Or, if these two tactics don't help, you can (3) shut your briefcase quietly and walk out. Let's examine these three options.

Asking questions about resistance. The most common reason a customer will not help you move a sale forward is that he sees the "progress" as a personal Lose or just doesn't see it as a Win. Asking questions to determine whether or not that's the case—and, if it's the case, whether or not there's anything you can do about it—is a radical and illuminating way of cutting through the garbage and allowing you to focus on the cause of the customer's resistance. If you're getting to the end of your thirty minutes with Jeffries and it's clear he's not even going to agree to your Minimum Acceptable Action, then it's time to find out what is making him so uncooperative. We'll talk more about this option in Part 5 of the book, when we discuss the relationship between commitment and Basic Issues.

Revising downward. Revising the Minimum Acceptable Action downward is not something we heartily recommend since it's a tactic that can obviously be abused. Moving toward this option too quickly, in fact, means you could end up on each successive sales call with less and less. But in some situations it may be warranted.

Generally, you should consider revising downward when you walk into a meeting and you find that the scenario is significantly different from what you had thought it was going to be. If as you walk in the door you discover that Jeffries has just been promoted (or demoted), then obviously it's time to rethink your tactics—including your definition of Best Action Commitment and Minimum Acceptable Action. Or you walk into Jeffries's office a month after your last meeting and announce, "We were going to discuss delivery schedules today, correct?" Instead of nodding Yes, Jeffries snaps, "We're nowhere near that stage yet!" Obviously, in both these cases it would be time to revise your sales call plan.

Best Action Commitment and Minimum Acceptable Action are not meant to be taken as rigid, do-or-die propositions. Yes, when the situation warrants it, you can revise either one. But it's important not to do this frivolously, or in response to a merely "difficult" customer. If you're willing to lower your minimum every time you experience any difficulty, there's no point in having a minimum at all.

Walking. Walking out is a last-resort action, but it's not one you should avoid at all costs because if you set your Minimum Acceptable Actions realistically and in accord with the guidelines we've laid out, there should be very few sales calls where the customer balks at your minimum. If she does, you need to ask: Is she really committed? Does she really want to play Win-Win? If you can't answer Yes to those questions, you may be wasting both your time and hers by meeting further with her at this time.

Sometimes we are asked by skeptical salespeople, "Do you really walk away from the business if you don't get the Minimum Acceptable Action?" With the rare exceptions we've just discussed, our answer is Yes. We set our Minimum Acceptable Action based on the least we need to obtain to make spending any more time on this sale worthwhile. If we don't get that "least," then it's only reasonable to consider walking. Anything else is selling ourselves short. And it's saying to the no-commitment client: "My time isn't as valuable as yours. I'd rather wait for the crumbs you throw me than go out and hunt up real business." A client who gets that indirect message will have no qualms about playing you for a fool. You've actually invited him to do just that.

Three related provisos. One, we don't advise anyone to walk as an excuse for not selling and working hard. Be as straight with yourself as you are with your customer. If you didn't do your homework, or didn't answer her questions, or in any way didn't manage the sales call properly, you shouldn't expect to get a commitment—even a minimum acceptable one. But if you've done your job right and you still can't get the minimum, it's time to start thinking about the door.

The second proviso is common sense. If you're considering walking, it's reasonable to discuss your decision first with your manager. For every call you've made on the no-commitment prospect, remember, you've spent several hundred dollars of your company's money—and expended time that you might have spent more profitably elsewhere. Before you write that off as a bad investment, it makes sense to discuss the account with someone else: Your manager may have some insight as to whether another call is worth your while.

Third, walking away doesn't necessarily mean forever. Part of managing multiple accounts (like most of us have to do) is having continually to adjust your limited selling time so that you spend it, week by week, where it does the most good. Sometimes this means shifting time and resources away from an apparent no-commitment account to one where it's easier to maintain a Win-Win position. But that scenario could change in six months or six weeks, and you could find yourself revisiting the uncooperative customer—or another, more cooperative individual in the same account.

TRADING UP

In many cases, sales professionals find it easier to define Best Action Commitment—after all, that's what they really want—than to define a good Minimum Acceptable Action. If you have difficulty here, we suggest you try what one of our program participants once called a "trading up" technique. In trading up, when you know the best that you want but not the minimum, you make that best serve as the minimum and "trade up" for a new best.

For example, suppose the Best Action you can imagine actually happening is for Jeffries to organize a preliminary survey; at this stage in the selling cycle, you would take that as a real coup. But you cannot imagine a lesser commitment that would sustain your level of satisfaction, so "Set up survey" comes to stand as both Best *and* Minimum Acceptable. All right. Call that commitment outcome your Minimum Acceptable, and set your sights on a higher level of commitment to define a new Best Action. "Get him to introduce me to the final approval authority," perhaps, or "Get a promise for division general manager's written response by month's end."

The danger in trading up, of course, is that you will price yourself out of the running by setting the new Best Action Commitment too high. If you began by thinking of "final approval explanation" as the best of all possible worlds, then don't jump from that to "get the order" when you set your new top goal. The watchword, as always, is realism.

PERSONAL WORKSHOP #4: ACTION COMMITMENT

To apply these commitment principles to your own up-coming sales calls, write the heading "Action Commitment" at the top of a notebook page. Under the heading write the description of the Single Sales Objective you're working with and the name of a specific person you'll be calling on in the account. For this exercise you should choose a person you've called on once or twice before.

Step 1: Assess the customer's Concept. Begin by taking a few minutes to review your understanding of this customer's solution image as it relates to the Single Sales Objective you're pursuing. Can you describe clearly what you believe this customer wants to get accomplished? In her mind, is there:

- a perceived *discrepancy* between where she is right now and where she wants to go?
- a business issue she considers *important?*
- something she sees as an urgent *problem?*

If you cannot answer Yes to at least one of these questions, you may not have a sufficient understanding of how this customer sees the situation.

Step 2: Current level of Action Commitment. Now, to get a fix on the customer's current level of commitment, write down the specific actions this individual has performed for you in the past that moved the selling process forward. These might range from "Set up a survey" to "Sent my proposal to CEO with his positive recommendation." Be sure, as you're writing down these notes, that you include an identification of the last action the customer performed or was supposed to perform. If she's agreed to do something by the time of your next meeting, put that down. If she's never done anything for you up to now, put that down.

Step 3: Your current commitment. Now list the actions that you have performed for the customer as a way of moving things forward. List anything from drafting proposals to making presentations to simply giving her your time on an initial or subsequent sales call. Remember that for every time you have met with this client or prospect, you have made a commitment of time and money. You might want to add up the estimated money here and write down the ballpark figure.

Step 4: Are you sharing commitment? Now look at your two lists—the indications of the customer's commitment and the indications of yours—and compare them. Are you both making commitments to the selling process? If the commitment is unequal and you're the one who's holding back, you need to ask yourself what you can do on this upcoming sales call to better demonstrate your commitment. If the customer has been holding back, you need to ask yourself these questions:

- What specific actions could she have performed for me by now that have not been performed?
- What questions have I asked in the past to find out why this person is holding back? Do I have an understanding of why she may feel she is losing?
- What questions should I ask on this call to uncover the reasons for her lack of commitment?

And write those questions down. Asking them should be part of your actions for the next sales call.

Step 5: Define your Best Action Commitment. With the customer's current level of commitment in mind, and with an understanding of the specific action (if any) she has promised to do for you by your next meeting, set out your Best Action target. In other words, define the best thing that, during the call, she could agree to do by the following meeting. Remember that whatever she agrees to do has to indicate a higher (incremental) level of commitment than what she has already done or agreed to do. And remember also that every Action Commitment target has to be specific; has to focus on what the customer, not you, will do; has to be measurable after it's done; has to move the selling process forward; and has to be realistic.

Step 6: Define your Minimum Acceptable Action. Finally, define the low end of your acceptability scale by stating the least you will settle for. In other words, when you next sit down with this person, what is the minimum commitment you will accept at that time for her to perform for the following call? Again remember incremental commitment and our five guidelines. And if you have trouble defining a minimum, recall the trading-up technique that we described just before this Personal Workshop. Define your Minimum Acceptable Action in a sentence, and write it down in your notebook.

You've now defined two of the four prerequisites that you need before you actually walk into your customer's office. Together these two prerequisites—Single Sales Objective and Action Commitment—lay out what you, the salesperson, expect the call to deliver. But in order for that to happen, you've got to make the call—meaning that you've got to get in to see the customer, who at this point may have little or no interest in your Single Sales Objective. So the third thing you've got to define, the third pre-call requirement, is a reason for your customer to meet with you in the first place. We address this "foot in the door" topic in the next chapter.

CHAPTER 7

WHY SHOULD THE CUSTOMER SEE ME?

Before you walk into a sales call, you must ask yourself "What is the reason this person is meeting with me?" We don't mean *your* reason; we mean your customer's or potential customer's reason for agreeing to see you. Whenever an individual schedules time for you, he has taken time out of a crowded schedule that might have been better spent on other priorities. When you ask people to do that, they deserve to understand why.

This sounds obvious enough, and yet most salespeople don't get it. Instead of giving their clients sound business reasons for spending time with them, they focus on their own comfort area, the product pitch, or on nonproductive social calls and lunch dates. As a result, the sales process falters or stalls.

Valid Business Reason: Key Ideas

A Valid Business Reason is something that gives a potential buyer a reason for wanting to spend some of his or her valuable time in a meeting with you. It may reinforce your reasons for wanting to make the call, but it emphasizes his or her priorities, not yours. A Valid Business Reason accomplishes two major purposes:

1. It gives the potential customer *information* he needs in order to understand exactly who you are and why you want to schedule a meeting at this time.
2. It establishes a common *foundation* so that when you do meet, you will be able comfortably to begin the questioning process by concentrating on understanding the customer's Concept.

Given these two basic purposes, it should be clear that a Valid Business Reason—unlike *your* business reasons or the vague social reasons that salespeople often give for getting together—has got to be defined very precisely. It doesn't focus on the account in general or your business in general, but on an upcoming sales call with an individual or individuals. It defines why a particular customer or prospect should want to meet with you at this time—and to what end.

Here's an example. Kim Schneibolk is a senior account manager for TTC, which provides telecommunications testing solutions to Fortune 1000 clients. Kim is responsible for one of TTC's major accounts, a telecommunications leader throughout the Northeast. "At any given time," Kim reflects, "there may be any number of our products—from hand-held testers to rack-mounted test systems to process improvement software—in which this large account could be interested. The challenge is to focus each call on a single interest and then to craft a Valid Business Reason that addresses it. This is critical in executive-level calling, where having a Valid Business Reason helps you to think through the logic for why an executive would want to give you twenty minutes of his or her time in the first place.

"At that level, having a reason that the customer sees as important makes all the difference. Just before a recent call to this account, for example, we discovered that they were wrestling with an inventory problem that was clearly beyond the capacity of their old manual entry system. That fact suggested an obvious Valid Business Reason. I said that I would like a meeting where I could show them how our inventory software could dramatically improve the efficiency of that single process. I didn't have to mention anything else. 'Inventory efficiency' was exactly what was on their minds."

What was on *their* minds, not just hers. The same lesson can be drawn from the story that PDP executive vice president Jim Farmer told in Chapter 4. In that scenario, you may recall, one of Jim's sales reps was faced with trying to get back in the door of a large account after having made a disastrous product dump. In effect, he had just wasted three hours of the client's time, so the likelihood that they would want to see him again, for any reason, might have seemed pretty slim. But they did give him a second chance. Why? Because this time the rep presented them with a Valid Business Reason.

"In announcing his Valid Business Reason to these reluctant customers," Jim explains, "the rep began by acknowledging that his first call had missed the mark because it had failed to focus on anything that these individuals were interested in. He apologized for wasting their time, and then he laid out what we had since discovered about their concerns—their interest in an assessment solution to their employee turnover problem that could be implemented quickly, provided reliable information, and was easy to understand.

"The Valid Business Reason followed logically from that discovery. He phrased it like this: 'I'd like to show you how PDP can reduce your turnover with a software system that is fast, reliable, and easy to understand.' That's all they needed to hear. Even with the bad history of that previous call, they were willing to give our guy a second chance because he was now focusing so precisely on their business needs."

As both of these stories indicate, the point of every Valid Business Reason is to encourage your customers to meet with you because it makes sense in terms of *their* business reality. But there are other key ideas involved in this critical prerequisite. Here are six of the most important:

1. The Valid Business Reason sets forth the real *purpose* of the appointment, from the customer's perspective. When you use a Valid Business Reason as a way of getting in, there's no hidden agenda. What you have in mind is unambiguous; the customer never has to wonder "What is this lunch *really* about?"

2. Stating a Valid Business Reason shows you are *prepared.* You've been thinking about the client's problems (or potential problems), and you've begun to do your homework toward providing a solution.

3. Setting out a Valid Business Reason minimizes your *calling time.* The Valid Business Reason is a kind of screening device that enables you to cut down on the number of calls you have to make and to concentrate on those where there is a real chance for mutual success. To people who have been trained to make as many calls as possible, this will sound heretical. But in Conceptual Selling you go for quality, not quantity, and you realize

that the *maximum* number of calls is not necessarily the *optimum* number.

Stating a Valid Business Reason also eliminates wasted time once the call begins. When the client knows in advance why you're coming, you don't have to spend valuable time—yours and his—defining the purpose of the meeting. You can get down immediately to the business at hand.

4. Stating a Valid Business Reason decodes as "Time is valuable." In other words, it not only *saves* you both time; it lets the client know you consider it *important* to save this time. To a potential customer whose time is in short supply, this says you are *courteous* and *efficient*. Even if the person is not interested in doing business with you at the moment, that perception may still help your future sales.

5. The Valid Business Reason sets mutual *expectations* for the meeting. It lets clients know what you will be speaking about and also what you expect *them* to be ready to talk about. If the client knows in advance why you're coming, he has time to double-check his own information, to clarify his understanding of his problem, to pull out any data you'll need to see—so that when you sit down with him, there are no surprises.

6. Stating the Valid Business Reason in advance gives customers the *time* they need to do this kind of preparation. In good selling, both the buyer and the seller have a responsibility to participate in the sales call—to move the selling process forward so that it leads to mutual satisfaction. Your clients can do that effectively only if they understand *before* the call how you see the agenda—and if they are in agreement with that perception.

Let's look at how to put these key ideas into practice, by discussing how you can make sure you have a Valid Business Reason on every call.

VALID BUSINESS REASON: THE FIVE CRITERIA

Before you can state your reasons for wanting to see anyone, you first have to determine, in your own mind, whether you really do have a Valid Business Reason for the meeting. You do that by focusing on five criteria. We outline them here in the form of questions you should ask yourself in advance of every call.

1. *Will the client accept the reason I want to see her as having an impact on her Concept or solution image?* We assume that if you've accepted the basic principle of selling to Concept, you intend to manage every sales call by relating your product or service to what the customer wants to get done. But it's not enough just to address your prospects' problems. They have to *know* you're doing this. So in defining a Valid Business Reason, make sure the client understands up front that her solution image is your primary concern.

2. *Does this Valid Business Reason tell the customer or prospect why she should place this call at the top of her priority list?* The issue here is urgency. Whenever you try to set up a sales call, you're competing with a hundred other priorities: calls that your competition may want to set up, meetings within the buying organization, planes to catch, personal appointments—and on and on. Your Valid Business Reason must make the customer want to see you first, or at least soon. Therefore,

Valid Business Reasons with the highest likelihood of getting you in will be those that focus on current, pressing business concerns.

3. *Does the Valid Business Reason make it clear what's in the sales call for the customer?* The client already knows what's in the call for you, or he can figure it out easily enough: Since you're trying to set up an appointment, he can safely assume that, somewhere down the line, you'll want an order sheet signed. But will there be any benefit to the client and his or her company in doing so? And what's the immediate benefit in meeting with you now—whether or not a contract signature is in the offing? If it's not clear to the customer what he can gain from a meeting, you're asking him to risk his time on faith. That's not a Win for him, and it's not even rational.

This doesn't mean you have to give the entire show away in stating your Valid Business Reason. Obviously, the real selling only begins when you're sitting down face to face with the client. But in order to get face to face at all, you have to show him he might *benefit* from the call.

4. *Is it clear that my Valid Business Reason relates to the customer's business, not just my own?* This is a subtly different point from the previous one. Naturally you want to meet your customer for reasons that will enhance business opportunities for *both* of you. But in stating a Valid Business Reason, it's the potential buyer's business that really counts—even at the temporary "expense" of your own. By helping your customers to Win in their *own* businesses, you're building credibility, a history of mutual success—and a foundation for future business.

5. *Is this Valid Business Reason stated concisely and clearly enough to be left on voice mail or email or relayed by an*

assistant? This criterion is a matter of simple practicality. Today, most sales calls are arranged by telephone, and in a world of laptops and global shuttling, you can count yourself lucky if it takes you only two or three rounds of phone tag before you finally hook up with the person you're trying to see. That means the first indication she gets that you want to see her is likely to come in the form of a phone message. If that message isn't clear and concise, both you and your Valid Business Reason will come off looking fuzzy and nonprofessional. That's why we advise our clients to write down their Valid Business Reasons in simple, lean sentences—and why you'll do that yourself later in this chapter. If you can't write down your Valid Business Reason in the proverbial twenty-five words or less, it might not be a real business reason, and it might not be valid.

Our five Valid Business Reason criteria are outlined on page 142. Remember that each criterion must be met as perceived from the *customer's* point of view.

BEYOND THE COLD CALL

Implicit in all five of these criteria is the assumption that before you ever walk into a customer's office, you've already done some thinking about his business. In Conceptual Selling, there's really no such thing as a cold call because when you sell to Concept you do tactical planning before every call—even the first visit to a new prospect. In fact, if you don't do this planning—if you don't give some thought to whom you'll be meeting, what his or her likely problems are, and how your product or service might relate to them—

VALID BUSINESS REASON CRITERIA

☑ **Impacts the customer's Concept**

☑ **Explains why this sales call should be a high priority for the customer**

☑ **Tells what is in it for the customer**

☑ **Relates to the customer's interest**

☑ **Must be concise and clearly stated enough to be left as voice mail or with an assistant**

there's no way you can draft a Valid Business Reason at all. And you really will be selling "cold."

You don't have to know all the details of a customer's operation. Obviously, on a first call to a new prospect, you're going to know very little, and there's nothing wrong with that. But it's not an efficient use of anybody's time to set up appointments when you've done *no* preliminary research. It may be something as elementary as having read a newspaper article about the prospective client's industry that leads you to believe there's a potential match. Or you may have heard about a reorganization in the company that could lead to new suppliers (such as you) being considered. The specific information you have may be ultimately less important than the fact that you've thought enough about the prospect to be one step up on the cold caller.

Our research shows conclusively that many sales calls are too general—too "preliminary" and unfocused to be useful to either the buyer or the seller. Thinking about the specific client, and about her company, in advance is one way of bringing focus into the situation so that when you go into the sales call, you know you are calling on the right person and that you are *managing* your selling time, not gambling with it.

Our client Richard Brashier, who is vice president of sales at ATS, a Premiere Technologies Company, makes this point emphatically when he describes the importance of a Valid Business Reason in the ATS environment. "With our large accounts," he says, "we don't do telemarketing or one-shots. To our salespeople, having a Valid Business Reason is incredibly important—it's what makes the difference between getting a meeting and not getting it—so you've got to do your homework way in advance. We tell our people all the time: If you don't have a Valid Business Reason, don't pick up the phone.

"And when they do pick up the phone, we want them to make it very clear. Tell the prospect or customer up front: 'This is what we think the meeting should be about and why we think that this can be of some value to you.' That way you know where you're going—or where you're not. Usually our homework is pretty good, and the customer is happy to confirm the Valid Business Reason. Once in a while, we miss something, and a customer will say 'No, that's not it.' When that happens, you shut up and listen. Or you tell the customer, 'OK, let's start over.' Either way, the Valid Business Reason is a great tool for ensuring that you're starting the meeting on the same page."

There are three basic points in a selling cycle when the use of a Valid Business Reason can provide the kind of insurance Brashier is referring to: at the time when you make the appointment, at the beginning of the meeting itself, and when you encounter "surprise guests" in a previously arranged sales call.

SETTING APPOINTMENT EXPECTATIONS

Using a Valid Business Reason to get an appointment in the first place is the most obvious use of the principle and the place where its value will probably be most obvious to the seller. But it's important to emphasize that when you use a Valid Business Reason to get an appointment, you need to *state the Valid Business Reason* clearly on the phone when you actually make the appointment. As we've already explained, it can clarify for both you and the client what is *expected to happen* in the visit. Setting the stage in this way gives you an immediate benefit: *It reduces your potential buyer's uncertainty level,* which makes developing real communication easier for you. In doing this, you should observe the following guidelines:

- Clarify *your selling responsibilities* in the call. What are you going to be speaking about, which of the customer's areas of concern are you expected to address, and what specific information are you expected to bring to the meeting? The more of this you spell out on the phone, the less chance there will be that you will make a presentation he wasn't expecting or didn't want to hear.
- Clarify *the customer's responsibilities.* This follows logically from our insistence on getting commitment. In

every properly managed sales call, you and the client *share* responsibility for moving the sales process forward. If on a previous call your client has promised to "bring the finance department's written response," be sure to verify that responsibility on the phone. This will also help you to clarify what *information* you expect to receive on this call.

- State the *purpose* of the meeting from the customer's perspective, that is, what you hope the meeting will accomplish. Stating this when you make the appointment reconfirms your interest in the customer's needs and also clarifies your mutual agenda. Since people's agendas are constantly in flux, this brings clarity into a potentially uncertain situation. And it helps you avoid the minefield of "But I thought we were supposed to be talking about..."

- Identify the *people to be present*. There are two reasons you should identify the relevant individuals when making an appointment. It allows the person you're calling on to make the necessary arrangements, and it minimizes the chances that too many people, or too few, or the wrong people will be there when you arrive. If you were expecting to be talking to only one person, but at the meeting you find yourself surrounded by six unknowns, that can throw off the entire momentum of the call. On the other hand, if two people are crucial to the success of the meeting and one of them doesn't get invited, you'll end up spending two meetings to do the work you could have done in one. Guard against these traps by defining "the shape of the table" on the phone.

- Itemize the *materials* needed. If your presentation requires a blackboard, an overhead projector, or a special room, be sure the client understands that when you set up the appointment. If it's his responsibility to provide those materials, make sure he understands that. If it's your responsibility, tell him that too so he won't waste his valuable time hunting up something that you're bringing with you.

Just one more point. If you make an appointment well in advance and you later call to confirm it, it's definitely not inappropriate to run through these guidelines *again*. It might sound like repetition, but that beats false assumptions every time.

VERIFYING THE MEETING'S FOCUS

It's useful to state your Valid Business Reason again at the start of the meeting. The reasons for this are the same as those for stating it (and the other appointment guidelines) when you call to confirm the appointment. It's natural and easy to do so because there is no better or more logical opener than a confirmation of the purpose of the meeting: "We were going to address the circuitry problem this afternoon, correct?" Or: "Am I right in understanding, Jerry, that you wanted a run-down today of our service record in your industry?"

Stating at the outset your reason for being there signals your listeners that you know exactly *what you're doing*—and invites them to confirm, before anyone's time gets wasted, that it's *what they still want done.* If it's *not* what they want done, of course, you're well advised, as Richard Brashier puts it, to say "Let's start over" and perhaps to move the meeting to a time when your expectations are more in sync.

DEALING WITH SURPRISE GUESTS

It's especially important to say "Let's start over" when you enter a meeting room and discover that you're not facing the person or persons you thought you'd be facing. Always find out who your listeners are *before* you start a presentation. One way of doing that is to state your Valid Business Reason at the beginning so that customers know as well as you do that they're in the right place at the right time.

If you don't do this, you're asking for trouble. An acquaintance of ours recently gave a presentation to a roomful of middle managers from a large multinational. He neglected to state the Valid Business Reason that had brought him there, and he was ten minutes into his presentation when a visibly puzzled manager in the front row got up from his seat, mumbled "This isn't my area at all; I must be at the wrong meeting," and left sheepishly. The manager felt lousy, his colleagues were distracted and embarrassed for him, and our friend lost valuable time regaining his own bearings and composure. "It threw my timing completely off," he told us. "I felt like an idiot teacher who had been lecturing to a Greek class on chemistry." All of this confusion could have been avoided if he had stated the Valid Business Reason first, and checked its validity with each member of the surprise audience.

THREE COMMON RESERVATIONS—AND OUR RESPONSES

Virtually all of the people we work with see the value of presenting a Valid Business Reason on every call. But we do encounter occasional resistance, usually from people who were taught that "friendship" or "keeping in touch" can be an adequate reason to call on a client. Here's how we counter their objections.

Reservation 1: It can't be necessary on every call. "There are still some calls where socializing is the only agenda and where I don't really need a valid reason for meeting because I'm not doing business; I'm just keeping the fires warm."

Sure, there are scenarios like this. There are plenty of social situations where you just want to wine and dine a potential customer for the simple reason that you enjoy his or her company. *But you should not confuse these situations with sales calls.* In a sales call, you are asking someone to give you *professional time* so you can explore ways of advancing each other's business goals. When you're in this professional mode, no matter how close you are personally, you owe the person (and yourself) quality time. The only way you can be sure of giving that quality time is to have a Valid Business Reason defined whenever you meet. Every time. If you don't, the best personal friends in the world might back off from doing business with you—they won't be able to afford not to.

Reservation 2: I don't want to come across as a hard-nose. "I don't want to be so rigid in insisting on the business side of the relationship that she thinks I don't care about her as a person. Miller Heiman says I should seek ways to let all of my clients win, personally. How can I do that if I never talk about anything but business?"

This objection also confuses the personal and professional aspects of a business relationship. If you're relaxing at the pool or on the golf course with good old Joe, fine: relax. But a sales call is a very special situation, with its own exacting requirements. Obviously, even in this exacting environment you should avoid precipitous bluntness, as in statements like "Let's not waste each other's time" or "Hi, Joe, the purpose of this meeting is . . ." But this is a matter of style and of maintaining sensitivity to your individual customers. The pleasantries that open many sales calls are perfectly acceptable as icebreakers. But don't kid yourself: They are *not part of the sales call proper.* When the two of you get down to business, that's exactly what you have to do: focus on your mutual business needs.

Far from being "inconsiderate" or "hard-nosed," defining a Valid Business Reason on every call is actually a *very* considerate way of doing business. It indicates to the potential buyer—whether you've known her twenty years or ten minutes—that you've given some thought to her current position and that you're seeking ways to improve it. It shows, too, that you're open to revising your understanding—that you're comfortable having a meeting only if it's "valid" for her.

Reservation 3: I feel uncomfortable stating the reason out loud. "It seems too obvious, too direct, to blurt out, 'We're meeting today for the following reason.' It seems almost insulting, as if the person can't figure that out for himself. I prefer to feel my way into the situation, rather than being so blunt."

Whenever you feel uncomfortable about stating the purpose of your meeting, it's a pretty clear sign that your "valid" reason is in some way inappropriate. Perhaps you've phrased it (to yourself or to the buyer) incorrectly; or perhaps you don't really understand, yourself, why the two of you are getting together. If the Valid Business Reason is correctly stated, it will *never* be "insulting" to the client—and it should never make you want to "feel your way." If you have some anxiety about saying out loud why you're there, reexamine what you feel to be the purpose of the meeting. You may find it helpful, in doing this, to rephrase the Valid Business Reason in the form of a question: "Am I correct in understanding that the purpose of this meeting is to . . . ?"

There are three basic reasons that a seller may be uneasy about stating a Valid Business Reason: (1) He doesn't know the purpose of the meeting himself—in which case he's got no business being there. (2) He's not sure that the customer's understanding of that purpose is the same as his, and he doesn't want to discover the discrepancy—in which case he's putting blinders on himself. (3) He's afraid the buyer will jump down his throat for being "simple" and wasting his time.

In this last scenario, the salesperson makes the implicit assumption that the customer is both *smarter* than he is and so *impatient* that she cannot spare ten seconds to confirm why she has agreed to a meeting. If you meet a so-called "brilliant" tyrant like this, our advice is still the same. It's to stay Win-Win with the person by confirming the Valid Business Reason up front. If she wants to throw it back in your face, it should be evident to you that she may not be willing to stay Win-Win. And that you may not belong in her office.

It all comes back to mutual satisfaction and mutual respect. Clarifying a meeting's purpose with a Valid Business Reason is a straightforward and necessary technique for enhancing clarity and good information flow. Any buyer who wants to play straight with you will welcome the offer of such clarification. A person who rejects or mocks your stated purpose or who thinks the purpose is either "obvious" or "irrelevant"— that person is not going to bring you good business anyway. So why waste your time going after him?

THE LONG-TERM PAYBACK

In addition to the benefits of a Valid Business Reason that we've already described, one more benefit is so important and so unexpected that we need to highlight it specially. That benefit is the long-term payback you get in terms of *differentiation*.

We'll discuss differentiation in some detail later in the book. Here it's enough to point out that customers decide between options by identifying distinctions. A Valid Business Reason is a perfect way for you to make yourself distinct in the customer's mind for the simple reason that it is so rarely used. Most sales professionals still feel they have to manipulate their way into appointments by giving the client "social" or "nonthreatening" reasons for getting together, like the telemarketer who interrupts your dinner under the pretext that he's "taking a survey," or the corporate rep who pretends not to be interested in a client's business, but just wants to "take him to lunch." Against this kind of traditionally manipulative backdrop, the seller who announces a business interest up front and who gives the client a Valid Business Reason for meeting—that seller stands way apart from the crowd. He or she will be *remembered,* and *listened to* as clearly differentiated from the competition.

One Conceptual Selling participant makes the point well. "I can't tell you how many supposedly inaccessible people I've gotten in to see by stating a Valid Business Reason up front. The shock value is terriffc. People are so used to having sales reps weasel their way in that when I come out and say *why* I want to meet, it really clears the decks. Three or four clients have told me that nobody had ever done that with them before. So automatically I'm in a class by myself."

That's differentiation.

Personal Workshop #5: Valid
Business Reason

Here's a brief exercise to relate the concept of Valid Business Reason to your upcoming calls. Write the heading "Valid Business Reason" at the top of a notebook page. Then, for a call you plan to make in the near future but for which you haven't yet made an appointment, write down the name of the account, the name of the person or persons you expect to meet, and what you hope to accomplish in the meeting. By "what you hope to accomplish" we mean here the *purpose*, as you see it, for the meeting.

Step 1: State your Valid Business Reason. You've just defined what you believe (or hope) to be the purpose of this upcoming meeting: You know why you want to meet this person. Now define a reason that *he or she* should want to meet with *you*. This is harder, of course, because it means getting into the other person's head. Write it down in your notebook, and remember two things. An effectively defined Valid Business Reason is *short*, and it's phrased from the *customer's* point of view. "Valid" here means valid in his or her eyes. So review the five "customer-centric" criteria that we presented earlier, and put your "valid" reason to the test with the following questions:

- How will this Valid Business Reason have an impact— and be *perceived* as having an impact—on this customer's Concept? How will he understand that it addresses his solution image?
- Why will this Valid Business Reason cause this person to put me at (or at least near) the top of a priority list?
- How does this Valid Business Reason make it clear that

there's something in the meeting for him and his company? Does it spell out unambiguously what's in it for them?

- Is it crystal clear that this Valid Business Reason is related to this customer's business, not just mine? What current business concern does it address?

- If I left this Valid Business Reason on the person's voice mail or email or with an assistant, would its meaning and importance be instantly comprehensible?

Using these questions as a guide, redefine your Valid Business Reason where needed. The final version doesn't have to check out against all five of these criteria perfectly, but the more complete the match, the more likely it is that the validity will be apparent from the customer's perspective. What you're aiming for is a *real* reason—not a pie-in-the-sky hope— that this customer will be eager to meet you.

Step 2: Test this reason. After you've tested the validity against the five criteria, test it again by trying it out on your colleagues. Ask your peers and your sales manager whether or not your reason for arranging the call makes good business sense to them. Ask them to put themselves in your potential buyer's place, and imagine that you are asking for an appointment. Does your Valid Business Reason seem to them a good enough reason for a client to spend time with you? If they're not sure of its validity, you may not really have a Valid Business Reason—and you may want to think further about the meeting's purpose.

Step 3: What actions can I take next? Finally, identify the specific actions that you can take right now to better define and present your Valid Business Reason. Maybe you need to do more reading about the client's general field of business. Maybe you need some coaching, either from someone within the buying organization or from someone in yours, or from a person not associated with either company. Maybe your currently stated Valid Business Reason is already solid—maybe it already passes the criteria and the "peer review" tests—and the next action you should take is to call the client. Whatever actions you decide on to move you closer to a good meeting, be sure they improve your understanding of the customer's situation. Remember: Your ultimate purpose in stating the Valid Business Reason is to demonstrate to the person that you and your company can help him or her win.

Once you've completed this exercise, you should have not only a better understanding of Valid Business Reason, but one more tactical element in hand that can help you manage each sales call most effectively from the moment it begins. There's only one more preparatory question to ask before we turn to the sales call proper. That question is designed to verify your professional credibility.

CHAPTER 8

DO I HAVE CREDIBILITY?

During the Watergate hearings of the early 1970s, novelty stores carried a poster of Richard Nixon that depicted the beleaguered president over the caption "Would you buy a used car from this man?" The photograph made him look like the prototypically devious used car dealer. The implication was that "Tricky Dick" was no more to be trusted than Slippery Sam.

Whether or not this characterization was fair, the photograph drew vividly on the old folklore about shady used car dealers, and it made a valid point about customer perception. If you can't convince your potential buyers that you can be *trusted*, you're no better off than a president facing impeachment—or than the lemon peddler whose income is based on deceit. In all sound selling—in all selling where long-term success is important—establishing your personal credibility and that of your company is a must. At the end of our previous book, *The New Strategic Selling*, we suggested that it may even be *the* must—the "open secret of success that every sales leader knows." In this chapter we'll discuss this fourth essential piece of "Getting Started," showing you how to ask and answer the question of whether or not you have earned the trust of your customers.

A potential customer will be reluctant to agree to a sale for five basic reasons.

1. There's *no need* for the purchase—no clear fit between the product or service and the prospect's wants.
2. There's *no money*—or not enough money in the budget, or no way to get it allocated—to make the purchase.
3. There's no *desire* to make the change that the sale would represent.
4. There's no *urgency* to make the change at this particular time.
5. There's *no trust*—no basis for the potential buyer to believe that the seller is concerned with both their interests.

Any combination of these elements can prove to be the undoing of a potential sale. But one of them stands out. The last item, lack of trust, kills more sales than the other four reasons combined.

The implication for the professional seller is dramatic. No matter what else you do well, if you don't have credibility with your customers you're going to lose. Nobody buys from a person he doesn't think can be trusted.

There are exceptions. If you are the *only* available supplier for a given product or service and a customer is desperate to have it—in other words, if the customer thinks there's no alternative—then it's possible to make a no-credibility or low-credibility sale. You can also trick some inattentive or impulsive buyers into trusting you temporarily when common sense says they should not. But such situations are rare. And *you cannot build a business* on this basis. If you want to succeed in Win-Win selling—that is, if you want to develop satisfied customers, great referrals, repeat business, and enduring relationships—then you *must* have credibility.

ELEMENTS OF CREDIBILITY

Because different people will trust you for different reasons, it's useful to understand the common elements of credibility. There may be dozens of these operating in any given selling situation, but we can break them down into four basic areas: your *experience,* your *knowledge,* your *presentation* of yourself, and your *associations.*

Your experience. One of the first things a potential customer wants to know about you as a seller is your experience in your current business or a related one. Twenty-year veterans automatically have more credibility than the sales reps who pulled in their first commissions last month. And the more closely related your past work has been to the potential *customer's* type of business, the more reliable you will look to him or her.

But it's quality, not quantity, that counts. What your potential customers are looking for is not just twenty years of steady employment but a *track record* that says you can deliver. Even if you're the new kid on the block, you can earn credibility with customers if you've accomplished something solid for them or for someone with problems similar to theirs. Credibility means that you're *believable.* So if you've come through for Ms. Harris with exactly the performance-improvement figures you promised, she knows you can do what you say.

That's the kind of experience that counts. If you've been having that kind of experience—delivering what you've promised—for twenty years, so much the better.

Your knowledge. Even if you haven't yet delivered solid results to Harris, you may still earn her trust through your knowledge. Your educational background, your technical expertise, your demonstrated ability to understand her areas of expertise and responsibility—all these can be elements of credibility. Establishing trust through what you *know* is not quite as reliable as establishing it through what you've *done*, but it can be a good second *if* what you know eventually helps your customer to accomplish something she wants done.

Of course, that can be a big if. There's nothing wrong with showing off your knowledge. But be wary of *simply* flashing the Stanford degree or quoting from the technical journals. Knowledge by itself might give you a provisional credibility. But if you want to make it stick, you've got to prove it—that is, to demonstrate the value of your particular expertise to the individual customer's interests and needs.

Presentation. By presentation, we mean the manner in which you present *yourself*, not your product or service, to the customer or prospect. Some of this is obvious, such as the need to follow John Molloy's rule about dressing for success. T-shirts and jeans have their place, but not when you're trying to look trustworthy to a business associate. But "power dressing" is only the most immediately visible example. Also crucial can be your personal appearance, your language and patterns of speech, your personality and demeanor, and your general level of professional courtesy. Anything that affects the way you look and sound to the customer can affect your level of believability.

But appearances can be misleading, and we don't mean to suggest that credibility can be earned just by looking good. You can devour every "dress for success" and "business etiquette" manual on the market and still strike out with certain clients because they don't believe that you're *more* than your clothes and manner. Other things being equal, the person who presents himself in a clean, articulate, professional way is going to earn greater credibility than the guy in the green suit who speaks in grunts. But your appearance, like your knowledge, just gets you started: It says to your customers that you are savvy enough to play in their league. Once you're in, you've got to show them that you can perform.

There is one aspect of the way you present yourself, however, that can be an extremely important element on its own. We've mentioned professionalism as an aspect of appearance. It's also an aspect of an effective face-to-face selling process. The salesperson who shows up on time for the appointment, who is organized in presentation, and who listens attentively to what the prospective customer has to say is demonstrating more than mere "etiquette." He is showing a concern for the other person that defines good selling *and* good manners. When this method becomes an integral part of the way you deal with individual clients and is not merely a slick, polite facade, it can be invaluable in developing a customer's trust.

Your associations. Ms. Harris may not know you from Adam. But if she knows your company, if she knows about you from one of your other customers, or if she knows about you from friends she trusts, you have a better chance than Adam would of getting her to trust you up front.

Associations of this order will seldom get you past that initial trust level, and we are not saying that you should rely on "connections" to build credibility. The days of relationship selling—of "who you know" and the old boy network—are numbered; that kind of selling, by itself, is just not conducive to Win-Win outcomes. But like your knowledge and like your presentation, your relevant business and personal connections can have a good introductory effect. They can set up a temporary trust in situations where you otherwise wouldn't have it.

ELEMENTS OF CREDIBILITY

- *Your track record of delivering results*
- *Your track record of accomplishments*
- *Your experience in the customer's business or industry*
- *Your technical expertise*
- *Your educational background*
- *Your language and speech*
- *Your appearance, dress, grooming*
- *Your personality, demeanor*
- *Your professionalism—punctuality, organization, manners*
- *Your associations—company, contacts, other customers*

The emphasis here is on *temporary*. As hard as it can be sometimes to gain credibility with your customers, it's extremely easy to lose it unless you keep earning it every time. For this reason, credibility has to be *checked* constantly to be sure it is not being eroded.

We mean checked on *every* sales call. *The sales call where you assume you have credibility is the sales call where you will lose it.* So we urge you to adopt an ongoing checking procedure with every account and every individual you deal with. The initial step in this ongoing checking procedure is to be able to determine when you do and when you don't have credibility with an individual customer.

Do You Have Credibility? Weighing the Evidence

You're sitting across a desk from an important customer and you've determined that you can probably solve her problem. But you've never done business with this person before, so there's no history of mutual trust. Or it's been six months or six weeks since you last met with her, and you're not certain she *still* trusts you. What you need is evidence about your *current* level of credibility with this person.

Evidence that you *do* have credibility includes the following customer reactions and behaviors:

- The customer is ready to talk about your product or service and its relationship to her needs.
- The customer asks "how" questions rather than "why" questions, indicating that she is zeroing in on your solution.
- The customer tells you outright that you have her trust.
- The customer tells you highly personal data.
- The customer's attention is clearly and unambiguously on your meeting.

When you encounter signals like these, you're probably on fairly solid ground. You may not have the sale or even the specific sales call in your pocket. But at least the customer seems willing to meet you halfway: She is giving you the attention that implies she believes what you are saying.

Evidence that you do *not* have credibility includes the following reactions and behaviors:

- The customer makes you jump through hoops and questions your credentials.
- The customer will not let you get to what you understood to be the point of the meeting.
- The customer is silent or talks in guarded monosyllables.
- The customer questions your logic or train of thought.
- The customer is visibly antagonistic or defensive.

When you encounter these signals, no matter how great your preparation, you can bet you're missing a critical piece of the "Getting Started" puzzle.

What should be clear from these pieces of evidence is that there is a direct relationship between credibility and customer "ownership." When a prospective buyer believes you can be trusted, he naturally becomes more actively involved in the sales call than if he sees you as a threat or an unknown quantity. When you have credibility, your client is a partner in the call: He asks pertinent questions regarding what you're trying to do, volunteers information that will help you to move the sale forward, and gives you his undivided attention because he feels involved in something that he "owns."

When you lack credibility, the opposite happens. When a prospect is not convinced you can be trusted, she clams up or becomes antagonistic. She bombards you with questions *about* your credibility rather than about your possible solution to her problems. Rather than becoming a partner with you in the buy/sell process, she becomes an anti-sponsor instead, expending all her energy trying to find reasons your proposals won't work.

Because credibility has such a decisive effect on the way a prospective buyer is likely to interact with you face to face, it's essential to be attentive to these signals from the first moments of a sales call. The quicker you spot them, the quicker you can shift tactical gears where necessary, and begin developing the credibility you need.

But how do you do that? How do you get credibility if you don't already have it?

"Getting" Credibility

In a sense, this is a trick question. Credibility is as fragile as it is valuable, and nobody ever really "gets" it once and for all. That's why it's more accurate to say that the Conceptual salesperson *gains* credibility in an ongoing process rather than nailing it down for all time. Unless you pay constant attention to gaining and regaining it on every call, you can easily find yourself *assuming* a person's trust when it's long gone.

With that proviso in mind, there are three basic ways to gain credibility. It can be established by *reputation,* it can be *transferred* to you by somebody else, and it can be *earned* by you personally.

Credibility by reputation. You've heard of guilt by association. Gaining trust because of reputation is a type of credibility by association. It's possible to gain temporary credibility if your company or the product you represent has its own good track record with your prospective client. The John Deere or Kimberly-Clark salesperson has a built-in

THREE WAYS TO OBTAIN CREDIBILITY

- **Established by reputation**
- **Transferred**
- **Earned by you**

credibility with new accounts—a "credit rating" that a new kid on the block cannot count on. But note that word *temporary* again. Reps for market leaders retain their credibility edge only up to a point. It's the point at which the market leader drops the ball by failing to attend to its customers' changing needs—and therefore suffers an instant credibility loss. We can all cite instances where that's happened in recent years.

Credibility transferred. Sometimes it's useful to think of credibility as an equivalent to credit at the bank. The best of all possible scenarios is for you to earn a great credit rating yourself. But just as you can sometimes get bank credit by having someone else cosign a loan, so too you can gain temporary credibility on the strength of someone else's recommendation—whether it's in the form of an introduction, a letter, or a phone call. If you have such an entrée to the customer from a respected colleague, a business associate, a past satisfied customer, or someone else the customer trusts, that person's credibility can be transferred to you. It will never be as high or as solid as credibility you earn on your own merits, but it will still be "credit" you can draw on—another case of credibility by association.

Credibility earned. By far the *best* way to get credibility is to earn it yourself with each individual prospect and customer. As we mentioned above, "results delivered" is a chief component of this selling prerequisite. If you've delivered a solid Win-Win outcome to Mr. Williams in the past, he knows you care about his interests as well as your own—and someone who knows that will do business with you again. When you've delivered once to a customer, your performance becomes "money in the bank" to the client, and he's going to be much more eager to draw on it in the future than to run to a rival seller from whom he may not get the same satisfaction.

No matter which of the three ways you get it in the first place, though, in the end *all credibility has to be earned.* Gaining credibility by association, like getting a bank loan on somebody else's recommendation, is a temporary expedient —what a newcomer has to do before establishing a personal credit history. Customers, like banks, will take a first chance on you if you come backed by the best. But they will not do so a second time, *no matter how glowing your references,* unless you prove your own personal reliability with results.

Some of this proving can come only after the sale has been made. But some of it can come along the way—in the various face-to-face selling situations that make up the selling process. You can, and indeed must, earn credibility as you go, in each and every face-to-face encounter. Here are some guidelines for doing this.

EARNING CREDIBILITY: GUIDELINES

Ask precise questions. The more focused and specific your questioning, the clearer it will be to the client that you have done your homework. We'll discuss the questioning process in detail in Part 3. The main point here is that vague discussions that wander around the topic always hinder the salesperson's credibility. Since the client's time is just as valuable as yours, save both of you some aggravation by drafting precise questions in advance of your meeting. Doing this not only impresses the client with your preparation; it makes it much easier for you to get the specific information you need each time to move the selling process forward.

Listen intently. Demonstrate to the customer that you're actively listening, with the appropriate body language and supportive responses. The purpose here is twofold. One, intent listening helps you to understand the customer's Concept better—which is the bedrock of everything you do in Conceptual Selling. Two, it shows that you're concerned with *her* needs—with what she thinks and feels about the situation. Showing a real interest in what prospective customers are saying is also one of the simplest methods of getting *them* to listen to *you*.

Be yourself. This may sound like a cliché, but it's good advice. If you're trying to establish credibility, the last thing you should do is to play a role. Any role. Salespeople who put on phony fronts—all gleaming teeth and hand-pumping and soulful gazes full of concern—soon come off looking like fools. To today's customers, such game playing is increasingly transparent. Besides, if you've got a good product or service and you're honestly working toward a match to the customer's needs, you don't need such theatrics to make the point. To earn a potential customer's trust, demonstrate straight out that you trust *yourself.*

Don't be a know-it-all. Don't give your prospect pat answers, and don't under *any* circumstances suggest that you know more than he does. Maybe you do know more—but that's irrelevant. In fact, it's worse than irrelevant because customers who find you condescending will give you an order only when they have no other option. Millions of dollars are lost every year by reps who try to establish their credibility by showing off how brilliant they are. This is especially common in the high-tech field, where technobabblers finesse themselves out of sales every day by displaying their fluency in "Geek" to bewildered prospects. Speaking a language the customer doesn't understand is one of the surest ways we know to *lose* credibility.

This doesn't mean you should be a shrinking violet. If your product knowledge is solid and extensive, and if you really do have superior insights about how a customer's problem might be solved, of course you should let him know that. But the *manner* in which you do it is crucial. You don't get credibility by wowing the customer. You get it by giving clear, comprehensive answers and by giving them at the *customer's* pace and level of understanding.

Stay Win-Win. Demonstrate to the prospective buyer that you're not ignoring yourself, but you really care about *her* coming out ahead in this sale. This is particularly important when the prospect is negative or defensive. When a customer is finding excuses to shoot you down, the natural tendencies are to fight back or to be overly accommodating. Resist those tendencies. Real credibility is achieved only in Win-Win scenarios. And there's nothing wrong with being blunt about this with the customer. If she's being "difficult" or "resistant," find out why. Tell her, "Joan, I want us both to win here, and I have a feeling that's not clear to you. How could we make this situation become a Win for you?"

When you're faced with an antagonistic prospect, we also suggest the following:

- Ask for *specifics.* Defuse the antagonism by focusing on the what, where, when, and how much of the situation.
- Make it clear, by means of precise questioning, that you're not aiming simply to overcome objections, but to gain a fuller *understanding* of what's happening.
- *Hear the client out.* Don't interrupt or counterattack, but allow the customer to vent his or her feelings until the anger runs out.

Sometimes, of course, the anger won't run out. In these cases it's virtually impossible to get to Win-Win, and your best strategy may be to walk away. But these situations are rare. Most times, waiting out the antagonism is a necessary part of gaining trust. And you don't have to be a martyr to pull this off. If you can show by statement and example that you want both yourself *and* your client to win, your chances for gaining credibility are high.

Always remember that you have to deliver. You will get credibility for sure only after you have *earned* it. You get long-term trust from a customer only by delivering the results he needs—by producing the mutual wins that make you believable.

Personal Workshop #6: Credibility

To see how credibility has been a factor in your own selling up to now, we'd like you to write the heading "Credibility" at the top of a notebook page, and then select *two* sales calls from the recent past: one where you *did* have credibility with (that is, were clearly trusted by) the customer, and one where you did *not* have credibility. Then take fifteen minutes to review specific elements of these two calls. For the first call:

Step 1: List the evidence of credibility. Write down the name of the account and the name of the individual you met with. Then list the signals you noticed on the call indicating that this person trusted you. You can refer to the examples of evidence we gave earlier in this chapter, and briefly jot down your recollections. "He had all his calls held while I was there," for example. Or: "She asked specific questions about our solution." The point here is for you to make visible what we often take for granted: the clearly definable signals that a customer believes you can be trusted.

Step 2: How did you earn credibility? Identify *how* you came to be trusted by this particular person. Remember that credibility can be based on your company's *reputation,* is *transferred* to you from an associate, or is personally *earned.* If you earned the client's trust, write down in a few words *how:* what results did you deliver that enabled her to win in the past? If the credibility was transferred from someone else, write down the name of that person. And if it was gained by your company's reputation, write down those aspects of your company's track record—its special strengths or history of performance—that made this particular individual trust you.

Step 3: How did you build credibility? Now list the actions you took in this sales call to build on and maintain your credibility. Refer to our "Earning Credibility" guidelines laid out earlier in the chapter, and write down short identifying comments to remind yourself how you built trust. "Asked him very precise questions about quality control," for example, or "Let her know I wanted her to win in spite of her rejection of original specs." What you're aiming for here is an overview of how the good sales call went and what you did during it to maintain your trust position.

For the second call, the one where you had no credibility:

Step 1: Identify evidence of "no credibility." Again, write down the name of the account and the name of the person you met. Then list the signals that convinced you this particular person did *not* trust you. Use our evidence list as a guide, and make your comments specific. "She didn't say more than twenty words in half an hour." Or "He constantly attacked my reliability: said we couldn't possibly perform as I said."

Step 2: What could you have done to gain trust? Now, for the same sales call, list actions you could have taken to turn the person's perception of you around. Refer to our "Earning Credibility" guidelines again, and pay particular attention to the last one, which explains how to earn credibility by staying Win-Win in a hostile situation. Perhaps "more specific questions" might have been a key, or "meeting objections in a calmer, less defensive manner." Whatever you write down, check that it is a potential action that would have verified *your eagerness to play Win-Win*. One of the central elements of getting a person to trust you is demonstrating that you don't want *him* to lose, any more than you want yourself to.

Having reviewed your performance in these two sales calls, you should have a clearer notion of what it feels like—and what it means—both to have credibility and to lack it. We urge you to use that clearer understanding in managing every sales call in the future—in other words, in making this fourth selling prerequisite part of your tactical *planning* for every call.

But before you actually go into those calls, there is one more observation to be made. It relates to the fact that credibility can be lost as well as gained. And one of the principal facets in the *maintenance* of any salesperson's credibility is that intangible commodity, timing.

CREDIBILITY AND TIMING

Everybody in sales has a favorite story about deals that fell through in spite of competent selling simply because the timing was wrong. In selling, as in anything else, being in the right place at the right time is often a component of success, and being in the same right place at the wrong time can just as easily spell disaster.

We have no argument with the view that timing is critical to good selling. Where we differ from most analysts of the sales scene is in our conviction that you, the seller, can have far more *control* over timing than is usually imagined.

Most people tend to think of timing as something that just

"happens" to them—and to think of themselves as its power-less victims. This is a cop-out. In Conceptual Selling, it's your job *to find out if the timing is right,* and *to do that each time you meet with a customer.* If you don't do it every time, you're going to end up with a string of nonproductive meetings where you "just happened" to hit him on one bad day after another. That isn't fate. It's poor planning.

The one way to avoid being victimized by bad timing and to capitalize on good timing is to be sensitive to the individual buy/sell situation from the beginning of the sales call. We'll give you two examples to illustrate this, one positive and one negative. First, the negative example.

Alex was an industrious and persistent salesman who, a few years ago, managed to set up an appointment with the CEO of a major trucking firm. It had taken him months to arrange the top-level meeting, and he prepared for it with great care. But when he walked into the CEO's office, he made one mistake. He failed to pick up on the fact that the man was nervous and distracted. Even though he had honored the meeting time, it was clear that his mind was some-where else. Had Alex been sensitive to that fact, he would have asked if a different time would be better—and given him-self the opportunity of making this important presentation when the CEO could give him better attention. Instead, Alex bulldogged his way through the call and got nowhere. Later—too late to be useful—he found out that the CEO had been scheduled to undergo major surgery three days after their meeting. No wonder he had been distracted—and no wonder Alex had been ignored.

Now, maybe if he had allowed the preoccupied executive to reschedule, the eventual outcome would have been no better. But he would at least have had a fighting chance. As it was, by ignoring the signs of poor timing Alex virtually ensured a bad call. As he told us, "I realized an hour after I left that the guy hadn't heard a word I said." That's a typical outcome of badly timed sales calls.

Here's the positive example. Kate is a top-level field rep for a large office design firm. She recently encountered a situation very similar to Alex's, but she handled it entirely differently. When *her* fidgety, obviously distracted customer started to look like his mind was in Tahiti, she stopped the interview cold. "Mr. Hoskins," she said, "it seems as if you've got something else on your mind. If this is a bad time for us to talk, maybe you'd prefer that we reschedule the appointment."

Hoskins, Kate later told us, was "relieved, thankful, and impressed. He said he appreciated my thoughtfulness in picking up on his distraction. It turned out he had a meeting that afternoon about some recently purchased software and he was having trouble understanding the manual. Luckily, I knew that software, so I offered to give him a half-hour briefing on it in lieu of our scheduled interview. We didn't say two words about office design that day, but since then I've met him four times, and his firm has become my hottest account. What got him in my corner wasn't our products at all. It was being sensitive to where he was—spotting the symptoms that my timing was off."

TESTING THE WATERS

What Kate did with the fidgety Mr. Hoskins illustrates more than sensitivity. It illustrates the value, in every sales call, of testing the waters before you jump in. The credibility that Kate earned that day was the direct result of such testing: Before she got in over her head in the call, she tested where she was with a good question. In determining the rightness or wrongness of your timing, that is always a good model to follow.

You should always test the waters as *early* in the sales call as possible. In fact, it's not out of place to *begin* most sales calls with a timing question. Virtually every business call we make begins with an introductory confirmation that the timing for the call is all right. "Is this still a good time for you to talk?" or "Am I interrupting anything right now?" or "May I have ten minutes now or would it be better if I called you later?"

As you'll see in Chapter 10, these are examples of what we call Confirmation Questions. By asking them at the outset of the call, you gain two immediate advantages:

1. You demonstrate your courtesy—that you care about the client's needs and priorities. This signals the person that you are playing Win-Win—and instantly increases your credibility.
2. You give the client the opportunity to postpone or reschedule a call that is likely to end up as a Lose for you both because one of you will not really be "there." Thus you save yourself, and the client, from wasting time.

THE COURTESY TRAP—AND THE REVERSE

Two traps to look out for. The first might be called the courtesy trap. It's what happens when a busy or preoccupied client, not wanting to offend you or foul up your schedule, goes ahead with a prearranged sales call even though the timing is bad for her.

Don't mistake courtesy like this for proper timing. If a customer honors an appointment merely out of politeness, you stand a strong chance of making a presentation to someone who won't really be listening. Therefore, even if Mr. Hoskins says, "Yeah, I guess this time is as good as any," give him a second option to back out if you have any suspicion that he's just being polite. Be straight with him. "I appreciate that you're willing to go ahead at this time, but I think we'd get a lot more done if we could meet when it worked better for you. Are you sure you wouldn't prefer to reschedule?"

The second trap is the reverse of the first. It's mistaking a potential customer's *current* uneasiness about meeting with you or dealing with your proposal with a *general* rejection of the opportunities you might offer. If your proposal elicits nervousness, hostility, or silence, it's not necessarily because Hoskins hates your company and everything you stand for. Maybe you simply hit him on a bad day. To find out whether he's reacting to you and your proposal or merely to bad timing, follow the same course of action that you would when faced with the courtesy trap. Ask the necessary Confirmation Question.

WHEN TO CONFIRM AND RECONFIRM

We've said that checking your timing should be an ongoing procedure throughout the selling cycle. There are three important points when performing this check.

1. When you make and confirm the appointment. Nobody but a very disorganized person or a masochist will agree to meet you at a time that she knows is going to be terrible for her. But people *will* agree to appointments that are set at less than ideal times. When you call to set up an appointment, make sure you get it as close to the prospect's "ideal time slot" as you can—without, of course, wreaking havoc with your *own* schedule. If she agrees to Friday but seems uneasy about it, play it straight: "If there's a time for you that's better than Friday, tell me what it would be."

If you typically confirm your appointments by telephoning a day or two in advance of the sales call, this "setup" call is another time when you should verify the appropriateness of the timing. If you don't do this, we guarantee that you will run into cases where a time slot that was great when you made the initial appointment has in the meantime turned out to be all wrong.

2. At the beginning of the sales call. We stressed this earlier, but here's an additional point. It's often useful when you confirm the appropriateness of your timing at the opening of a call to establish the time *limits* also. "Is this still a convenient time for you to give me about half an hour?" If you don't verify the parameters of the meeting in this way, you may find yourself just getting down to business when Hoskins cuts you off in midstream. If your appointment is for 3 P.M. and you expect to be with him until 4, state that clearly at the outset so you won't be surprised by a 3:30 intruder.

3. Toward the end of the sales call. It is usually appropriate, before you end a sales call, to ask what we call a Commitment Question—that is, a question designed to elicit from the customer a promise to *do* something to move the sale forward. You can tie in questions like this with questions about her timing. "Will you be able to show these specs to the committee by the twenty-first, Jan?" Or "We can begin the installation process in March. Will that be a good match to your schedule?" Asking questions like these helps to move the selling process forward by defining *future* timing requirements.

In short, by checking your timing throughout the selling process, you stay in constant touch with the customer's inevitably changing priorities and needs. That does more than keep you alert to where you are in the sales call. By reminding the customer continually that you are thinking about his or her scheduling requirements, you also enhance the possibility of a Win-Win outcome and thus provide further assurance of your business credibility.

You've now been introduced to the four questions you must ask yourself before every sales call. In the next part of the book we move to questions that you must ask your customer as the first step in establishing superior customer communication.

PART III

THE SALES CALL: GETTING INFORMATION

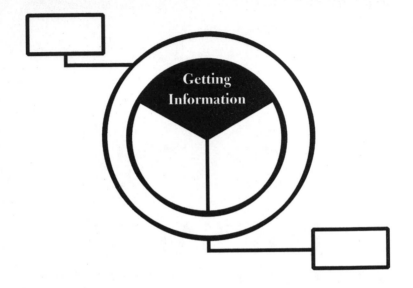

Getting
Information

CHAPTER 9

LEARNING TO LISTEN

Effective selling is the art of establishing *dialogue*. Because this is so, the greatest salespeople are seldom the fastest mouths in the West. In the vast majority of cases, sales success begins with the ability to ask good questions and then listen—really listen—to the answers.

There are plenty of reasons for asking good questions on a sales call. To cite only the most important:

- Good questioning allows you to identify clearly, and to qualify early in the selling process, not only the individual people you deal with but also their companies. It helps you get a handle at the outset on whether a given company is an appropriate account match for your company.

- It helps you to understand the current customer situation. Good questions can uncover the fact, for example, that a given customer, although a good bet in general, is not an appropriate prospect at the present time or for your Single Sales Objective.

- Good questioning at the outset of a sales call helps to establish the rapport that is so helpful in fostering fluid communication between buyer and seller: It helps to establish a comfort level between the two of you.

- Good questioning lets you determine where you do and where you do not understand the decision-making process of a given customer. It helps you avoid the all too common selling error of wasting your own and your customer's time by making the perfect presentation to the wrong person, in the wrong place, or at the wrong moment.

- It enables you to identify significant differences between your own capabilities and those of your competition. Good questioning can help you uncover your competitors' weaknesses and highlight your own strengths.

- Good questioning can reinforce your credibility with a customer by demonstrating to him that you are in fact interested in his needs and opinions, and not just in pushing your product.

- Finally, and arguably most important, good questioning can motivate and sustain your customer's interest, stimulate her thinking, and modify her attitudes—her Concept—regarding you and your product or service. In other words, it can generate a fluid communication process that gives both you and your customer the information that needs to be laid on the table to get you to a Win-Win conclusion.

Given these obvious advantages, you'd think most sales professionals would spend the bulk of their time planning good questions prior to the sales call, learning how to phrase

questions properly, and in general focusing on getting information. They don't. In fact, just the opposite occurs.

THE 80 PERCENT SYNDROME

Imagine popping your head in at random to observe 100 sales
calls. The focus of one call might be a $30 pair of shoes;
another might be about a $3 million computer system. One
call might be an initial meeting with a prospect, while on
another the salesperson might be two minutes from getting
the contract. Whatever the situations, we'll bet that 80 percent of the time, the person who's going to be talking when
you look in will be not the customer but the salesperson. This
is what we call the 80 Percent Syndrome.

It's a typical pattern in sales calls: Four out of every five
minutes the seller and the buyer are together, it's the seller
who is talking. Moreover, 80 percent of the time that the seller
is talking, guess what he's talking *about*. Is he focusing on the
customer or asking questions to uncover her Concept?
Rarely. Actually, 80 percent of the time the seller is talking, he
is *telling* the customer something—in other words, he's
making statements, not asking questions.

It gets worse. To take the 80 Percent Syndrome to its last,
fatal step, we'll make this observation: 80 percent of the time,
the statements the seller is making have to do not with the
customer's interests or needs, but with the virtues of the
seller's product or service. Most of the time, it's product pitch
with a vengeance: The seller spends the bulk of this valuable
face-to-face time pointing to bells and whistles, whether or
not the customer wants to see them.

What does this mean in terms of the average sales call?
Suppose you have an hour to spend with a given customer,

and you fall into the common 80 Percent Syndrome. In that precious hour, your time will be divided in the following way:

- About thirty-one minutes will be spent in telling the customer about your product or service.
- Another eight minutes will be spent in telling her something else—that is, in making other statements.
- About nine minutes will be spent in asking her questions.
- The remaining twelve minutes will be spent in listening to the customer.

The pie chart on page 185 indicates the total sixty minutes in our hypothetical sales call, and the breakdown indicates how much time, according to the 80 Percent Syndrome, the average salesperson will spend on each activity.

On calls lasting less than an hour, it gets even worse than that. In fact, the less time the average salesperson has to spend with the prospect or client, the greater chance he will spend the bulk of that time talking. If you've got only twenty minutes to tell your story and you have a headful of data to deliver, the natural temptation is to talk nonstop. The result can be disastrous. If you allow a customer only one minute out of every five to get a word in edgewise, the information you receive from him is naturally going to be inferior to what you would receive if you said less and listened more.

Why? Because it's a psychological fact that you cannot talk and listen at the same time. You may be able to vaguely "hear" background noise; you may convince yourself that you're picking up on body language and nonverbal cues; but if you're honest with yourself you'll admit that you can't really listen intelligently when you're giving a spiel. If you doubt that, ask a friend to read you a magazine article while you're

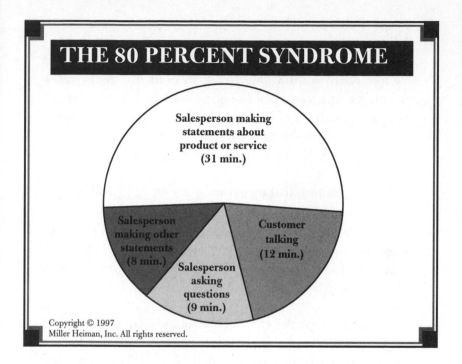

THE 80 PERCENT SYNDROME

Salesperson making statements about product or service (31 min.)

Salesperson making other statements (8 min.)

Salesperson asking questions (9 min.)

Customer talking (12 min.)

reading him or her another one. The only words either of you will hear will be those that sneak through when you pause for breath.

It's inevitable, therefore, that when you fall into the 80 Percent Syndrome *you will miss information you need* to make the sale work. Good selling begins not with Show and Tell, but with Getting Information—in other words, with learning. And you cannot learn effectively when you're talking.

WHY DO SALESPEOPLE TALK SO MUCH?

Why do sales professionals indulge themselves so frequently in this counterproductive habit? When we ask this question in our Conceptual Selling programs, we get answers like the following:

"I feel more comfortable being in control." Many salespeople fall into the trap of assuming that when they're talking, they are in control of the sale. Yet this equation of "talking" with "control" is almost always an illusion. It's a comforting illusion, however, and therefore a very common one.

"It's my job to tell the customer about the product." In other words, it's my job to engage in a product pitch—whoever the prospective client and no matter what his real need for what I might have to sell. The fatal assumption here is that *everybody* has a need for your product and that incessant chatter will make the need obvious.

"Talking is what the customer usually wants you to do." This chestnut is one of the most common excuses for not finding out what the customer is thinking. There is a tradition, we admit, of letting the seller do the talking, and there are many customers who are guilty of encouraging the 80 Percent Syndrome. Customers have to be educated, just like salespeople, to avoid it. But no matter what she says and no matter how sympathetic she may seem to your jabbering, no customer ever really *wants* the seller to do all the talking. If your quiet client didn't have anything else to say to you, after all, you'd already have her order in your pocket.

"Talking takes less planning." This is certainly true, and we're always gratified to hear this "explanation" from a program participant: It means she's already begun to think about planning her sales tactics in advance and has begun to realize that planning a sound questioning process often does take more work than doing one more review of the product specs. Many salespeople avoid questioning for this reason: It's much easier to run down the same old product line with every customer than it is to "customerize" a new set of questions for every encounter.

"Sometimes you're afraid to hear the answers." This honest response goes back to the seller's comfort level and to the illusion of control. It's true that when you ask a question, you might get an answer you don't want to hear. But the way to avoid this unpleasant possibility should never be to avoid asking the question. It should be to establish a questioning process that enables you to use *whatever* answers you get to better understand the situation.

THE QUESTIONING PROCESS

We say questioning *process* rather than questioning *techniques*. The distinction is crucial. Most sales training programs teach what the trainers call "questioning," but it's not really questioning at all. The "questioning skills" most programs teach are really only a series of manipulative tricks designed to make statements *sound* like questions.

You know the kind of "questions" we're talking about. The rhetorical come-ons like "Wouldn't you agree that's a good deal, Ms. Jones?"—where the only acceptable answer is Yes. The false-choice trial closes such as "Would you like to sign the contract today or this Friday?" And the whole game of "asking" for the order—which isn't asking at all, but only a sophisticated form of manipulation. This approach is summed up in the traditional selling advice: "Never ask a question to which you don't already know the answer."

Not only is this seemingly clever observation dead wrong, it can be dramatically counterproductive. What lies behind it are two related fears: the fear of being thought ignorant, and the fear of having the buy/sell dialogue go somewhere you hadn't anticipated. When you learn to listen, however, both of these fears soon vanish. You're happy to acknowledge your ignorance because you accept that as a necessary step in acquiring information. And you're comfortable with the dialogue going "off track" because you know that such "diversions" may help you to clarify your understanding. So the Conceptual Selling watchword is the reverse of the traditional one: "Never ask a question to which you already know the answer."

Traditional "questioning" teaches you how to *force answers*. That's the last thing we want to encourage. The point of asking good questions, as we define them, is never to "rephrase" a client's resistance or to "redirect" the course of an interview or to put the customer in a position where he's only allowed to say Yes. It's for you, the seller, to find out something you *don't* already know.

There's an irony here. Salespeople who are primarily interested in "asking for the order"—that is, forcing an answer—often find that getting the Yes answer they want is an uphill battle all the way. But when you use an effective questioning process, you often don't even have to ask for the order: The order happens almost automatically as a result of the other questions you've asked, your customer's responses to them, and the ensuing dialogue. In the words of one of our clients, health care executive Margaret Shiver, when you establish a real dialogue with a customer a mutually beneficial solution often "bubbles to the surface."

A sound questioning process enables you to maximize your cognition of the customer's situation as she perceives it.

This cognition, as we said in Chapter 2, is the first step in understanding the Concept. Working with this understanding, and using the questioning process we'll outline, you will be able to do something the traditional "go for the order" type of questioning actually *prevents* you from doing: You will be able to create a fluid communication process between you and your customer so that both of you always have the information you need to get yourselves, mutually, to Win-Win.

PERSONAL WORKSHOP #7: IDENTIFYING MISSING INFORMATION

Our questioning process begins with identifying those areas of the sale where you are currently lacking information. A number of areas are typically information-poor for sellers, and we'll present them to you here, as an informal laundry list that you can use as a reference point throughout the rest of the book. In our programs we find that this exercise in exposing information gaps provides a helpful starting point for people unfamiliar with our kind of questioning. So set aside about ten or fifteen minutes and ask yourself the questions that follow. In thinking about each of these questions, keep your Single Sales Objective in mind. You might want to write down brief comments to yourself, under a heading "Missing Information."

Step 1: Do I need information about the customers involved? In our Strategic Selling programs, we use the term *Buying Influence* to refer to anyone who can have a positive or negative impact on your selling—whatever his position, whatever his company, and whatever his role in a given sale. You should look at each customer you call on as a Buying Influence. And because the roles played by these Buying Influences are diverse and frequently changing, you should begin your information analysis by determining whether you know *all* the Buying Influences for each upcoming sales call. To do that, ask yourself:

- Who will have final *approval authority* for the Single Sales Objective I'm currently pursuing?
- Which person or persons in the buying organization will actually *use* (or manage the use of) the product or service I'm selling?
- Which person or persons will be *judging* my proposal?
- Do I have a *guide*—that is, someone who can provide me with reliable information—for this sale?
- With regard to the individual I'm going to be calling on next: What is this person's *degree of influence* in the sale?

Step 2: Do I need information about the customer's Concept? Each of the various people involved in a sale will, of course, have his or her own solution image regarding your proposal. With regard to the person you're going to be calling on in your next sales call, ask:

- Is this person's Concept *clear* to me and to the customer himself or herself?
- What is this person trying to *accomplish, fix,* or *avoid?*
- What are the specific, measurable *results* that he or she expects to gain from doing business with me?
- What *degree of risk* does this person perceive in our potential transaction?

Step 3: Do I need information about the account's buying process? Since corporate purchasing structures and buying procedures vary dramatically from company to company, and since they may even change from time to time within the same company, you need to be clear on how decisions are being made, right now, within this account. Ask yourself: What do I need to find out about:

- the money that needs to be allocated for my sale
- the urgency of my proposal to the company or customer—that is, whether or not my timing is right
- "political" factors in the buying organization, such as turf battles that may affect how decisions are made
- any other factors that may be currently beyond my control

Step 4: Do I need information about possible new players? In Strategic Selling we identify typical Red Flag, or danger, areas in managing sales. One of these danger areas is the appearance of new players or the rearrangement of existing players. To locate potential problems here, ask:

- Have there been any recent changes in the lineup of key decision-makers for this sale? Is there a new face on the scene, and if so, do I understand his possible influence on the sale?
- Has there been reorganization recently in the customer's organization—no matter how seemingly "trivial" or "irrelevant" to my proposal?
- Am I certain that the person giving final approval for this sale has not changed?

Step 5: Do I need information about the competition? Since you don't sell in a vacuum, and since your customer's Concept can always be influenced by your competition, you need to ask:

- Who does the customer see as my main competitors for this sale?
- What are these competitors' primary strengths and weaknesses?
- What is the price differential between their likely solution and mine—and is price a major factor to the customer?
- What is the availability of the principal competitors' products?
- How are they positioned with the customer? Are they new players, running neck and neck with me, or firmly entrenched?

Step 6: Do I need information about my own uncertainties or worries? One of the deadliest sales errors is to ignore gray areas in the vain hope that the problems will go away if you don't think about them too much. Be particularly attentive to exposing information gaps in this area. If you're feeling at all uncertain or worried about an upcoming sales call, ask yourself:

- In what areas could I profit from having more information? Or, to put it negatively, where is a lack of information contributing to my uncertainty?
- Is there an uncovered base here? That is, is there a decision-maker or influence for this sale I haven't identified, I feel uncomfortable about, or I can't get to?
- Does the sales picture include a strong anti-sponsor— someone who feels he or she will lose if I achieve my objective?
- What's my credibility level with key people in the buying organization and, specifically, with the person I'll be meeting in this call?

- What's the *real* fit (not a wish-fulfillment one) between my product or service and the customer's needs? If there's not a real fit, what am I doing here?

The point of going through a checklist like this one, and in doing so before every sales call, is to make clear to yourself where you are missing the information you need to manage the sale and the call well. The first order of business on every sales call should be to seek out that information. You do that, naturally enough, by asking your customer questions.

DEVELOPING QUESTIONS: THREE GUIDELINES

But you don't ask just any questions. We recommend that you follow three criteria in developing questions for an upcoming sales call. You can improve the quality of your calls 100 percent just by spending five minutes before each call thinking about these three points. The questions you ask must:

1. Elicit the information you need. We mean the most urgent and important facts. Obviously, Ms. Jones is not going to have the time or the interest or probably the expertise to fill in every gap on your checklist herself—at least not in a single sales call. That's why, as you're focusing on what you need to find out, you should narrow the gaps down to a manageable five or six. Choose missing pieces of information that you can reasonably expect to get and that are urgent in terms of the way you perceive the sale to be going.

2. Be phrased in an effective manner. You can identify very precisely what you need to find out, but you'll still fail to get that information if you phrase your questions badly. In developing questions it's important to word them so that you don't get loaded, self-serving, or defensive answers.

3. Be presented in an appropriate sequence. What would happen in a sales call if the first question you presented to the customer was "How about signing this order?" Or if the last one was "How do you do?" No matter how appropriate your questions, and no matter how well they are phrased, you can still come up dry on the needed information if you ask the questions in the wrong order.

The checklist we presented in this chapter will help you think in a more focused manner about the first criterion, the areas where you're missing information. In the following chapter we'll zero in more closely on those areas and provide a detailed explanation of how to use the second and third criteria. We'll show you (a) how to select the most appropriate questions for a given sales call, (b) how to phrase those questions most effectively, and (c) how to arrange them in a sequence that will create a positive flow of information between you and each of your customers.

CHAPTER 10

THE FIVE QUESTION TYPES

Since good selling means searching for a fit between your product or service and the customer's Concept, your principal attitude in a sales call should be that of an interviewer—a specialist in the art of asking questions. In Conceptual Selling we define five types of questions that should be asked in every sales call interview. Each type has its own distinctive purpose; that is, each one is designed to elicit a unique and specific kind of information. Each type is phrased in a specific manner, using distinctive key words. And as you put the five types of questions together into an effective interviewing process, you should also give some attention to their sequence.

Before we go into detail about the purpose, phrasing, and sequencing of the five question types, here are some thumbnail definitions.

1. *Confirmation Questions* validate your data or reveal inaccuracies in what you thought was true.

2. *New Information Questions* force you to listen and accept the reality of current data; they help you clarify the customer's Concept and desired business results.
3. *Attitude Questions* identify the customer's personal needs, values, and attitudes.
4. *Commitment Questions* help you locate your current position in the sale by identifying what action the customer is willing to take to move things forward.
5. *Basic Issue Questions* are specialized Commitment Questions that help you identify customer concerns that could result in the loss of the sale.

We'll discuss Commitment Questions and Basic Issue Questions in Part 5. This chapter concentrates on the first three types of questions. We begin with the one type that should always be asked near the beginning of a sales call, but that few salespeople ever ask at all: the Confirmation Question.

CONFIRMATION QUESTIONS

As our thumbnail definition illustrates, Confirmation Questions have a dual purpose. They help you to verify information you already have—or think you have—and they help you to discern discrepancies in it. The answer you get to a Confirmation Question, therefore, can either validate or invalidate the data you think you have as you enter the sales call. Either way, these questions provide you with the up-to-date picture you need to be able to proceed effectively with the call. It's especially important to be current with regard to

- your customer's Concept
- business issues that may have arisen since your last meeting
- any possible changes in organizational structure

But these are only three of the most common areas. You should use Confirmation Questions to check the accuracy of *any* and *all* data.

As an example of a good Confirmation Question, think back to the story we told in the first chapter about our friend Gene, the food service sales representative who secured a major contract by doing more asking than telling. Going into the initial call, he knew the potential client had been having trouble with its current food service supplier and was looking for a replacement. To check the validity of this basic "entry data," Gene began the sales call by asking: "Do I understand correctly that you're dissatisfied with the way your food service operation is currently being run?"

As it happened, the answer he got to that question confirmed what he already believed. In a different scenario, the customer might have told him, "No, we don't have any service complaints—we're just looking for a better price." But that invalidation, no less than the confirmation he actually got, would have told him right at the outset what he was dealing with. Whatever answers you get to your Confirmation Questions, they will always give you more up-to-date information than you could possibly have if you didn't ask. That is why it is foolish to avoid Confirmation Questions and why it is usually appropriate to begin a sales call by asking one.

CONFIRMATION QUESTIONS

PURPOSE:
- **Verify what is known about:**
    - **Each customer's Concept**
    - **Business issues**
    - **Organizational structure**
    - **Data accuracy**
- **Reveal discrepancies in the current information**

WHEN USED:
- **At the beginning of a sales call**
- **Before presenting any new product/service**
- **To build a foundation before moving forward**

PHRASING CONFIRMATION QUESTIONS

The focus of a good Confirmation Question is always the *current* situation. By asking a Confirmation Question, you're trying to determine what's happening right now—and by implication, whether what's happening now is different from what was happening a week or a month ago.

Three phrasing techniques can help you accomplish this. First, always phrase your Confirmation Questions in the *present tense*. Second, use *key words* that signal the customer that you are asking for information about the present. "Does inventory *continue* to be a problem?" "Are you *still* using the

X4000 models?" Other key words that are useful in phrasing Confirmation Questions are *remain, as usual, now, currently,* and *at the present time.* Third, phrase Confirmation Questions

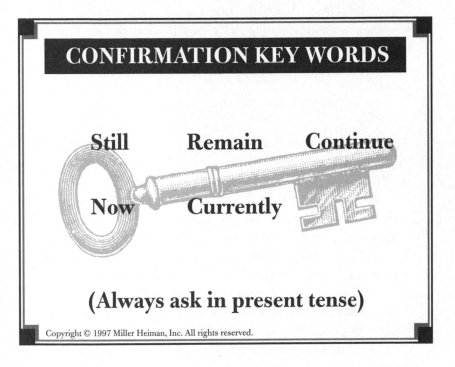

CONFIRMATION KEY WORDS

Still   **Remain**   **Continue**

Now   **Currently**

(Always ask in present tense)

so they can be answered by a simple Yes or No. When you ask a Confirmation Question, you already have an idea in your mind as to what the current situation is. Either that idea is correct, or it isn't. Hence Yes or No.

Many times, when you're having trouble phrasing an appropriate Confirmation Question you can shift to a statement-question combination by first making a statement that you believe to be true about the past and then asking, "Is this still the case?" If Mr. Johnson has been having inventory control problems, for example, you could begin the sales call by saying, "The last time I was here, you were experiencing database problems with the inventory system. Are you still having those problems?" Again, the point is that you want accurate information about possible discrepancies between your view of the situation and what that situation actually is right now.

WHEN TO USE CONFIRMATION QUESTIONS

In emphasizing the value of Confirmation Questions early in the sales call, we have suggested that you may want to open most sales calls by asking this type of question. One good way of doing this is to verify the *purpose of the meeting,* as you understand it, in the form of a Confirmation Question: "As I understand it, Sarah, what we had planned to do today is assess your finance committee's reaction to my last presentation. Is that your understanding?" This has the double advantage of confirming the situation *and* confirming the agenda.

We realize that to salespeople who have been trained to open with polite chitchat in order to establish "rapport," the suggestion that they open with a question may sound iconoclastic. So it is—but we're not saying you should avoid the customary "How's the family?" exchanges. If it makes you comfortable to open with these pleasantries, fine; we don't advise you to drop anything that puts you or your customers at ease. But remember that the chitchat is preliminary. It's not part of the sales call proper. Once you're ready to get down to business, you've got to verify your information quickly. Never assume that because you've established rapport with Mr. Johnson, you can jump safely into a product demonstration and skip the data confirmation.

Salespeople sometimes make this mistake because they imagine that customers buy from them out of friendship. "I got that contract," you'll hear, "because they like me." Wrong. Nobody buys anything simply because the salesperson is "well liked." So begin the conversation, if you wish, with the chitchat that makes you both relaxed. But (a) keep it short because your time is valuable, and so is your customer's, and (b) once you begin the substantive part of the sales call—once the emphasis shifts from the social niceties to the business at hand—always consider beginning with a Confirmation Question.

You should also use Confirmation Questions immediately before presenting the customer with any new product or service data. This will maximize the chances that a possible fit actually exists between the product or service you're going to describe and the real needs of the customer, as she understands them. A pre-presentation Confirmation Question helps you clarify the customer's Concept; if you fail to ask one, you may default into product pushing.

Confirmation Questions are also valuable when you are building a foundation for moving the sale forward. As you get closer to taking a customer's order, two things happen. One, your own confidence begins to rise. Two, your vulnerability rises precisely because you're becoming more confident. As they proceed through all the complexities of a drawn-out selling process and it looks as though the order is a certainty, many salespeople fall prey to a dangerous assumption: that the customer's needs have not substantially changed since the first sales call. Since customers' needs are in fact changing all the time, it's important to keep asking Confirmation Questions all the way through the process, from prospecting to close.

New Information Questions

The second type of question to be asked on every sales call is the New Information Question. Usually, these questions follow up and build on Confirmation Questions by asking for more clarification.

The purpose of New Information Questions is threefold: (1) to clarify your understanding of what your customer is trying to accomplish, fix, or avoid; (2) to update your information; and (3) to resolve your information discrepancies by filling in the gaps. On the Chicago food service call, Gene followed up his Confirmation Question with the following New Information Questions: "What's been happening in your current operation that you'd like to see not happening?" and "Would you describe what a good food service contract would look like to you?" Other examples might include questions like the following:

- "How do you intend to approach that problem?"
- "When do you see this decision happening?"
- "Where is the project likely to be situated?"

PHRASING NEW INFORMATION QUESTIONS

As these examples suggest, there's a similarity between our recommendation that you ask New Information Questions and the traditional journalistic advice that a lead paragraph focus on the "Five Ws": the *who, what, when, where,* and *why* of the situation. In formulating New Information Questions, we advise you to use the same key words—with one important exception. Instead of asking "why," we say you should ask "how" or "how much" or "how many." "Why" can be useful

NEW INFORMATION QUESTIONS

PURPOSE:
- Better understand what the customer is trying to accomplish, fix, or avoid
- Update information
- Identify missing information

WHEN USED:
- When encouraging a customer to explore his/her Concept openly
- In response to an unexpected No answser to a Confirmation Question
- When information is missing or unclear

as a kind of second-level probe, to follow up on an insufficiently answered New Information Question; but as an opener it can be confrontational, and it seldom gets you the information you need. We'll talk more about "why" in the following chapter.

New Information Questions that begin with the key words *who, what, when, where,* and *how* make up only one subset of this question type, however. They are what we call *explicit* questions since they ask the customer to provide very specific new information: "Where will the new plant be located?" "How many units are processed per month?" A second subset includes what we call *exploratory* questions.

Exploratory questions invite the customer to explore, at

her own level of detail, an area where you need more information. They begin with key words like *tell, explain, demonstrate,* and *show.* Like explicit questions, these questions seek further information, but they do so in a more open, expansive manner. To understand the distinction, look at the two questions Gene asked the food service selection committee. The first one ("What's been happening . . .?") is an explicit question that begins with one of the journalist's opening key words. The second one ("Would you describe . . .?") is an exploratory question that begins with a modified form of the key words *explain* or *show.*

Since people are sometimes resistant to being told "Show me," we suggest using a technique that makes exploratory New Information Questions sound less confrontational. You can mute the perceived aggressiveness of a question—and this goes for any question, not just New Information Questions—by phrasing it indirectly, by employing such structures as "I'd like to . . ." or "I'd appreciate it if you would . . ." or simply "Could you . . . ?" Gene's second question is an example. To a customer who is sensitive to being told to do something, the expression "I'd appreciate hearing more" may get you better results than the direct "Tell me more."

WHEN TO USE NEW INFORMATION QUESTIONS

You use a New Information Question whenever you discover that you are missing specific information regarding the current status of the sale. Obviously this can occur at any point in the sales call. We've already emphasized that New Information Questions can be valuable in following up on Confirmation Questions, and this is especially so when you get an unexpected No answer to the Confirmation Question. If you've just asked your customer whether or not she's still using 1,400 units a week and you find out she's upped it to 2,000, it's time for you to get New Information: The follow-up question might be something like "What's happened since the last time I saw you?" or "Could you tell me some more about the reasons for the increase?" Whenever you discover that the data you thought you had is inaccurate, it's time to ask a New Information Question.

New Information Questions are also appropriate whenever you want to encourage the customer to explore the situation freely, on his own terms. As we've emphasized earlier, contrary to popular opinion, customers generally want to talk and will do so at length if you give them the opportunity. Because of this, New Information Questions often give you an added benefit on top of the missing information: They tend to put people more at ease. And someone who is at ease with you is more likely to *keep* giving you information.

In short, it is appropriate to ask a New Information Question at any point you feel you have exposed a gap in your information. Your prospect's pen may be poised above the contract, but if he says something at that moment that isn't crystal clear to you, ask a New Information Question fast, or expect trouble down the line.

Here's a concrete example. A friend of ours recently was literally seconds away from having a major customer sign a contract for a multimillion-dollar industrial sale. The customer was a regional development manager, and as he was putting pen to paper he casually mentioned, "Now this just has to go to Division for the rubber stamp, and we're all set." At that point our friend *should* have said, "Just a second, Phil. Who do you mean by Division, and could you tell me some

NEW INFORMATION KEY WORDS

What	Where	When
How	How much	How many
Elaborate	Show me	Explain to me
Describe to me	Demonstrate	Tell me

(Be cautious when using "Why")

more about the 'rubber stamp' mechanism?" He didn't. He let Phil sign the paper and send it on to Division—and he never saw a commission. By failing to ask a New Information Question at a point where he obviously lacked a crucial piece of information, our friend assumed his way out of the sale.

ATTITUDE QUESTIONS

While New Information Questions focus chiefly on the customer's desired results, Attitude Questions focus on how she

ATTITUDE QUESTIONS

PURPOSE:
- **Uncover individual needs, desires, concerns, and feelings**
- **Discover unidentified issues**
- **Understand attitudes and values**

WHEN USED:
- **To understand the customer's feelings**
- **To get the customer's perspective on the feelings of others involved**
- **To understand the real issues**

personally *feels* about those results. The purpose of an Attitude Question is to get the customer to reveal personal information—information about how she, individually, will win or lose in this sale. Such questions seek to discover the individual customer's values and attitudes, which are so important in determining Concept. Because these questions get at those values and attitudes, they also frequently serve to uncover unidentified personal concerns that an "objective" New Information Question can't uncover.

Many salespeople resist asking Attitude Questions for a variety of reasons. They may believe that personal feelings are irrelevant in a work situation or that what a customer feels is none of their business. They may say it's just not their "style" to ask such questions, or they may feel uncomfortable or embarrassed about asking them. For many salespeople, the old *Dragnet* line, "Just the facts, ma'am," seems to serve as an unwritten motto.

Stephanie Kuhnel, who supervises the implementation of Conceptual Selling at our corporate client SAS Institute, is extremely familiar with this reaction. "For some salespeople," she says, "asking an Attitude Question clashes with their personal selling pattern. In practice sessions, many of them will argue against a 'warm-and-fuzzy' approach, or they'll claim— and this is really common—that it's considered *unprofessional* to ask such questions. Often, even when they do uncover a customer's feelings about a problem, their immediate response isn't to acknowledge the feelings but to jump right into solution mode: 'What do you want me to *do* about this problem?' They're very results-oriented, and you'll hear any number of so-called reasons why you shouldn't go beyond that."

Gender may be a factor here. As Stephanie acknowledges, "In our society, women get a lot more practice in exchanging their feelings, and so women in sales may be somewhat more comfortable than their male counterparts in exploring the attitudinal elements of a selling encounter." Like the men described in Deborah Tannen's best-selling study of male and female conversational styles, *You Just Don't Understand,* many salesmen tend to gravitate to a "fix the problem" approach, while women may be quicker to understand that a customer's feelings are, in almost all cases, *part* of the problem.

Whatever role gender may play, however, ignoring the customer's attitudes is always a mistake. No single factor in sales is more important than what your customer is feeling, personally, about what you're trying to sell him. Personal feelings are central to a customer's Concept, and if you do not understand the Concept, you're not even at square one.

That's one reason Attitude Questions are so important: They expose gaps in your information about the one thing that drives the sale: the customer's mental picture of what buying from you can do for him or her. There's also a second, related reason—one that also overturns the conventional wisdom about customers' feelings. It's that the vast majority of customers *want* to talk about their feelings. They welcome the opportunity to react personally to a sales proposal, and the salesperson who gives them that opportunity has an immediate and enormous advantage over the competition.

We don't mean that people want you to be their therapist, and we're well aware that some people are reluctant to tell you anything but "the facts." But when we advise you to ask Attitude Questions, we're not talking about in-depth psychology or about the old "I'm your pal, Joe, you can level with me" line that is a favorite ploy of manipulative salespeople. We mean simply that you should take a customer's attitude about your product or service as a critical factor in the sale and that you should no more ignore it than you would ignore your own product specs or service capabilities.

It's especially important to remember this when you sense an uneasiness or reluctance that your New Information Questions have not been able to explain. A good example occurred in Gene's food service call.

Typically, food service is partially subsidized by the employees' corporation: It is an overhead cost that is budgeted as part of employee benefits. "When we started talking about subsidies," Gene told us after his Chicago call, "the committee just grimaced, and I realized it was time for an Attitude Question. I asked them how they felt about having to subsidize the food service operation. What I got was amazing. They went on for fifteen minutes expressing their resentment at the subsidy structure, and that gave me a lot of information about the operation that I hadn't even asked for. In the course of their gripe session, for example, all kinds of new information surfaced about the pricing schedule, the in-house supervision arrangement, employee relations—I obviously had tapped a nerve, and it turned into an information bonanza."

As Gene's description indicates, not only do Attitude Questions often open up the discussion with regard to the customer's feelings, but they also bring the salesperson a great deal of "hard," nonsubjective information that the Attitude Question wasn't even asking for. So by using New Information Questions and Attitude Questions together, you can generate an enormous amount of information in a relatively short period of time.

PHRASING ATTITUDE QUESTIONS

Since the goal of Attitude Questions is to elicit information about personal values and attitudes, these questions typically use key words like *what, which, why,* and *how* in conjunction with phrasing that encourages a judgment: "What is your opinion about . . .?" "How did Kate in Finance react to the prospectus?" And, most commonly, "How do you feel . . .?" New Information Questions and Attitude Questions, therefore, both use the journalist's openers. But the Attitude Ques-

ATTITUDE KEY WORDS

What   **Which**
How   **Describe**

Use these words in conjunction with words that
solicit a feeling or opinion, such as:

Opinion   **Feeling**
Reaction   **Attitude**

(Be cautious when using "Why")

tion uses these key words to set up a probe for a value judgment. As we said, it's not appropriate to use the key word *why* to solicit New Information, but it's fine in an Attitude Question.

A cautionary note, though. When you use *why* in forming an Attitude Question, remember that you are seeking out the person's judgment, not challenging or questioning it. As any parent of a three-year-old will tell you, this little word can be one of the most aggravating sounds in the language if it is overused or if it is used in a teasing, interrogative manner. Since every good sale starts with your customer's Concept, the last thing you want to do with a *why* question is to give anyone the message that you think his Concept is invalid or that he has "no good reason" for his opinion. Therefore, use the *why* format sparingly, and make it clear by your tone of voice that you are trying to understand, not criticize.

One other proviso. Although these tips for framing Attitude Questions have proved useful for most of our clients, you should use whatever makes you and your customers most comfortable. The phrasing of questions can be a personal thing, as one of our instructors, Liz Zagorodney, discovered in a recent workshop when she asked a group to frame practice Attitude Questions. These participants sold drilling equipment to Texas oil companies, and they weren't very comfortable asking how their customers "felt."

"Well, what would you do," Liz challenged them, "if you promised to deliver some equipment and the shipment was late? How would you determine whether the customer was angry or not?"

They thought about it for a few moments, puzzled, until one of them finally came up with this suggested Attitude Question: "I reckon just about now you want to shoot my dog, don't you?" It probably wouldn't have played too well in Boston, but somewhere west of Dallas it came out just fine. The point is to use what *you* need in *your* selling situations to gauge *your* customer's state of mind.

WHEN TO USE ATTITUDE QUESTIONS

Use an Attitude Question whenever you need a better understanding of how your customer feels about your being there and about what you're trying to sell her. You can also use Attitude Questions to solicit information about the personal feelings of *other* people in the buying organization whose attitudes and Concepts might affect your sale. Although it's best to find out about each individual's feelings directly, sometimes the only way to discover someone's attitude is to ask someone else. Finally, you can use Attitude Questions to help you understand the real issues—both corporate and personal—that may be involved in your selling proposal.

Attitude Questions are important specifically when you need to identify how a given individual will "win" or "lose" with your sale. Since in a complicated corporate sale there may be many individuals involved, and since no two of them will "win" in the same way, it's important to keep on top of each person's personal reasons for wanting or not wanting to buy. Attitude Questions help you to accomplish that.

Attitude Questions also help you determine what's behind the results a given customer wants—or says she wants. Different customers will want the same result for different reasons, and this means that each one's Concept of the result you can deliver is going to be different. Therefore, Attitude Questions should always be used when you know that Jill wants the Model 1205 but aren't sure exactly why. If you sell her the Model 1205 without understanding what that does for her personally, you're still selling with inadequate information, and that may undermine your relationship with her, if not on this sale then on future ones.

Better than any other kind of question, Attitude Questions help you focus, on every sales call and through all the stages of a long selling cycle, on the person behind the title on the door. So they are always appropriate when you need to know more about what makes that person tick.

As we've mentioned, we'll discuss the fourth and fifth types of question—the Commitment Question and the Basic Issue Question—in Part 5, "The Sales Call: Getting Commitment." Now it's time for you to apply the lessons of Confirmation Questions, New Information Questions, and Attitude Questions to your own selling situations.

Personal Workshop #8: Questioning

In Personal Workshop #7 we presented you with a checklist of common problem areas—areas where salespeople typically lack information—and asked you to identify, with regard to your own sales situations, the areas where you were information-poor. You're now going to take that process of identifying gaps one step further by drafting questions that you can use on your next sales call to get the information you're missing. The following exercise, which includes four steps, should take you about fifteen minutes.

Step 1: Select your critical areas. First, taking a closer look at the information-poor areas you identified on the checklist, zero in on no more than five or six areas where you are (a) most in need of information now, and (b) most likely to get that information from the person you're next calling on. In other words, select a manageable handful of problem areas that are both urgent and feasible areas to attack, given the sales call coming up.

By "urgent" we mean something you need to know now—something you need to know before you can move the call toward the next level of commitment. If you're about to make a second call on Mr. Chadwick, and you know that the typical selling process to a company like his takes six months, it's not urgent for you to know now all the details of the final contract review process. If you're two weeks from a close and you still don't know those details, that is an urgent area of missing information.

	Confirmation	New Information	Attitude
Buying Influences			
Customer's Concept			
Buying Process			
New Players			
Competition			
Uncertainties			

By "feasible" we mean information the specific person you're calling on can actually get his hands on and will be willing to give to you. There's no point in asking a vice president in charge of operations how many units rolled off Line 32 last week and no point in asking a plant manager details about the corporate P&L profile. You know who your customers are, and you know (or should know) their individual areas of expertise and responsibility. As you're zeroing in on the five or six areas where you need information on the next sales call, be sure the person you're calling on has responsibility in those areas—or at least can point you to someone who does.

Once you've selected the five or six most important areas, write them down in your notebook. You don't need to go into detail, and you don't need to phrase questions at this point. Just make yourself some notes about the areas where you're lacking in information. The list might include things like "Need to know more about purchasing decisions in Louisville plant" or "Need information about competitor's new line." When you're finished, you'll have a brief and very focused list of problem (and opportunity) areas.

Step 2: Construct your Question Grid. Now that you've narrowed down the areas where you need information to the five or six most important, the next step is to construct a planning device that will help you organize those problem areas most effectively so that you can ask the right questions in the upcoming sales call. We call that device a Question Grid.

First, down the left-hand edge of a page, write the brief descriptions of the problem areas that we laid out in Personal Workshop #7; see the sample on page 215. Then divide the rest of the page vertically into three columns, and at the head of the columns, write the first three question types: Confirmation, New Information, and Attitude.

Step 3: Categorize your problem areas. Now, go back to the checklist and put each of your five or six critical problem areas under the appropriate category in the lefthand vertical column. We've written in a couple of examples on page 218 to show you what we mean.

Step 4: Phrase appropriate questions. Now, using appropriate key words, draft questions designed to get you the information you need in each of your five or six information-poor areas. Write them in on the Question Grid, as in the examples given on page 219.

This exercise isn't "20 Questions," and you shouldn't be trying to fill in all the boxes. The goal is not quantity or "completeness" but quality. You may come up with questions in every question-type category and you may not; you may come up with no questions in a given category and several questions in another. That's fine. As long as each question you draft is phrased so that it will be most likely to elicit the information you need, then this exercise will have its maximum effect.

To check the effectiveness of your questions, we suggest you ask yourself the following:

- For every Confirmation Question: Is this question phrased to help me verify (validate or invalidate) the data I already have?
- For every New Information Question: Is this question designed to help me update my information, fill in the gaps, resolve discrepancies, and/or get information about my customer's desired results?
- For every Attitude Question: Is this question likely to give me information about this person's individual

	Confirmation	New Information	Attitude
Buying Influences			
Customer's Concept			
Buying Process *Purchasing in Louisville plant			
New Players			
Competition *Their new line			
Uncertainties			

	Confirmation	New Information	Attitude
Buying Influences			
Customer's Concept			
Buying Process *Purchasing in Louisville plant	"Is Charley still involved in this type of purchase?"	"What's his current role?"	
New Players			
Competition *Their new line	"Am I correct that you now have a second supplier?"		"How do the quality control people feel about this line?"
Uncertainties			

values, attitudes, needs, and opinions regarding my current proposal?

Although we don't advise you to simply "fill in the grid," we do suggest that you try to come up with at least one well-phrased question in each of the three question categories. We say this because if left to their own "traditional" questioning, many sales professionals spend the majority of their time drafting nothing but New Information Questions. Those questions are essential, but you cannot manage a sales call profitably by relying on them alone.

With the questions you've written in on the Question Grid, you should now be in a much better position to get the information you need to get on your upcoming sales call. As we've said, though, before you actually ask those questions you need to do some thinking about sequence.

SEQUENCE GUIDELINES

You should think about sequence before the sales call begins in order to avoid the common error of subjecting your customer to a barrage of disconnected queries—and to be able to direct the dialogue in a way that is profitable to you both. In ordering your questions in the most effective sequence, remember the following:

- It is almost always safe to *begin* a sales call interview with a Confirmation Question. These questions can also be used before presenting new product data and in building a foundation for a close.
- New Information Questions are an appropriate *follow-up* to Confirmation Questions, especially when the response

to the Confirmation Question is unexpected. They are also appropriate when you are missing information or want to open up the interview.

- Attitude Questions are used when you want to identify the personal needs, interests, and concerns of an individual customer or prospect: that is, when you want to get more information about the *feelings* behind someone's answers.

An important proviso is in order here, however. We present the first three question types in this sequence because we have found that, as a general guide, this 1-2-3 sequence is an appropriate one. But this is not an "ideal" sequence, and it's certainly not meant to be viewed as a "best practice" game plan. In an actual sales call, for example, you may have to ask several of one type of question before going on to another type. Or the answer to an Attitude Question may suggest that you have misunderstood something basic about the situation—and lead you to a Confirmation Question to clarify your understanding. In addition, of course, your prospect or customer will have his own agenda and will be asking you questions. All of which will make it unlikely that you can follow any rigid model with success.

We've criticized track selling for exactly this kind of rigidity, and we need to emphasize that sticking to any prepared list and ticking off items as you go is an almost ironclad guarantee that you will not get the information you need. Good sales call management, like good interviewing, is always a matter of being responsive to the individual situation—and to the moment-to-moment changes in that situation. So the best way to know when to ask a given question is to *remain attentive to what your customer is telling you.* The best sequence of questions in the world can still turn into a non-productive monologue unless the questioner puts constant energy into listening.

We'll talk more about the art of listening now.

CHAPTER 11

ESTABLISHING SUPERB COMMUNICATION

The best questions in the world won't do you a bit of good if you don't listen, and listen carefully, to the answers. We made this point in a general way in Chapter 9. In this chapter we're going to get more specific by providing you with tested techniques to improve your listening. We begin by suggesting that selling is a form of *teaching*, and we encourage you to follow the example of the world's best teachers—precisely because those teachers are such expert listeners.

According to studies done by educational researchers a number of years ago, the most effective teachers almost invariably employ an instructional style with the following characteristics:

- The teacher and student participate in a mutual *dialogue*, rather than one being the "sender" and another the "receiver."
- There are longer and more numerous *pauses* between

questions and answers   than you typically see in less effective teaching styles.

Since we are convinced that the teaching process and the Getting Information phase of a good selling process are very similar in terms of information flow, we long ago incorporated these findings into our own area of expertise and made them a basic element of Conceptual Selling.

The results have been extremely encouraging. By employing the best teachers' dialogue style, we have found, our clients are able to dramatically improve the flow between themselves and their customers and are able consistently to achieve Superb Communication. In this chapter we'll be describing Superb Communication more fully and explaining how you can make it happen in every face-to-face encounter.

QUESTION SHOCK

We say that the dialogue teaching style involves longer pauses between questions and answers than other teaching styles. That's not an incidental observation. Nor is that seemingly simple feature—the extending of the length of time between questions and answer—merely a teaching or conversational gimmick. It is a universally reliable technique for creating Superb Communication. But unfortunately this simple technique is not popular among salespeople.

Many salespeople, when they take the time to ask questions at all, seem less interested in hearing the customer's responses than in getting as quickly as possible to the end of a list. You know the kind of rhetorical, rapid-fire questioning we mean. It's the style the Music Man uses when he asks and then answers his own question: "Am I right? You know I am." It's the style the old-time drummer uses when he asks "What can I sell you today?" and immediately responds "How about a nice bottle of Sam Slick's Superfine Snake Oil #31?" And it's the style that seems to be favored by journalists in political press conferences: "I have a follow up question, Mr. President, and then a follow-up to the follow-up."

This type of questioning style—throwing all your queries in the listener's lap at the same time—may be unavoidable in a thirty-minute press conference, where each questioner is jockeying for position with twenty competitors. But it seldom leads to Superb Communication. In fact, what this machine-gun interrogation style usually leads to is exactly the opposite. It leads to the person being questioned clamming up or dodging the question or scratching her head in bewilderment.

You see this all the time in press conferences, and it doesn't necessarily happen because the person being questioned is being evasive (although that's obviously sometimes a factor). Sometimes it happens because he is suffering Question Shock. Question Shock is what happens when Sam Donaldson strings together fourteen probing queries in one sentence and asks the politician to field them all at once. Sam's got the questions written down and he's rehearsed them, so there's little chance that *he'll* be confused. But the politician doesn't have them written down, and he hasn't rehearsed fourteen replies, so there's a better than even chance that he *will* be confused. No matter how bright you are and how experienced you are at thinking on your feet, if somebody zaps you with more demands for information than you can adequately process on the spur of the moment, you are going to experience some level of cognitive confusion. That confusion is what we call Question Shock.

This is just as relevant to selling as it is to politics. If you assault your customers with a steady barrage of questions, if you are continually ready to pounce with a follow-up probe, if you anticipate their answers or answer your own questions, you are going to send your customers into Question Shock. And you are going to throw a logjam into the information flow.

Our application of educational research to selling has revealed some startling statistics. We actually measured, with a stopwatch, the conversational pauses in sales transactions. This is what we found to be typical:

- In many sales encounters, sellers who are questioning their customers can deliver *five or more questions every minute.*
- After asking a question, sellers often wait only about *one second or less* before either rephrasing the question, asking another question, answering the question themselves, or making some other comment.
- After receiving a reply to a question, many salespeople tend to wait *less than one second* before commenting and moving on to another point.

These findings suggest that in probably the majority of selling situations, salespeople inhibit the positive flow of information by trying to move things forward much too rapidly. How much real thought can you expect a customer to give to your question if you give her only one second to answer it? How much thought can you be giving to her responses if you spend less than a second analyzing them before moving on? Very little. As a result, the typical, rapid-fire questioning style has no connection to Superb Communication.

It's not surprising that the figures we've given here are so low. Salespeople have traditionally been told that silence is the death of a sales call. Keep it moving, we're always told. Don't give him too much time to think. And—probably most pointedly of all—if your mouth is moving, you're in control of the sale; if the conversation "lags," you've lost control.

But these slogans are as wrongheaded as they are common. They arise from a confusion about "control" vs. "domination." In a sales call dialogue, the person who does most of the talking may be dominating the call, but it is the person who is doing the listening who is actually in control. The key to really "controlling" the call and the key to creating Superb Communication, therefore, are the same: to ask one question at a time and then *wait* for the answer.

Golden Silence

This insight can be put to practical use with a technique that we refer to as Golden Silence. Golden Silence is the only reliable cure for Question Shock we have ever seen. As you can see from the diagram on page 228, it is a straightforward and elegantly simple one.

In using Golden Silence, you, the salesperson, simply pause for approximately *three or four seconds* at two different points in the questioning process: after you ask a question, and after your customer responds. The first three-to-four-second pause is what we call Golden Silence I; the second one we call Golden Silence II. Introducing these two pauses into your sales call questioning will, we guarantee you, dramatically—and immediately—improve the quality and the quantity of the information you get.

The reason is simple. When you practice Golden Silence I by giving your customer a moment to think about what you've

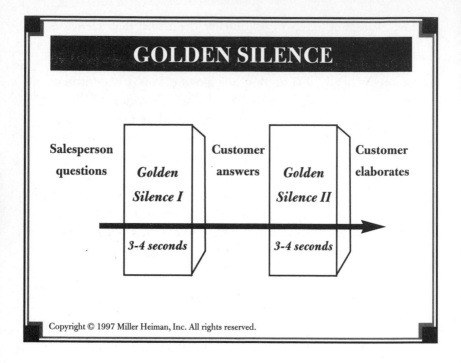

asked her, the information she gives you is much more likely to be solid information than if you had given her half as much time. When you practice Golden Silence II by waiting after she speaks, you are giving *yourself* a better chance of understanding what she has told you than you would if you'd spent half the time. Furthermore, during that second pause the customer will often reflect further and then provide additional information. The result of using Golden Silence I and II together is a more leisurely, more thoughtful, and ultimately far more productive flow of information.

We're not saying that you should carry a stopwatch into your selling encounters, that you should follow this technique slavishly to the exact second, or that you should use it in every question-answer exchange on every sales call. Each selling encounter has its own rhythm and pace, and you need to adjust to that reality each time you sit down with an individual customer. But as a model to aim for, Golden Silence is, quite simply, invaluable. As you practice the technique in actual sales calls, you will learn how to adjust the pace to a given situation, that is, when to speed up and when to slow down. Ideally, you will slow down far more frequently than you speed up. In any event, the point of the technique is to introduce into your selling situations those essential periods of silence without which Superb Communication cannot develop.

Admittedly, the Golden Silence technique may make you uncomfortable at first. Salespeople are so used to talking their way through obstacles that waiting after a question can seem unnatural: It can easily give you a case of "silence nerves." But this is a problem that diminishes quickly with practice, especially as you come to see that Golden Silence is not a gimmick.

When we say "Ask the question and then keep quiet," we don't mean you should stare stonily ahead, as if you're challenging the person to open up. And we're not talking about the manipulative closing advice that says "He who blinks first, loses." Good selling is never a game where you try to overpower or psych out your customer. When you use Golden Silence, you still have access to all the body language and nonverbal cues that any good salesperson (or teacher, or conversationalist) uses in a one-to-one exchange, and those techniques continue to be important. If you're uncomfortable "just sitting there," you can nod, lean forward, establish eye contact, and so on—just as you would if you weren't using this technique.

Furthermore, when you're using the Golden Silence method, you have to be sensitive to those instances where the client simply doesn't understand you and where "waiting him out" leads to nothing but a Leaden Silence. If you ask a question and after four or five seconds you have still gotten no response, the chances are good that he didn't comprehend what you asked. At that point it's appropriate—indeed, it's essential—to rephrase the question or ask another one. One very effective technique of doing that is to say, "My intention in asking that question was to . . ." and then to rephrase what you were trying to find out. This broadens the focus of the original question and makes it clear that you are working at a dialogue, not a drill.

The Golden Silence technique is meant to expand, not limit, the possibilities of Superb Communication. When it's used with discretion and flexibility, it does more for creating positive information flow than any other communication skill we know. But it's not a magic wand and, yes, it can be used too rigidly. You avoid that misuse by being sensitive to what your customer is saying—and that includes what she's saying non-verbally. Silence is not golden in itself: it's golden because of the information it brings you. If it's not bringing you the right information, it's time to adjust.

When Golden Silence is used with close attention to how the customer is reacting, it vastly improves your chances of making a Win-Win sale. This is particularly the case when you're presenting something to a group or committee rather than to an individual. Many of our program participants have told us that before learning the Golden Silence technique, they had been terrified of presenting to a group; the technique, they've said, enables them to set up a communication dynamic where the committee ends up doing most of the work. In the words of a colleague who makes a lot of presentations to government review boards: "You ask a committee one question and you give them five seconds to respond; I guarantee you it will be another five minutes before you have to ask them anything else."

BENEFITS OF GOLDEN SILENCE

We've said that Golden Silence cures the common disease of Question Shock. There are numerous other benefits of using the technique. Among the most common ones are these:

The number of customer reactions increases. When you use Golden Silence, you are much less likely to be stonewalled by people who feel pressured by fast-talking salespeople or who are too deliberate to be able to respond well to a rapid-fire style. Giving your customers the courtesy of a pause after your questions tends to increase their comfort level and make it easier for them to respond. This is especially useful with those who process information slowly. Some people need more time to think than others—which doesn't mean they're stupid. Golden Silence gives them that time.

The length of responses increases. Since Golden Silence gives your customer time to think, it also gives her time to formulate more comprehensive answers. It offers her the opportunity to expand on her feelings about the sale, the results she needs, and her Concept of what you're trying to do for her.

The reliability of the information you get increases. Since the customer is being given more time to reflect on the situation, he is more likely to come up with considered responses, not just ad lib speculations. In a Golden Silence format, answers tend to be more objective as well as fuller.

The number of relevant unsolicited responses increases. The person who is given adequate reflection time is more apt to provide you with information you haven't specifically asked for but that can still be crucial to your understanding of the situation.

The number of customers' questions increases. Here's another logical outcome of being afforded more thinking time. People who are given this time tend to ask you more questions regarding your product or service, and such questions may help to move the sale toward closure.

Open-ended, speculative thinking increases. The customer tends to explore more alternatives, more possibilities of a fit between your product or service and her needs. This obviously sets up a golden opportunity for you to proceed toward a mutually satisfying sale.

The focus of the dialogue shifts. Golden Silence tends to shift the focus of the discussion, during that critical pause period, onto the customer's real wants and needs, as opposed to what the seller initially "wants" or "needs" to sell. Again, this increases the exploratory possibilities, helps you to better understand the customer's Concept, and creates better chances for a Win-Win outcome.

It gives you more time to think. Last, but certainly not least, Golden Silence gives the salesperson additional time to think about what information is still missing, to formulate additional questions, and to make those questions pertinent to the specific situation and specific customer. Invariably the Golden Silence technique improves the quality of the salesperson's questioning—and this in turn improves the quality of the information received.

"Techniques" to Avoid: Dangerous Verbal Signals

We said at the end of the preceding chapter that there are right ways and wrong ways to phrase questions. We've just explained one technique, Golden Silence, that will enable you to present your questions in a more productive manner. But there are also several techniques you should avoid because they interfere with Golden Silence, impede the positive flow of information, and drastically undermine Superb Communication. We caution you in particular against issuing the following five signals.

"Think about it." There are two basic problems with this extremely popular "pre-closure" directive. First, it's vague. The phrase "Think about it"—whether it's used in the middle of a call or as a parting gesture—gives the customer nothing specific to do. Someone who has been asked to think about a proposal or a set of specs for your product has every right to do just that and nothing more; he has every right to say to you, when you return for a follow-up meeting, "I've been thinking about it, as you asked, but I just haven't made up my mind."

The second problem with "Think about it" is that it is a subtle put-down. When you direct somebody to do some (more) thinking about a topic, you're implying that he hasn't done any so far—or that the thinking he has already done has been so inconclusive that he'd better get "serious" about his thinking from now on. We do not help people to think better by asking or telling them to do so. The only way to get your customers to do the kind of thinking you want them to do before the next meeting is to give them specific information or materials around which to organize their thoughts. We'll be talking extensively about how to do this in the next chapter.

Mimicry. Somewhere along the line in sales training, the "experts" embraced the idea that one good way to indicate to a person that you've heard and understood what she just said is to give it back to her verbatim. Ms. Hardwick ends a lament about her accounts receivable situation with the observation "So as a result we have a constant cash flow problem," and the listener responds, "You have a cash flow problem?"

This may sound sympathetic, but it risks coming off as either dense or condescending, or both. That's why we advise our clients never to parrot back a comment unless there's a pressing need to verify factual information or clarify very complex ideas. At other times, if you want to demonstrate to your customer that you've gotten the point of what she's just said, a nod will do quite well. An exploratory New Information Question is even better. In the example we just gave, an appropriate and productive response to Ms. Hardwick might be "When did the receivables situation start to deteriorate?" or "Can you tell me a little more about your billing procedures?"

"Yes . . . but." When a conversation includes a high level of "Yes . . . but" or other "give and take back" statements, the probability is good that the dialogue is stalled. When a sales call is going nowhere, this phrase becomes a frequent refrain—on both the customer's and the salesperson's part. Usually it indicates the rejection of a just proposed idea or train of thought. For this reason, it tends to derail productive exploration and to set up a broken-record syndrome where the customer's objections are countered by the seller's, and vice versa—and no real information gets exchanged.

You cannot control your customer's "Yes . . . but" statements, but you can control your own, and you should. Because good selling relies on information flow, because you find the proper fit in any sale largely through exploratory discussion, and because the exploration of possibilities is always impeded by a "Yes . . . but" interjection, avoid this phrase and instead, use an alternate phrasing that does not retract with the left hand what you've just offered with the right. Good alternate phrases include: "If that's the way it is, then how . . .?" or "What kind of data do you have on that point?" Also, you can always move a potentially confrontational discussion in the direction of a Win-Win outcome by asking the exploratory New Information Questions we mentioned in the discussion of mimicry. Instead of "Yes . . . but," try "I don't understand fully yet what you mean. Could you expand on your production downtime problem?" Or: "I'm not sure I see what you're getting at, Joyce; could you tell me some more?"

Rhetorical questions/tags. A rhetorical question is one to which you don't expect an answer or to which you think the answer is obvious. Examples would include "Sure is hot, isn't it?" and "Isn't this new tax proposal outrageous?" Often such so-called questions (they're really not questions, but statements in question form) are preceded by, or followed by, traditional "tags." The introductory "Don't you think that . . ." and the suffixes "Isn't it?" and "Right?" are among the most common.

The not-so-subtle purpose behind the use of such verbal persuaders is to get the listener to agree with what the questioner has already decided. The question "Don't you think you'd profit from a higher-density alloy?" does not mean "Would you profit from a higher-density alloy?" It means "I have a higher-density alloy to sell you, and I'd like you to sign here." The purpose is to close off the customer's options rather than opening them out. The use of such tags is at best a merely useless filler tactic. At worst it's an irritating presumption that serves to alienate any potential customers who do not want you to make their minds up for them.

The "Right?" and "Isn't it?" tags are often used in telemarketing today. We have a friend whose method of countering this technique is brutal but appropriate. "When a phone solicitor calls me to say that they've got something that will solve all my problems, I listen quietly up to the point where they make the first 'commitment break.' I let them say, 'Now that sounds like a pretty good deal, doesn't it?' Then I say, 'No, it doesn't' and hang up." Today, more and more customers are responding this way. So we warn you away from these tags completely. They do not lead to finding a fit, but only to some customers (like our friend) throwing a fit.

"Why?" We've already explained how this little word can put people on the defensive, and we've explained why it should be kept to a minimum. This has a particular relevance to the development of Superb Communication, for nothing can so immediately and disastrously impede the flow of information as making a person feel she's on the defensive.

If you are uncertain about why a client has said or done something, therefore, we advise you not to phrase your clarifying questions in the "Why" or "Why did you" form. Instead, use the equivalent, but not nearly so challenging, "How." The change may seem insignificant, but it's not. Communications research indicates that a questioner can nearly *double* the amount of useful information elicited by a question if he prefaces it with the setup word "How" rather than the potentially offensive "Why." "Why did you decide to change the monthly schedule?" comes off as a demand for justification. "How did you decide to change the monthly schedule?" merely asks the person to describe his or her actions.

Because this phrasing is perceived as less threatening, it can actually get you the information, while asking somebody to explain "why" a given decision was made may get you nothing but evasion, rationalization, and defensiveness. The difference between the two words is perceived by the person being questioned as the difference between conversation and interrogation.

Of course, a conversation, as opposed to an interrogation, always has two parties involved. Up to now we've been focusing on Phase One of the sales call—the phase where you, the salesperson, elicit the information you need. We're going to move now to Phase Two—that equally essential part of the sales call where the other party to the conversation, your customer, gets the information that he or she needs.

PART IV

THE SALES CALL: GIVING INFORMATION

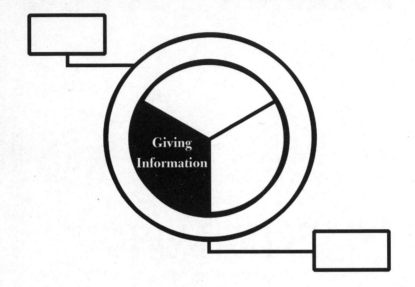

Giving
Information

CHAPTER 12

THE IMPORTANCE OF DIFFERENTIATION

Giving information is supposed to be what salespeople do best. Just as selling is often considered the art of persuasion—of telling customers why they should want what you have—the display of your product information is often considered the most important part of the sales call. The heart of any pitch worth its salt, it's sometimes assumed, is an extensive rundown of a product's features and benefits.

But there's a problem with this approach. Of course you have to know your product well, and of course letting the customer in on the product's impressive catalog of capabilities is a necessary part of many sales calls. The difficulty is that the information you have about your product, the information you consider important, may or may not be the information your potential customer needs in order to make a sensible purchasing decision. And giving out the wrong information, in many cases, can be quite a bit worse than giving out no information at all. That's why, in the Giving Information phase, you need to dispense your wisdom selectively so that it facilitates a better understanding of the customer's situation and enables you to work together toward appropriate solutions.

In order to be effective, the information you give your customer has to do two related things:

1. It has to help you identify the fit—if indeed there is one—between your product or service and the customer's Concept.
2. It has to make it clear that your solution to his problem is significantly different from the solutions being offered by your competition. The information you give out must do more than prove you're a candidate for the business; it must demonstrate that you're offering the best solution.

This second, critical point about Giving Information is what puts the Conceptual Selling approach so far ahead of the old-fashioned features-and-benefits game. We're saying that when you get down to showing off your product or service, it's never enough to establish that you can do the job; you have to give the customer information that *differentiates* you and your company from everybody else. That means you have to be an expert in a very special, and specialized, kind of "telling."

DIFFERENTIATING: WHY IT'S IMPORTANT

Buying, as we explained in Chapter 2, is an exercise in decision-making. Some buying decisions are made impulsively and almost unconsciously; others are made after long and careful consideration of all the variables. But all decisions to buy—that is, all logical decisions—are ultimately the end result of a mental selection process by which the buyer converges on a "best" option. Buyers can perform that selection process in one of two ways. They can make the selection at random—by throwing dice, drawing straws, or just guessing. Or they can make the selection by differentiating—by acting on a *perceived distinction* between one option and all the others.

Of these two ways of deciding, differentiating is by far the more "natural" one because the ability to sort and select is one of the things that make us rational. Nobody makes a decision—especially a potentially costly buying decision—by random choice unless he can see no difference in the available options. Whenever possible, people decide by differentiating.

Think back to the last major purchase you made yourself—your car, an insurance policy, a messaging system. Think about how you came to buy that particular car or policy or messaging system from that particular seller at that particular time. Chances are you didn't throw darts at the Yellow Pages. If you're like most informed buyers, you did some comparison shopping first. You checked out a few car dealers, you sounded out friends and business associates about their experiences with different insurance companies, you asked for information from several telecommunications providers—all of this as a way of seeking out a distinctive feature or capability so that you could make a wise decision. That's typical of intelligent buying. And it's precisely the kind of decision-making you want to help your customers to perform; the fundamental purpose of the Giving Information phase should always be to help them see a distinction.

The reason it's critical to provide this kind of help is that if you don't help your customers to see a distinction, they will create one of their own—one that may not work in your favor. This point merits some clarification.

Let's suppose you're in the carpeting business, and you've been given an opportunity to bid on a subcontract for a new office building. You're one of three carpet vendors being considered for the job—not the biggest or most prestigious of the three, but still one of the chief contenders. Let's suppose further that because you've already done the necessary groundwork in defining the customer's Concept, you're confident your company can do the job: the carpet your company can install will meet the design specifications. It's time now to link the customer's Concept to your particular product line by giving him product and service information that he must have in order to make a decision. There are three basic ways you could go about this.

First, you could lay out your product specs and service capabilities exclusively on their own merits and assume that their excellence will automatically incline the customer in your favor. In other words, you could simply ignore the competition, tell your story as fully as possible, and let the buyer decide. This is what we call "letting the buyer do the sorting," or "buyer differentiation." It's a common, and deadly, approach.

Second, you could size up the capabilities of the competition and try to convince the customer that you can do everything they can do—that your carpet installation is as good as anyone else's in the business. This is what we call the "me too" or "We're just as good as Microsoft" approach. Like the approach that ignores the competition, it asks the buyer to do his or her own sorting. Faced with three "identical" vendors in this kind of scenario, which one is the buyer is going to select? Unless he loves to spend money, it's going to be the cheapest. That works in your favor only if you're consistently the low bidder.

Third, you could help the buyer with the sorting, by

emphasizing something that is different about you—*and* that connects directly to his or her Concept. Not what's "good" or "just as good" as somebody else, but what is in fact unique to your company and its capabilities. Maybe it's a quarterly cleaning program that nobody else can match, or a recently developed-stain resistant formula, or the widest available color selection. Whatever it is, the thing that's significantly different about you is what we call a Unique Strength. Or, to be more precise, a *possible* Unique Strength. As we'll explain in a moment, a differentiator is only really a strength when the customer considers it to be of importance. For now we'll just say that in giving your customers information, it's only by emphasizing the Unique Strengths of your proposed solution that you can make differentiation work in your favor.

We realize that, strictly speaking, *unique* means "one of a kind." But we use the word more flexibly than Webster does. In selling, there can be, and often is, such a thing as "relative uniqueness," where a company is able to offer a product or service or package that is different *to a significant degree* from what everybody else is offering. Linguistic purists notwithstanding, it's reasonable to speak of such a degree of difference as a Unique Strength too.

SAS Institute's Stephanie Kuhnel adds an interesting footnote to the linguistic quibble when she observes that a composite of relatives can sometimes equal a "unique." "I once had a dictionary-quoter tell me, a little huffily, that unique was 'binary': Something is either unique or it isn't. I admitted he was right, but that in practice, you can sometimes bring two or three 'almost unique' strengths together to create a composite uniqueness. In computers, maybe only you and one competitor offer the ability to run on all platforms, and maybe only you and another competitor offer a full spectrum of consulting services. If you put those things together, you might position yourself as the only supplier—the unique supplier—who is able to provide full consulting for all platforms. Whatever the semantics say, that's as good as being 'truly' unique because it allows you to demonstrate the necessary differentiation."

Differentiation is exactly the point. To sum up what we've been saying: Buying is an exercise in decision-making, and people make decisions, whenever possible, by differentiating. In order to do that intelligently, they need to perceive a distinction. If they don't, they will create one of their own. Your fundamental task in the Giving Information phase of the sales call, therefore, is to highlight those areas where you are different—your Unique Strengths.

UNIQUE STRENGTHS

You can see that our concept of Unique Strengths is quite different from the traditional, product-related notion of features and benefits. The basic difference between the two approaches to giving product information is that the features-and-benefits idea starts with the product, while Unique Strengths starts with the customer's Concept and then enables you to relate the product to that Concept.

This is a subtle but crucial distinction. The flaw of features-and-benefits selling may be summed up very simply: It assumes that every product feature has a benefit and thus that if you describe the feature glowingly enough, the benefit will be obvious to the customer. But this works only when the prospect has *already* recognized and accepted the value of the benefit—that is, when it's already a part of her Concept. The feature "tenderness" in a T-bone steak has absolutely no benefit to a vegetarian. That's why pushing any product's "inherent" benefits is a self-defeating proposition unless you first determine that those benefits link up to the prospective buyer's Concept.

The value of the Unique Strengths approach is that it begins by asking "What is this customer's solution image?" and then proceeds logically to the next step: "How can I, uniquely, speak to that image?" Features-and-benefits selling begins (and often ends) with the product. Unique Strengths lets you look for a fit.

There's another reason Unique Strengths is a more reliable method of Giving Information about your product than even the best features-and-benefits pitch. Many features and benefits are common to a number of competitors, and so they do not provide true differentiation. Your stain-resistant feature may be attractive to your customer, but if everybody in the carpet business offers it, it's hardly a Unique Strength.

Product strengths alone are never enough. You've got to be able to give information about those product strengths that make you stand out from all the others. In any competitive environment, unless you move beyond product specs you're going to default to the "me too" scenario, where the customer is forced to do his own sorting—and where he will do it, usually on the basis of price or availability alone.

One of the great advantages of emphasizing Unique Strengths, in fact, is that it diminishes the importance of price competition: It has the ability to level the playing field when your company is not the lowest bidder.

Consider a scenario faced by one of our clients. Kim Schneibolk is a senior account manager at TTC. Recently, in proposing a software solution to improve a major account's inventory system, TTC encountered an "internal competitor." The account's management was considering shelving their outsourcing plans and having their own technical people solve the problem in-house. "They were very budget-conscious," Kim says, "and so they had to be shown that we could offer them something that could be more valuable to them than a low initial cost.

"That turned out to be our detailed experience in precisely the kind of problem they were encountering. Our division at TTC has been solving this kind of inventory problem for fourteen years. For this customer's in-house people to come up with anything comparable, it would take them years rather than months, and it would end up costing them *more* than our higher-end solution. So that's what became our Unique Strength: our capability of doing for them, quickly, exactly what we had been doing in similar situations for fourteen years. That's what we brought to the table that nobody else could match."

One clarification. The strength that Kim identified here was not a Unique Strength in itself, but was a strength by virtue of the fact that it fit with this customer's Concept at this time. If the solution image had been different—if, for example, the customer had had perfect confidence that his in-house people could duplicate TTC's ability on a tight schedule— then that enviable track record would have been merely a feature. A great feature, sure. But it became a Unique Strength only because the *customer* saw it as differentiating in TTC's favor.

A fourteen-year track record is something that is "relatively unique" to TTC, and of course to many other value-adding companies. It may not be your Unique Strength, however. You can have (and develop) Unique Strengths in any number of different areas. We've highlighted some of the most important ones on page 249.

AREAS OF POSSIBLE UNIQUE STRENGTH

- People
- Product
- Process
- Knowledge
- Service
- Implementation
- Delivery
- Experience
- Organization
- Customer base
- Technology
- Reputation
- Application
- Training
- Logistics

It all comes back to customer Concept. In the Giving Information phase of the sales call, no less than in the Getting Information phase, you always need to begin with what the customer expects your product or service to accomplish. In selecting which of your possible Unique Strengths to emphasize in any given sales call, you should always start by asking yourself: "How does this Unique Strength meet this person's individual need? How does it hook up to her solution image?"

To put this all into an immediate, practical focus, we'll give you the chance to do a Personal Workshop on the concepts of differentiation and Unique Strengths.

Personal Workshop #9:
Unique Strengths

First, at the top of a sheet of notebook paper, write the heading "Unique Strengths." Then, underneath that title, write down the following information:

- the name of the customer you're going to be calling on in an upcoming sales call
- your Single Sales Objective with regard to that person and his company: that is, what you want to sell him, how much of it you want to sell, and by when
- your current understanding of the customer's Concept as it relates to your Single Sales Objective
- the solution that is being offered, or can be offered, by your chief competitors for this business

Obviously, this last point may involve some speculation. You're never going to know as much about your competitors' solutions as you know about your own. But when you're totally in the dark about them, you're selling from a position of weakness. If you know nothing about what your competition has to offer, you need to highlight this as an area of missing information, to be tackled by outside research or by asking New Information Questions on your next sales call.

Keep in mind also that other companies represent only one type of competition. As we explain in *The New Strategic Selling*, you should consider as "competition" *any alternative* to the solution your company is offering. For example, your competition might include these options:

- Your customer's company adopts an in-house solution.
- They decide to use the budget potentially allocated for your solution for something else entirely.
- They decide to stick with the status quo.

Whenever you try to sell someone something, you're telling that person in effect, "I can help you get results that are better than the results you're getting now." To get those better results, the customer has to accept the *change* that is represented by your solution—and many people are highly resistant to change. So always consider your account's multiple options—including its current state of affairs—as alternatives that may compete with yours.

Once you've written this basic information down in your notebook, take fifteen minutes to focus on your Unique Strengths.

Step 1: Draw your Unique Strengths chart. Underneath the heading and the information you've just identified, divide the page into four columns. At the top of each column, place a heading, as we've done in the example on page 252. Also as in the example, list in the left-hand column the fifteen areas of possible differentiation that we mentioned in the box on page 249. And add to that list, at the bottom, the catchall "Other" category to cover things that may be relevant to your business but that we haven't mentioned. When you're done, your worksheet will look like the one on page 252.

Step 2: Identify your Unique Strengths. Now, using the left-hand column as a guide, write down in the second column any Unique Strengths you possess, for this Single Sales Objective to this customer. You're not going to find an entry to write in for each category—if you could, you'd probably already have the order. Try to come up with several areas

Area	Unique Strengths	"So What?"	"Prove It"
People			
Product			
Process			
Knowledge			
Service			
Implementa-tion			
Delivery			
Experience			
Organiza-tion			
Customer base			
Technology			
Reputation			
Application			
Training			
Logistics			
Other			

where the solution you're offering this customer can be clearly differentiated, in your own and the customer's mind, from the solution your competition is offering.

Two provisos for this step: (1) Avoid listing "strengths" that are no different from those of your competition We've emphasized the hazards of "me too" selling and marketing; don't fall into the "as good as Microsoft" trap. Avoid listing "strengths" like "Our great service capability" and "Our rock-bottom cost" unless you have an impeccable service record and your prices really are below everyone else's.

(2) Keep in mind our concept of "relative uniqueness." You don't have to confine yourself to those areas of possible differentiation in which you're absolutely distinct from everyone else. Being truly, grammatically "unique" is only an ideal. In listing your own Unique Strengths for this sale, focus on capabilities that approach the ideal and that therefore put as much distance as possible between you and the "me too" suppliers. Concentrate on those areas where you are "unique" to a greater degree than anyone else offering solutions.

Step 3: "So what?" Now, for every Unique Strength you've listed, put yourself in your customer's place and ask yourself the question "So what?" This exercise, which often reveals some startling gaps in information when our program participants perform it, is designed as a first-level test of the validity of your information. You're testing validity by focusing on your customer's Concept. You can bring out the most impressive list of Unique Strengths in the world, but if they don't relate to the solution image a client wants, they're going to be useless—even worse than useless because they'll distract her and you from finding an appropriate fit.

As an exercise in relating each of your Unique Strengths to

her Concept, therefore, write down in the third column of the chart the answer you would give this person if she asked you "So what?" State clearly and concisely how you would demonstrate that the Unique Strengths you're highlighting do actually tie in with her needs.

For example, let's say you're trying to sell a production line maintenance program to a large industrial manufacturer. Among the Unique Strengths you've listed are "Dramatic reduction of machine downtime" and "Our unique training program for line operators." The plant manager you're dealing with in this sale has been consistently plagued by machine breakdowns, but he is also a fanatic about his company's training its own people. Putting yourself in his place, you ask yourself "So what?" about the two items we've mentioned. In doing that, you'll discover that the first Unique Strength—reduction of downtime—will tie in perfectly to his needs. But you'll also discover that the second Unique Strength—your ability to train his people—isn't a strength at all in his eyes. And if it isn't a strength to him, then by definition it's not the kind of information you want to be giving this customer. So you'd scratch it from your list.

Filling in this third, testing column will probably leave you with fewer Unique Strengths than you had (or thought you had) before. But the remaining ones will be real. They will focus much more directly—and therefore, for you, more productively—on relating your product or service to this individual customer's Concept.

Step 4: "Prove it" Finally, a second and even more demanding test, to further focus your Unique Strengths listing. In the fourth column of the chart, write a brief sentence for each Unique Strength entry that proves its value for this sale. Our program participants do this by completing two sentences, and we'll ask you to do the same. For each Unique Strength you've listed, write an ending to these two sentences:

- "We are the only ones who . . ."
- "We are different because . . ."

There are no right or wrong answers here, and your "proofs" don't have to be elaborate. In fact, they shouldn't be. You ought to be able to say very briefly why you're the "only ones who" for this sale, and why you're different from the competition. If you can't, then you need to do some more thinking about what your Unique Strengths really are.

In proving the validity of your solution to your actual customers, of course, you're not necessarily going to produce a written statement like the ones we're suggesting here. You can prove your validity by giving references from satisfied customers, by offering a written guarantee, by bringing in an expert witness to vouch for your capabilities, and/or by actually demonstrating them with presentations, examples, or previous successes. If any of these "proofs" are what you would normally offer a customer, fine: Write that down in the fourth column of the Unique Strengths chart. For example, you might say "We're the only ones who will give you a six-month written guarantee" or "We're different because of past success; we can provide testimony to our effectiveness from ten satisfied customers."

Once you've made sure that each of your potential Unique Strengths is in fact related to your client's Concept, and once you've further tested the value of each Unique Strength by "proving it," you'll have gotten your list of differentiating qualities down, probably, to three or four. That may seem like a small amount of information to be providing on the next sales call, but it's not. When you've clearly identified the Unique Strengths you want to highlight, you're already miles ahead of the salesperson who goes in with a headful of dynamite data but no plan for relating it to the customer. Giving your customer just three or four pieces of concrete information that effectively link your product or service to his Concept is a far more efficient use of your time and his than winging it with a satchel of bells and whistles. And it always gets you better results.

Of course, once you meet the person, you will also be asking further questions, and these questions will no doubt expose further gaps in your information, which will necessitate a reexamination of your Unique Strengths. To stress once again a point that is central to the use of our system, the three phases of the ideal sales call are not to be seen as sequential Parts One, Two, and Three. They are to be seen, collectively, as a framework within which you can move freely and effectively from asking, to listening, to telling, and back again.

When you do that, consciously and consistently, you're practicing a form of selling we call Joint Venture. We mentioned Joint Venture briefly in Chapter 2, when we described your customers' natural decision-making process. It's time now to move to a fuller discussion.

CHAPTER 13

USING THE JOINT VENTURE APPROACH

In Chapter 2, we said that in making buying decisions, people follow a natural thought process. That process begins with cognition thinking, or understanding; moves to divergent thinking, or the consideration of options; and ends with convergent thinking, or the selection of the best option. In traditional selling, we said, the salesperson often undermines or ignores this natural process. In the approach to selling that we recommend, Joint Venture Selling, the salesperson facilitates the process, which makes buying infinitely easier for the customer.

The comparison diagram on page 258 summarizes the differences between the two approaches. In this chapter we'll give you more detail on Joint Venture selling, show how it enables you to link the Getting Information and Giving Information phases of the sales call, and have you apply it to your own sales situations. We'll begin by clarifying the advantages of Joint Venture Selling.

COMPARISON

Joint Venture Approach	Traditional Sales Approach

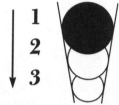

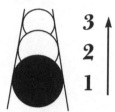

- Asking, learning, exploring
- Searching for a fit
- Customer-focused

- Showing, telling, explaining
- Assuming a need
- Product/service-focused

MAKING IT EASY ON YOURSELF

The most obvious advantage of Joint Venture Selling is that it makes the sales call easier—not only for your customer, but for you too. Because it's a natural, fluid method, salespeople who adopt Joint Venture Selling typically report that their sales calls become far less stressful and far more predictable. There'a a psychic boost that comes with the realization, as our friend Gene recalled about his Chicago meeting, that he "didn't have to sell these guys." All he had to do was to make buying logical and easy for them.

Gene's case is typical because searching for a match—as

exacting and challenging as that can be—is infinitely less of a burden than cramming product. As many of our program participants tell us, Joint Venture mentally liberates you. It frees you from the strictures of traditional sales rules, and especially from the oldest rule of all: the idea that your job is to make someone need your product. With the deadweight of that rule lifted, you're free to get down to the real business of selling, which is to provide your customers with solutions.

We're not saying that providing solutions is easy or that if you practice Joint Venture Selling the orders will fall into your lap. Joint Venture salespeople work as hard as anyone else. But they work with greater efficiency. The energy they put into sales calls isn't misdirected, beat-your-head-against-the-wall energy. It's energy that leads, logically and naturally, to results. In the words of another colleague, "For most people, making a tough sale is like driving a hundred miles with the emergency brake on. Joint Venture takes the brake off."

INPUT, "OWNERSHIP," AND COMMITMENT

Another advantage of Joint Venture over traditional selling is that it facilitates customer input into the solution. Traditional, product-pitching selling by its very nature cuts down on the client's involvement. This is hazardous because it allows you to push through sales that can easily become derailed later on. As one savvy executive puts it, "People don't resist their own ideas." The opposite of that dictum is also true. People do actively and vociferously resist ideas that they do not "own"— even when they've ostensibly accepted them by purchasing a product or service.

When you make a sale without developing customer ownership, you set yourself up to lose down the line when the person discovers he has been "sold." But when you actively encourage the buyer's input in the decision-making process, you allow him to buy in to a mutual solution. When a customer owns a solution in this way, he will fight to keep it in place.

And not just for the present. When you work with a customer through all the necessary stages of a Joint Venture Selling process, you lay the groundwork for a long-term commitment that will be far more profitable to you over the years than any one-time commission could ever be. Here's just one example.

A friend of ours, Dave, had some carpentry work done several years ago. It was complicated trim work, and the carpenter he hired was at the time the new kid on the block. Dave wasn't entirely confident about the outcome, but the young carpenter came through beautifully. It wasn't just that he knew how to handle a hammer and saw. He actively involved Dave and his wife in the design and construction of the work. He went over blueprints with them, invited them to inspect the work in progress frequently, and made absolutely sure at every step of the decision-making process that the trim was a perfect fit to their mental picture. "When he put on the finishing touches," Dave told us, "it was exactly what had been in our mind's eye. He had done the cutting and the planing, but the finished product was ours."

That's ownership. But it was only half of the story. About two years later, after the carpenter had become well established, Dave hired him again. This time the work wasn't so great. The carpenter had by then taken on three helpers, and one of them was not up to scratch. Halfway through the second project, Dave started to spot obvious defects in the workmanship. But because the carpenter had established such a sound Win-Win relationship with Dave on the previous job, his reaction was very different from what it might have been with someone else.

"If anybody else had put that kind of work in my house," he confided to us, "I would have canceled the contract on the spot. With Jim, I had such a good history of working together that I bent over backwards trying to keep him on board. I went to him directly, pointed out my concerns, and gave his firm a week longer than I would have given anybody else to resolve the problems. We worked it out together so that a project that once looked like terminal trouble has turned out great."

The lesson is clear. By making your customers part of their own solutions, you make an investment in the future that no amount of quick fixes could ever match. In Conceptual Selling, the input of the customer leads to ownership—and ownership leads to long-term business commitments.

THE JOINT VENTURE MATRIX

The basic difference between Joint Venture and traditional selling is the difference between exploring solutions and pushing product. But in championing Joint Venture, we're not saying you should never talk about your product or service. In order to relate it to the customer's Concept, in fact, you'll have to talk about it at some point. We're only cautioning you against getting stuck in the telling mode, as traditionally trained salespeople are tempted to do. Adopting a Joint Venture approach insulates you from that temptation. It also makes you alert to the *dynamics* of the call so that you're better able to determine when it's right to be laying out product specs and when it's more appropriate to be listening to your customer—in other words, when you should be shifting from Giving Information to Getting Information.

Every time you go into a sales call, you have two essential tasks to perform: First, you have to understand the customer's Concept. Then, when appropriate, you have to connect your product or service to that Concept. To perform these two tasks, you have access to two basic conversational modes, Getting Information and Giving Information. You're always going to get the best results in sales calls when you spend some time in advance thinking out which combination of tasks and methods you want to be using in the call. We lay out the four possible combinations in a Joint Venture Selling Matrix below.

JOINT VENTURE SELLING

	Getting Information Asking, Learning, Exploring, Discussing	Giving Information Showing, Telling, Explaining
Understand the customer's Concept	"What does higher efficiency look like to you?"	"Let me show you how this will help your company in achieving higher efficiency."
Connect your product/service	"What specific features will help you achieve higher efficiency."	"Let me show you the features we have that will help you achieve higher efficiency."

You may notice a surface similarity between this matrix and the Win-Win Matrix we introduced in Chapter 3. That's all it is—surface. In the Win-Win Matrix there's an ideal quadrant, the Win-Win quadrant, where you want to have all your sales end up, every time. Here, there's no ideal quadrant. Although we have been emphasizing the importance of understanding your customer's Concept and of listening rather than telling, it doesn't follow that you can—or should—be in the upper-left-hand quadrant of this matrix at all times.

In fact, depending on where you are in the selling process, and depending on what specific information you need to cover in a given sales call, you may want to start the call in any one of the four Joint Venture quadrants. Moreover, within the time frame of a single sales call, it will almost always be appropriate to move into more than one quadrant, as the information requirements of the situation change. We'll explain this more fully now, by examining each of the quadrants in turn.

QUADRANT 1: CONCEPT/GETTING INFORMATION

When you and your customer choose to operate in the Concept/Getting Information quadrant at a particular point in a sales call, the major emphasis is placed on what we have called cognition thinking. In this quadrant, you spend much of your time asking questions—and probably your customer does too—so that you both get a complete understanding of the current problems, opportunities, and situation. You also work with the person in an exploratory, mutual fashion to find out what results he or she needs and to determine how you can help to provide them. The focus is on the customer's Concept, not on your product or service, and your questioning should be designed to elicit information about that Concept. Typical Concept/Getting Information questions address the broad picture, not details: "If you could wave a magic wand here, Sarah, what would this organization look like?" Or: "What does higher efficiency look like to you?"

Because it's essential to understand the Concept first, and because listening to a customer is more likely to get you information about Concept than any amount of telling, this first quadrant is usually an appropriate one to aim for at the *beginning* of a call if for no other reason than to confirm your current understanding of the customer's Concept. This is crucial when you don't know the customer well—for example, on an initial prospecting call—or when you're unsure of his interests and concerns. It's also appropriate to work toward the Concept/Getting Information format whenever an information gap surfaces during the call. Since everything in Conceptual Selling begins and ends with the Concept, and since you can understand Concept only by exploration, it's advisable to spend some time in this quadrant on every sales call to every customer. But you don't want to be there all the time.

QUADRANT 2: PRODUCT/GETTING INFORMATION

When you're Getting Information to help you connect your product or service to the customer's Concept, you shift the focus toward what you have to sell, but you do so in a way that still invites maximum participation from the customer. Questioning here would focus on the product itself but would seek to determine how the product ties in with the customer's stated needs. "Do you feel comfortable with our scanning capability as a way of addressing your QC problem?" Or

"What features will help you achieve greater efficiency?" In this quadrant you also explore a customer's level of satisfaction with the products or services she's using now. So you move in the direction of nuts and bolts, but you are constantly checking—asking, exploring, learning—to be sure that every nut and bolt you're discussing can provide a match to what the client really needs.

Notice that when you're in this quadrant, it's assumed you have already made headway on understanding the customer's Concept. That always comes first. Even if you're toward the end of a drawn-out selling cycle, it's not appropriate to begin a sales call by pitching the product. The ideal pattern is to cover Concept/Getting Information up front and then move to Product/Getting Information so you can discuss in more detail how your solution may address the customer's problem.

QUADRANT 3: CONCEPT/GIVING INFORMATION

Here the focus of attention is on what the customer thinks the product or service will be able to do, but the bulk of the talking is done by you. We realize this may sound self-contradictory since we have continually emphasized the importance of listening and minimized the value of simply telling. But, as we just pointed out, that doesn't mean it's never appropriate for a seller to be doing the talking. As long as you don't monopolize a sales call interview, and as long as you remain alert to your customer's responses, there are situations where it is highly appropriate for you to be telling him about Concept.

Now, since the Concept is by definition something that's in the customer's mind, not yours, we don't mean you should be telling him about *his* Concept. But you can use this method effectively to describe how *other* customers, with similar Concepts, have benefited from your company's solutions. Say your customer is concerned about assembly line efficiency. If you've addressed such a problem successfully in the past with another company's assembly line, then it's entirely appropriate to tell the customer that directly. "One of our Bay City clients had a similar problem two months ago; this is what he wanted to accomplish." Or: "Let me show you how this will help you achieve higher efficiency."

There's a possibility of fuzziness here on both your part and the customer's. On the one hand, you're telling him about what you've already been able to accomplish; in a sense, that's a type of product sale because you're focusing on your own company's solutions. On the other hand, you're relating those solutions to what you believe to be his real needs; in that sense, you're definitely zeroing in on Concept. The terminology is less important than remembering what it is you're trying to do. In the Concept/Giving Information quadrant, you're doing the talking, but you are constantly checking, with questions, that what you're saying relates to this individual's Concept. If you've already clearly identified the Concept, there really isn't anything wrong with running through a show-and-tell session. At some point in many sales calls, that may be exactly what the customer wants or needs to hear.

The danger is in slipping prematurely from this tricky third quadrant into the seemingly less tricky fourth quadrant.

QUADRANT 4: PRODUCT/GIVING INFORMATION

This quadrant is home base for traditional selling. When you're here, you're tempted to fall back on the supposedly time-tested basic sales tactic, which is to tell everything you know about the product or service so that you dazzle the customer into buying. When you move to the Product/Giving Information quadrant, you drag out everything you've ever learned about the levers and buttons, capacity and horsepower, safety checks and warranties and service specs. Whether you're selling airplane parts or banking services or answering machines, the bottom-line message is the same: "Let me plug this baby in and show you how great it runs."

We've already described at length how limiting and dangerous it can be to rely on this kind of product-pitch philosophy, and in fact the entire thrust of Conceptual Selling works against this approach. To highlight the basic point we made about this method in Chapter 4, the product-oriented approach is effective only *when you have already determined a match* to the customer's real needs and when the feature or benefit you're describing actually speaks to that need. Many salespeople never make this prior determination, and so they end up working against themselves in one of two ways: Either they pitch their great product to people who don't really need it, or they describe the *wrong* feature or benefit to a customer who may be desperate for the product, but for another reason.

Obviously, we're not saying it's never appropriate to sell in the Product/Giving Information quadrant. Introducing your product specs may be helpful to the customer in generating divergent thinking or in selecting a best choice through convergent thinking. Certainly it can help you as a seller to place emphasis on your Unique Strengths. And of course if a prospect has asked for a demonstration or fuller description—if she in effect says "Show me the bells and whistles now"—you may want to consider doing so. But there's a danger in adopting this tell-all approach. We can explain why by telling a story on ourselves.

THE FOURTH-QUADRANT TRAP

Years ago, when we had just started our business, we were asked to give a presentation to a large pharmaceutical company. There was good potential revenue involved, so we were there bright and early, raring to go. When we walked into the presentation room, we found a group of eight executives, only half of whom we had met, waiting for us to begin. The vice president for sales, who had invited us in to make the presentation, introduced us to the group and then said, "OK, why don't you tell us what you do?"

With that invitation to "hit it," we launched into the greatest product spiel of our careers. For twenty-five minutes they sat enraptured as we described all our programs in infinite detail, explained how every one of them was perfect for their type of business, and gave them a slide show that would have made Hollywood envious. And what was the result of this world-class performance? Not only did we not make the sale, but we weren't even invited back for a second round. The reason was that we had made at least two major blunders.

First, we didn't clarify who we were talking to. The first thing we should have said was, "We've only met Don, Jane, Rebecca, and Arnie. Would the rest of you mind introducing yourselves and giving us some preliminary idea of your concerns?" Then we should have sat back and practiced a lot of Golden Silence while we found out why the eight of them were there—and, therefore, why *we* were there. By jumping headfirst into the presentation before we knew anything about the audience, we had simply set ourselves up for a fall. Instead of being able to tailor a presentation to the individual interests of this group, we forced ourselves into a dog-and-pony show that may have had nothing to do with the individual interests of our listeners.

Second, we ignored the individual Concepts entirely and concentrated solely on pitching our product. We figured at the time that this was an acceptable tactical approach because, after all, it was what the client had asked for. But going along with that seemingly reasonable request proved to be a big mistake. It forced us into the Product/Giving Information quadrant and kept us trapped there throughout the whole sales call.

The outcome was disastrously one-sided. The pharmaceutical managers learned more than they ever wanted to know about our operation, but we learned nothing about them—nothing about their current needs, their problems, their reasons for calling us—that we hadn't known before we got there. When you go through an entire presentation without finding out anything new about the client, what you get is exactly what we got: nothing. We learned some valuable lessons from that experience:

- You should never, absolutely *never,* give a dog-and-pony presentation to a group whose members you don't know. If there are surprise guests in your audience, find out *before you start* who they are and why they might want to listen to you.
- Even if you're speaking to only one individual, *never start with a product pitch.* Find out early in each sales call interview what the current situation is regarding his Concept, and move to describing your product or service only when the customer is clearly ready for that information.
- Even when you're convinced that he is ready for product information, *test* that assessment periodically by asking questions: "Is this what we should be discussing?" or "Am I addressing your concerns?"

- Finally, when you find yourself trapped in the Product/Giving Information quadrant, stop and *ask for feedback* from the customer. Even when you're invited to make a product pitch, involve the customer in the discussion and keep the presentation tied to the customer's Concept.

We don't say that any of this will come naturally. Most salespeople feel more comfortable when they are talking than when they are listening. Besides, the traditions of selling are tenacious, and there are plenty of face-to-face situations where the customer seems to *want* you to keep talking, describing all the bells and whistles, even though the match between product and Concept has not yet been identified. You've got to be attentive to those situations and strive constantly to redirect the discussion so that it puts both you and the customer where you need to be.

There's no surefire way of saying exactly where you should be at a given moment in a call or of saying when you're in danger of being caught in the fourth-quadrant trap. But as a general guideline, *four or five minutes* is the maximum amount of time you should allow yourself to pitch product without moving from Giving Information to Getting Information, that is, without asking for the customer's input about how the call is going. If you've been talking for six or seven minutes without getting any feedback, you're already trapped and may not even know it.

The feedback may be a precisely worded question that asks you to expand on a certain area, or it may be a rephrasing of something you've said. Whatever it is, you want some indication that the customer is involved in the call—that she considers it her call too. Win-Win says you and the customer share responsibility for how the buy/sell process moves forward. This means you don't simply follow orders when someone says "Give me a thirty-minute demo next Friday." Instead, you strive throughout the presentation to make it truly a Joint Venture.

You determine how you want a sales call to evolve by thinking through in advance which quadrant of the matrix you should be in and how, if it becomes necessary during the call, you can move comfortably from one quadrant to another. We'll give you the opportunity to see this in practical terms now.

PERSONAL WORKSHOP #10: JOINT VENTURE

In this Personal Workshop you'll relate the concept of Joint Venture to your own selling. Pick one of the model calls you've been working with, and be sure that for this call you have a clear Single Sales Objective in mind. When you've chosen the objective and the specific sales call, write the heading "Joint Venture" at the top of a notebook page, and write down the name of the individual you're going to be calling on. You'll probably need two full pages in your notebook and about half an hour of workshop time.

PART A: JOINT VENTURE APPRAISAL

This Personal Workshop is divided into two parts. In the first one, you'll appraise your current Joint Venture status.

Step 1: Cognition. Put yourself in your customer's place, and write down a brief description of his or her cognition of the situation. You're trying here to think with your customer's

mindset, and we know that isn't easy. Our program participants often find they can come to a clearer understanding of
this mindset if they complete the following sentences *as they
believe the customer would complete them*:

- The timing is right because . . .
- The situation today is . . .
- The budget is . . .
- I need to get approval from . . .
- My key supporters/detractors are . . .
- An important thing to accomplish is . . .

Write down the completed sentences in your notebook. Keep
in mind that although you're trying to think with the customer's mind, the answers you put down must also relate to
your Single Sales Objective. In fact, when we say "situation"
here, we include the fact that you are trying to get the customer to decide in favor of your sales objective.

Step 2: Divergent thinking. Now, still thinking with your customer's mindset, generate the alternative solutions that he or
she is likely to be considering with regard to the current situation. To help you do that, complete the following sentences.

- I've thought about . . .
- Another solution would be . . .
- We've already ruled out . . .

Fill in one or more of these sentences the way you believe the
customer would fill them in, and write down the completed
sentences in your notebook.

One subtle point: Remember that when potential buyers
consider alternative options, they look not just at a range of
possible purchases and possible vendors, but also at modifi-

cation of existing procedures—and at the very real possibility that the best course of action may be to stay with the status quo. For this reason the status quo is always a kind of "competitor," and you should therefore consider the possibility that as your customer weighs different actions, one action will be to take no action at all.

Step 3: Convergent thinking. Finally, still with your customer's thinking cap on, consider the selection process he or she will probably be going through in converging on a "best choice" solution. You can do this by completing the following sentences:

- This is important because . . .
- The final solution here will have to . . .
- I will only be satisfied if . . .

Again, write down your customer's probable answers in your notebook. Be especially attentive in this step to how well or how poorly these answers relate to your Single Sales Objective. If a customer's convergent thinking does not relate in some way to the objective you're trying to accomplish, then the chances are good that you and/or the customer have missed something earlier in the thinking process. It may be useful for you to review the cognition stage of that process again to see if you have clearly understood what you're in this selling situation for and whether or not it relates clearly to the client's Concept.

PART B: JOINT VENTURE MATRIX

Now you'll review your history with this customer and determine where you want to start your next sales call with him or her.

Step 4: Identify the last quadrant. Think of the last call you made on this customer. Where were you positioned at the end of that call? Or, alternatively, in which of the four Joint Venture Matrix quadrants did you spend most of your time on that call? To determine your most recent matrix position, use these guidelines:

- If you spent most of your time asking questions and together discussing options to determine the customer's Concept, you were probably in the Concept/Getting Information quadrant.
- If you spent most of your time showing how your product or service would be likely to relieve his or her problem, you were in the Product/Getting Information quadrant.
- If you spent most of your time discussing ways your other customers have solved problems similar to his or hers, you were in the Concept/Giving Information quadrant.
- If you spent most of your time telling how your product or service works, you were in the Product/Giving Information quadrant.

Write down "Last Call," and next to it the name of the quadrant (or quadrants) where you spent most of your time. You're defining your current or latest position so that you can more realistically plan where you want to go next.

Step 5: Where is the customer now? Now think about where the customer was at the end of that same sales call, by asking yourself:

- What is this person's current solution image regarding the problem or situation he or she is facing?

- What is his or her current understanding of my product or service as it relates to that solution image? What kind of information does he or she now have regarding the relationship of my product or service to the problem?
- What kind of information does he or she still need in order to make an intelligent buying decision?
- Given the dynamics of the last call, in what quadrant of the Joint Venture Matrix does the customer expect us to begin the upcoming sales call?

We realize we're asking you to speculate on what's in your customer's mind. There are no right answers here. Our purpose in asking you to think about where your customer now stands is to help you focus on those areas where your information about his or her thinking is still deficient. Write down whatever you have to in order to clarify your understanding. If you don't know the answers to these questions, write *that* down.

Step 6: Plan the next call. Once you've thought about where both you and your customer were at the end of the previous meeting, sketch out a Joint Venture plan for the upcoming meeting. Remember that you can make a conscious choice about which quadrant of the matrix you are in. So decide which quadrant or quadrants you should be in with this customer the next time you meet so that at the end of that call, both of you will be closer to a Win-Win conclusion than you are at the present time.

Begin by noting where this customer was at the end of the previous meeting and where he or she expects the next call to start. Is that where *you* want it to start? If the answer is Yes, write down a Confirmation Question that you can ask at the beginning of the call to verify that you're both working from the same page. If it's No, then you'll have to draft statements or questions that will help you understand why the two of you may not be on the same page. Take each of the four quadrants in turn and write down two or three good questions that you need to ask the client when you are selling in that quadrant.

Whatever questions you write down, be sure it is clear in your mind how each one will keep you where it would be most helpful for you to be in order to better understand this individual's Concept. Be sure, too, that whatever questions you devise will help you manage the call in a Win-Win fashion.

This is really the whole point of using the Joint Venture Matrix. We say you should manage your sales calls, not command or dominate or push them. Good sales call management, like good management of any kind, means being constantly attentive to the needs of all parties involved so that "joint ownership" is sustained and so that you and your customer can come to the end of the selling cycle with a complete understanding of how and why you have gotten there.

Again it comes back to the Concept. Whatever time you intend to spend in a given quadrant on a sales call, and no matter what questions you draft to get you from one quadrant to another, the fundamental thing to remember is that in any Win-Win selling venture, the customer is encouraged to buy for his or her own reasons.

By asking you to use the Joint Venture Matrix as a way of "rehearsing" your next sales call, we're really saying not only that you should figure out where you want to be, but that you should manage the call so your customer is positioned with you in the quadrant(s) where he or she can go through the decision-making process most efficiently. The ultimate reason you want to prepare any sales call in advance is so that at the end of that call, no matter where you are in this matrix, you and your customer will both be moving toward a Win-Win outcome.

For that to happen, however, you need mutual commitment. That's why the third phase of every sales call, Getting Commitment, is essential to both immediate and long-term success. We move now to a discussion of that third phase.

PART V

THE SALES CALL: GETTING COMMITMENT

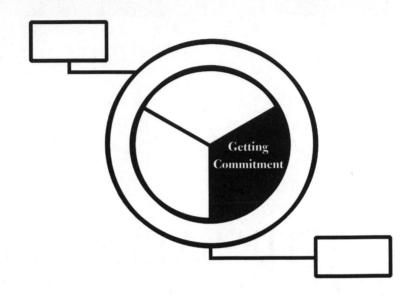

CHAPTER 14

BEYOND THE CHUMMING EXERCISE

The average face-to-face sales call today may cost a selling organization $1,000 or more. This cost, which includes such major items as accommodation and transportation expenses, has escalated tremendously in the past decade or so, and that's one reason so many large organizations are moving toward less expensive selling methods like 800 lines and Web-based marketing.

But there is still no substitute for face-to-face interaction, provided the expected sales revenues justify it, and so the salesperson who actually sits down with the customer is still the mainstay of the selling profession. But how can professional salespeople utilize their time and resources most efficiently to get the best possible return from every individual call?

At a thousand dollars a call, it's obvious that cost-wise companies are going to be increasingly concerned with how the salesperson spends his or her valuable selling time—and their money. A successful sales call today means, above all, ensuring that every time you go out, you come back with something to show for that time and money. As we said earlier, that something doesn't have to be the order. Because of the nature of their business, some salespeople do write first-call orders, but many do not. What you do have to get, on every call, is a measurable degree of Action Commitment.

COMMITMENT REVISITED: KEY IDEAS

As we discussed in Chapter 6, every time you go out on a sales call, by definition you have committed your own and your company's time and resources to a possible buy/sell relationship. You should not be the only person in that relationship who has extended himself or herself in this way. Unless your customer commits also, you do not have a Win-Win relationship.

On the first call to a new customer, you have no choice but to commit yourself. If you're going to write any business at all, you have to spend that initial $1,000: It's seed money, and you have to be willing to risk it with no guarantee of customer commitment. But that's the *first and last* time you should sell from this position of unilateral risk. That initial call, and every subsequent call, must end with the customer agreeing to do something to help move the sales process forward. Customers must know, in other words, that if they are considering doing business with you, there is no free lunch.

Vague promises to "think about the proposal" or "get back to you sometime next month" are not signs of commitment. What you want before the end of every sales call is the customer's promise to *do* something by a specified date. For example: "I will present your proposal to the planning board this Friday." Or "After I've had a chance to review these figures, I'd like to meet with you again before the end of the month to discuss our budget requirements." Specific actions, specific dates. Not an evasive "sometime" or "soon."

The commitment can be the kind of "high-end" commitment that we defined as your Best Action Commitment, it can be the "low end," your Minimum Acceptable Action, or it can be something in between. But whatever level of commitment your customer agrees to, it should indicate unambiguously that he is willing to spend some of his company's time and resources, just as you have. If that's not the case, then you're being asked to carry the ball by yourself. Sooner or later, for you that's a losing proposition.

INCREMENTAL COMMITMENT

You start by getting commitment on every call. But that's just the beginning. As your expenditure of time and energy increases throughout the selling process, your customer's degree of commitment must also increase. If commitment isn't *mutual* and *incremental,* you're spinning your wheels.

At the initial stages of a selling process, the degree of customer commitment can, and probably will, be modest. If it's the first sales call you've ever made on Mr. Stein, you might be satisfied with the input you get about his organization's needs and his agreement to set up a second meeting with other key individuals. There's nothing wrong with that kind of low-level commitment as long as you're just getting started.

But when you go back to Mr. Stein the next time and you deal with the concerns he has about your warranty structure, and you spend another hour of your time trying to zero in on his Concept, then his commitment at the end of that second call must be more substantial. By the end of that second call, you may have put in another thousand dollars of your company's time. That should be worth something concrete to Mr. Stein.

If you've been in selling for more than a few months, you've probably been involved in "limbo" sales—sales where you're never quite sure, from one sales call to the next, how close you are to getting the business, or whether the customer is "giving you the business." You've met the person three or four times, and you seem to be getting along well. She's seen your material, she's "thinking about" what you've told her, you've taken her to lunch a couple of times, your conversations are always pleasant—but the whole thing doesn't seem to be moving anywhere.

Every salesperson we know has found himself in these situations, and very often the response is to let things slide—to put the pleasant but noncommittal customer on the back burner for a while, and to check back periodically in the hope that, eventually, something will break and you'll get an order.

Forget it. These situations are what our friend Mike Joyce, who has been selling for Miller Heiman for several years, calls "chumming exercises." His wordplay is as apropos as it is clever. Whether you think of chumming as socialzing or as throwing bait on the waters to attract fish, it's not something you should be doing with your customers. As friendly as you may be with them, becoming their "chum" can't be the goal of your sales calls. And as for using your resources as bait to "reel them in," that's a classic case of a no-Win, manipulative attitude. Mike correctly ridicules chumming in both these senses. And he's right on target when he observes about getting commitment, "You cannot think of this as something extra. Getting commitment is the whole point of going into a sales call. When you don't get it, you realize there's been a disconnect."

The only way to ensure that you don't fall into a chumming situation is to strive for incremental Commitment every time you go out. Remember this especially if a potential customer asks for a proposal.

We often see salespeople commit to submitting a proposal without asking for any specific action in return. Yet you know how long drafting a proposal can take. You can't knock it off in half an hour while you're unwinding at the nineteenth hole. So if a customer, toward the end of a sales call, says, "That sounds good; why don't you send me a proposal?" you have every right to respond, "I'll be happy to do that; what will the next step be when you receive it?" In other words, "What will you *do* with it?" Not asking for this kind of commitment means you are setting yourself up to lose.

The fundamental issue here is time. Every salesperson's single most valuable resource is that precious commodity—not time in general, but the time you actually spend face to face with your prospects and clients. Nobody ever has enough of it—certainly not enough to use it recklessly. When you agree to commit your time to a customer without getting something in return, you're saying, "My time is not as valuable as yours is. I'll do all the work on this sale if you'll just give me an order." If you establish that kind of relationship, even if you do get the order, eventually with this person you're going to lose.

COMMITMENT QUESTIONS

We've said that commitment isn't free. It also isn't automatic. If you want commitment on every call, you've got to ask for it.

The way you do that is by crafting Commitment Questions.

At first glance it might seem that for sales professionals, asking Commitment Questions would be the most natural thing in the world. A main thrust of traditional sales training, in fact, is to show salespeople ever more ingenious ways of "asking for the order." But when we speak about commitment, we do not mean simply going for the order.

In a good selling process, with each sales call you should move the sale closer to an ultimate Win-Win commitment in a series of graduated steps. Getting the order is only the final evidence of commitment—and you cannot secure that final evidence unless on previous sales calls with this customer you have secured consistent evidence of forward motion. That's why we emphasize that commitment must be incremental.

Because it's incremental, the level of commitment may vary considerably from one sales call to the next. And the purpose of a Commitment Question, as we define it, is to tell you at exactly what level you are positioned at any given point in the selling process and, at the same time, to make it possible for you to move toward the next higher level.

A good Commitment Question does more than simply move you toward the close. It also gives you information that tells you how far away you are from the close, suggests the timing of events that have to happen to move things forward, and tells you what aspects of your customer's Concept you may have to explore further before you can hope to secure the necessary incremental progress. Commitment Questions serve as a kind of compass to keep you aware of your current position and of the rate and direction of your movement.

COMMITMENT QUESTIONS

PURPOSE:
- **Move toward closure**
- **Determine where you are in the sale**
- **Obtain the customer's agreement to take action that moves the sale forward**

WHEN USED:
- **Before the end of every sales call, to ensure that the customer will take action**
- **To learn what remains to be done**

WHEN TO USE COMMITMENT QUESTIONS

Because of their value as compasses, Commitment Questions often function well at or toward the end of a sales call. In our friend Gene's Chicago call, for example, after he had confirmed the manufacturer's problems and asked New Information and Attitude Questions to clarify his understanding of those problems, he posed this end-of-the-call question: "Are we in agreement that the next logical step is for you to set up a date when we can survey your food service patrons and analyze the current operation?" That question looked both backward and forward. It summed up his understanding of the meeting—that Gene's company was going to be a prime candidate for the replacement contract—and it defined exactly what had to be done next to move the selling process forward.

But beware of asking Commitment Questions only at the end of the sales call. A Commitment Question is appropriate *whenever* you need a check on your current position, and one benefit of asking these questions frequently is avoiding coming to the ink-on-the-paper call only to discover that the rubber stamp is not a rubber stamp, or that Janice in Accounting hates your company, or that there's still a review committee that needs to be heard from before a decision can be reached on your proposal.

As we mentioned in Chapter 10, you should not follow our five-question-type format in a strict 1-2-3-4-5 pattern; that kind of rigidly sequential thinking is a legacy and a fallacy of track selling. Whenever you feel uncertain about your current position vis-à-vis a given individual, and whenever you are uncertain about what needs to be done to move a selling process forward—that is the time to ask your customer a Commitment Question.

PHRASING COMMITMENT QUESTIONS

The key words that are most appropriate in phrasing Commitment Questions are those that relate to *future* efforts—verbs like *determine, plan, schedule, propose*—in constructions that focus on what still needs to be done in order to keep moving toward Win-Win. We've given other examples on page 289.

Like Confirmation Questions, Commitment Questions can often be phrased effectively in the form of a statement-plus-question combination. Gene's Commitment Question, for example, might have been phrased: "It seems that the next

COMMITMENT KEY WORDS

Decide   Plan   Share

Commit   Direct   Schedule

Determine   Propose   Provide

Recommend   Agree   Secure

logical step would be for us to survey your patrons and analyze your operation. Are we in agreement that you'll set a date
for that now?"

There's a critical point to remember here, which is implicit
in the sample questions we have mentioned. We say that
Commitment Questions relate to future efforts. We mean the
customer's efforts, not yours alone. A good Commitment
Question focuses on what the customer has to do, or be
involved in doing, to move the sales process forward. "Do you
plan to approve?" "Will you set a date?" and so on.

MUTUAL COMMITMENT

The bottom line here is *mutual* commitment. That's why we stress getting the customer to do something. Obviously, there's going to be plenty for you, the seller, to do too, but you already know that, and if you want the business, you've committed yourself to doing it. What you don't know is whether or not your customer is also committed to carrying the buy/sell process forward. It's unrealistic to suppose that you can manage any selling process to a Win-Win conclusion unless you get some commitment to action on every call you make.

If you've just spent twenty minutes with Mr. Hackford and he seems delighted with your general presentation, but all he will say is "Give me a call sometime," then you might as well forget it. Commitment means a time, a date, and a specific agenda. It means Mr. Hackford is interested enough in what you've said to dedicate a given amount of time on a given day to cooperating with you to move the sale forward. If he's not willing to make at least that commitment, you should consider discussing the situation with your sales manager to determine whether "giving him another call" is worth the effort.

With that understanding in mind, you can now move to a Personal Workshop in which you draft Commitment Questions for an upcoming sales call.

PERSONAL WORKSHOP #11: COMMITMENT QUESTIONS

In this workshop you'll add to the planning you developed in Chapter 6, in the Personal Workshop on Action Commitment. So turn to the "Action Commitment" page in your notebook. Spend a few minutes reviewing what you wrote there, paying particular attention to the level of commitment this individual has demonstrated to you on previous sales calls. Then, as a way of ensuring incremental commitment on the upcoming call, work toward developing appropriate Commitment Questions.

Step 1. Review your Action Commitments. In Personal Workshop #4, you defined a Best Action Commitment and a Minimum Acceptable Action for this sales call. Look at those actions again now. With regard to the approaching sales call, make certain that

- each Action Commitment is *specific*
- it focuses on something that the customer, not you, will *do*
- it can be *documented* objectively once it has been accomplished
- given the current scenario as you understand it, it is still *realistic* from the customer's point of view.

If your Action Commitments don't fulfill all four of these criteria, consider how to revise them so that they do.

Step 2. Write corresponding Commitment Questions. In the Action Commitment workshop, you wrote down your Best Action Commitment and your Minimum Acceptable Action. Now draft and write down one carefully phrased Commitment Question for each of these two possible customer actions. Remember that a good Commitment Question may or may not verify your customer's willingness to perform the speciffc action you've defined. But it will, at the very least, verify her willingness to move the sales process forward in a Win-Win fashion.

Step 3. Test these questions. A good Commitment Question should be answerable by a simple Yes or No. Is that true of the questions you have drafted? For each Commitment Question you have drafted, ask yourself the following:

- Does this question *match* the Action Commitment? That is, if the customer answers Yes, will he or she be committing respectively to my Best Action Commitment or my Minimum Acceptable Action?
- Does this question ask the customer to take a reasonable action? That is, am I asking for something that the customer will *do* and that he or she realistically *can* do?
- Does this question indicate a specific *date* for the completion of the Action Commitment?

If you can't answer these three questions with an unqualified Yes, then you may not have a true Commitment Question. Using the key words we have indicated, revise as necessary. When you're finished with this final step, you should have two effective questions to use on your next sales call to help verify your position in the sale and to move the process forward.

WHEN YOU CAN'T GET COMMITMENT

What do you do when your customer simply won't agree to do anything more substantial than "think about it and get back to you"? Everybody runs into situations where the sale just seems to be stalled, and nothing you can do or say seems to be able to move it forward. Sales reps have a million reasons for explaining why this happens. "The timing isn't right now, I guess." "Our price must be too high." "They're strong for our competition." "The guy is stubborn; he just won't see reason." And our personal favorite, "It's politics."

These excuses are usually accompanied by the sound of madly spinning wheels. Sometimes they're fairly close to reality; many times they're light-years away. Never do they describe the real reason any sale slows down. No matter what the excuse, and no matter what the particular situation, there is always only *one* reason a person won't give commitment. It's because she perceives a personal Lose in the acceptance of your solution—or, at the very least, does not see a Win.

That's the bottom line, every time. You can have the best product in the world, it can be perfectly suited to a given person's real needs, and you can spend half the national budget taking her to lunch—all to no avail if she doesn't perceive that the sale you're trying to make is going to be a personal Win. In every case where the selling process is stalled by a "stubborn" or "difficult" or "price-sensitive" buyer, the reluctance can be translated into the same perception: "I don't see what's in this sale for me."

Because a customer's Lose or No-Win perception can spell death for the most "surefire" sale, being able to pick up on a customer's "I'm losing" signals is a valuable part of sales call management. The sooner you as a seller are able to spot and deal with a potential buyer's Lose feelings, the sooner you'll be able to move the selling process forward. Until you get to that point, you'll just be taking the excuses for the reality.

That's why an essential step in getting commitment when that seems impossible is digging for why the person feels he's losing. In Conceptual Selling, we define that digging process in a very particular terminology. We say that whenever a customer feels that he is losing, there is a Basic Issue involved. The next chapter discusses these Basic Issues.

CHAPTER 15

DON'T CALL THEM OBJECTIONS

A Basic Issue is any *personal* feeling a customer may have that results in his or her believing "I'm losing." Note the emphasis on *personal*. Basic Issues are not concrete, quantifiable, "objective" realities, waiting to be tinkered with and fixed up by the savvy, product-wise salesperson. Basic Issues arise from deep within the customer's individual experiences and value system. So they cannot be "overcome" or talked around like a reluctant buyer's objection.

In fact, a Basic Issue and an objection, although they may both impede the selling process, are two very different things. An objection is merely the manifestation of an underlying Basic Issue; or, to put it in more exact terms, the Basic Issue is the hidden cause of the customer's reluctance, while the objection is the visible effect. When someone raises an objection, he's always giving you a signal that something underneath is troubling him. That "something" is a Basic Issue.

Another difference between an objection and a Basic Issue

is that an objection is usually something tangible about the product or service or its implementation. Basic Issues, on the other hand, are related to the customer's mental picture, or Concept. They may involve negative feelings about you, about your proposal, about your company, or about something else apparently unrelated to the sales situation. But whatever their ostensible focus, Basic Issues, like any mental picture, are subjective, intangible, and personal.

Overcoming an objection, therefore, is very different from dealing with a Basic Issue. It's no less than the difference between cause and effect, and sellers who consistently achieve Win-Win outcomes are never content simply to deal with effects. They know that dealing with causes is fundamental not only to Getting Commitment, but also to any long-term business relationship.

In the box on page 297 we've listed some possible Basic Issues you may encounter in your selling situations. These are, of course, only examples since the sources of Basic Issues are really unlimited. But they should be enough to give you the idea of what we mean. The list indicates how personal Basic Issues can be. That's the fundamental point to remember about them, and it's why they're often so difficult to resolve. Two related points deserve some emphasis:

First, you should never *judge* a Basic Issue. A Basic Issue is what someone is feeling, deep down, about what working with you will mean to her. There are ways to analyze and discuss and work with those feelings, but the one thing you should not do, ever, is to deny their validity. One of the surest ways we know to kill a sale on the spot is to suggest to someone with a Basic Issue, "You shouldn't be feeling that way."

Second, never assume that you know what the particular Basic Issue is. Since the "I'm losing" perception and non-

POSSIBLE BASIC ISSUES

- loss of power
- loss of control
- less leisure time
- lack of skill
  development
- decrease of personal
  productivity
- not seen as problem
  solver
- lack of recognition
- stuck in a rut

- loss of security
- being seen as malcontent
- not invented here
- seen as sub-par
  performer
- loss of credibility
- lose freedom of choice
- seen as me-too
- decrease responsibility
- loss of self-esteem
- less time with family

commitment are always linked, it's safe to assume when you cannot get commitment that there's *some* Basic Issue involved. But it's hazardous to assume that you know exactly what it is. Dealing with Mr. Franklin's fear that he's going to lose power, when in fact he's not worried about power at all but about a family situation, will do nothing for either of you but waste your time. As this example suggests, it's easy for a salesperson to confuse one possible Basic Issue for another. That's why we stress the principle of "No assumptions" and why we say that identifying specific Basic Issues is critical to Getting Commitment.

BASIC ISSUE SIGNALS

Before you can identify a specific Basic Issue, however, you need to be able to recognize that a Basic Issue exists—in other words, to recognize when your customer feels he or she is losing. You do that by attending to Basic Issue Signals, as indicated in the box below.

The signals identified there are fairly self-explanatory, and we're sure you can understand why we say a hesitant or argumentative customer is likely to be concealing a Basic Issue. One thing about this list that's not self-evident is that the severity of the signals increases as you go down the list and the probability of a good sale decreases. If you're dealing with a merely hesitant client, you generally still have time to iden-

---

BASIC ISSUE SIGNALS

- **Hesitation**

- **Questioning attitude**

- **Repeated objections**

- **Argument**

- **Passive resistance**

tify and resolve her Basic Issues before the situation deteriorates. By the time you are encountering arguments or passive resistance, it's unlikely you can save the sale.

In many sales situations, moreover, the severity of the customer's Basic Issue Signals will follow a kind of natural downward trajectory over time, going from bad to worse, *unless you consciously intervene.* In the early stages, you have a certain level of control over where the dialogue is going, but this level inevitably decreases the longer you ignore the Basic Issue. Since every sales call is unique, there is no absolute "signal level" at which you lose control of the sale. Generally, though, once responses have gotten beyond the "repeated objections" stage, it's very hard to turn things around. If you don't intervene by this point, the situation is almost certain to deteriorate further.

When we say "intervene," we mean something very specific. We mean that you need to ask a particular type of question to search out the hidden reason this individual feels he or she is going to lose. We call this fifth type of question a Basic Issue Question.

BASIC ISSUE QUESTIONS

A Basic Issue Question is a specialized type of Commitment Question. As one of our client associates, Stephanie Kuhnel, pointed out to us recently, Basic Issue Questions seek to uncover negative feelings, and thus they may also be seen as a subset of Attitude Questions. Like Attitude Questions too, they're often uncomfortable or unfamiliar territory for many salespeople, who may shy away from asking them because they're not used to them.

In our description of Commitment Questions in Chapter

14, we said their purpose was to show you where you were in the sale and what still needed to be done to move it forward. A Basic Issue Question does exactly that, in the context of a customer's reluctance. Basic Issue Questions have a dual purpose. On the downside, they help you to understand your customer's reasons for feeling that the situation is a Lose. On the positive side, they help you to uncover what still needs to be done to turn the situation into a Win.

PHRASING BASIC ISSUE QUESTIONS

But however you look at them, Basic Issue Questions are designed to reveal the customer's sense of uncertainty or con-

---

BASIC ISSUE QUESTIONS

PURPOSE:
- **Uncover why the sale is not moving forward**
- **Discover unidentified issues**
- **Learn how a customer may lose**

WHEN TO USE:
- **After a No response to a Commitment Question**
- **As a final test to ensure customer commitment**
- **When signals arise**

cern that has led to the reluctance in the first place. This is reflected in the key words you should use in phrasing these questions. Since you're trying to elicit information about a potentially gray area in the buy/sell encounter, it's appropriate to use key words like *doubtful, puzzled,* and *unclear.* See the box below for more examples.

BASIC ISSUE KEY WORDS

Uncertain	Issue
Questioning	Uncomfortable
Puzzled	Hesitant
Concern	Lose
Doubtful	Unclear

WHEN TO USE BASIC ISSUE QUESTIONS

When should you ask a Basic Issue Question? One of the most crucial places to do this is when you get an unexpected No answer to a Commitment Question. But that's only one example. Actually, you should ask a Basic Issue Question at *any* point in the call where you sense your customer is in an

"I'm losing" frame of mind. Whenever you spot a Basic Issue Signal, no matter how trivial it may seem, it's time to head off future trouble by immediately seeking the cause of the problem. The earlier you do this in the sales call, the better.

Better late than not at all, however. Another common place to ask a Basic Issue Question is toward the end of a call, when you sense that something about the call just didn't feel right. Every sales call should end with an understanding of what the customer will do before the next call—her commitment. Asking a Basic Issue Question toward the end of a call is one good way of determining just what the current level of commitment is. It's a solid way for you to make sure, before you walk out the door, that your customer understands not only what you're going to do for her, but what she's expected to do for you.

THE "UNSTUCK" SALE, OR BUYER'S REMORSE REVISITED

What you're going to do for the customer, at a point in the sale where you uncover a Basic Issue, should certainly include an attempt to understand and resolve it. We'll speak more about this in the Personal Workshop on Basic Issues. The essential point is that when a Basic Issue surfaces, the only way you can move the sale forward is to address the customer's Lose perception.

If you are unable to do that, if you don't have the authority to do it, or if you don't understand how to do it, then the smart response is to acknowledge the reality of the problem and to indicate to the customer that you're committed to finding a solution but that you cannot provide it on the spot. "Let me work on this, Lisa," you might say, "and I'll get back to you as soon as I can give you the kind of answer that would make you more comfortable."

Traditionally trained salespeople often don't do this. Instead, they ignore Basic Issue Signals, hoping they will go away, or they proceed under the false assumption that they need to deal with Basic Issues only when they surface as objections. This is a self-defeating tactic because it leaves you knowing less than you need to know to keep all the variables of the sale under control. Failing to address Basic Issue Questions is just asking for misinformation; when you're burdened with misinformation, you're in an even worse position than the salesperson with no information at all.

Can you make a sale without resolving a Basic Issue? Sure. Salespeople do it all the time when they ignore a customer's puzzled or uneasy looks and close the deal in spite of his resistance. Not all customers, after all, have a conscious handle on their Basic Issues. Often a customer will have only a vague sense of uncertainty or dissatisfaction and won't be able to articulate what's causing it. A salesperson who is solely concerned with getting the order and getting out can "help" a prospect to ignore these feelings.

But the long-term outcome of such sales is not good. Typically, two weeks or two months down the line, the customer finds out that the product didn't solve his problem, or that he's lost credibility with his colleagues because of the deal, or that the sale has made his job more rather than less difficult— in short, that for any one of dozens of reasons, the sale has become a personal Lose.

The implication for the seller is always bad. Even if the customer doesn't send your product back to the factory or make your service manager's life a nightmare, the very least he's going to do is to back away from doing future business with you. At worst, Buyer's Remorse will lead to Buyer's

Revenge. You'll have taken the order and run, all right, but just like the old-time snake oil drummers, you'll soon find that you can't stop running. This can happen even if you're not trying to win at your customer's expense.

Because of their hidden power to undo your good work, you have to make a conscious and active effort to seek out and deal with Basic Issues. We emphasize *active* to highlight the critical distinction between a Basic Issue and an objection. Sales reps are taught to overcome or ignore objections. It's never enough to "overcome" a Basic Issue—in fact, trying to do so can be dangerous—and it's often deadly to ignore it. Basic Issues are the hidden weapons threatening every sales relationship. You've got to go after them before they surface. You're going to do that now, in a Personal Workshop.

PERSONAL WORKSHOP #12: BASIC ISSUES

We've said that not all Basic Issues are clear to the potential buyer himself; they can be hidden and poorly understood. Even when the customer is conscious of them, though, they can still be hidden from you. So we break this Personal Workshop into two parts. In Part A, you'll clarify your understanding of those Basic Issues you've already identified. In Part B you'll work at identifying those that are still unknown to you.

At the top of a notebook page, write the heading "Basic Issues." Then, with a specific customer and a specific Single Sales Objective in mind, complete the following exercise.

PART A: KNOWN BASIC ISSUES

Step 1: Describe the customer's Basic Issues. Using as a guide the list of possible Basic Issues that we presented earlier in this chapter, start by jotting down all the areas of concern that this person has already expressed to you regarding the Single Sales Objective you're proposing. You're aiming here to identify areas of your customer's *distress,* and you can focus on the appropriate areas by asking yourself the general question, "How is this individual losing right now—or how does she think she's losing?"

You may come up with one or two or ten areas of concern here: Every one, if left unattended, can eventually undermine your sale, so don't be shy about listing even areas of "marginal" concern. A marginal concern can become a major one unless you bring it to the surface and resolve it.

Step 2: Confirm these Basic Issues. Since you will be meeting this person in the near future, and since the selling process can be stalled if you go in there with false assumptions, it's important to think out in advance how you will verify your current understanding of his concerns. You'll remember from the chapter on questioning that verification is accomplished with Confirmation Questions. So for each of the Basic Issues you've just listed, write down one Confirmation Question that you can ask on your next sales call with this individual to validate or invalidate your understanding.

For example, if Jane Beddoes in quality control has expressed concern about the security of her position, you might begin the next call on her with this Confirmation Question: "You had shown a little uncertainty about the effect of my proposal on job security. Do you still feel that's a possible problem?" The goal is to have a specific and properly phrased Confirmation Question to address each of your customer's known Basic Issues the next time you get together.

Step 3: Can you help? Just because you know what's bothering your customer doesn't necessarily mean you can solve his or her problem. In this step, for each known Basic Issue you've listed ask yourself the following question: "Am I in a realistic position to help this customer reduce or eliminate the Lose perception?"

If the package you're offering Ms. Beddoes will bring her instant recognition and thus enhance her job security, then the answer may be Yes—provided that this is indeed the area where she's feeling distress. If her feeling of uneasiness is related to something that's outside your control, then the answer is No. Being as realistic as you can about your own capabilities, identify which Basic Issues are within your power to affect and which are not.

One way to check your understanding in this step is to refer to the Unique Strengths workshop you did in Chapter 12. There you highlighted areas where your proposal and your company could have a positive impact at this time on your customer's problem or problems. In addressing a customer's Basic Issues, it's always best to work from a position of strength. Reviewing your Unique Strengths in a specific scenario is a way of ensuring you're doing that.

Don't be surprised if you uncover Basic Issues that you aren't capable of resolving—areas where you can't eliminate the Lose for your customer. Don't be disappointed either. Finding out there are aspects of a sale that you are not able to handle at this time can be just as valuable a discovery as finding out you've got an answer for everything.

In fact, it can be far more valuable. Let's face it—nobody has an answer for everything every time, and the salespeople who say that they do are the "refrigerators to Eskimos" types who rarely deal with the same customer twice. We've already mentioned that in some sales scenarios the wisest course of action may be to recognize that you can't help—and walk away. Identifying your customer's currently unresolvable Basic Issues is a step toward that sadder but wiser understanding.

Step 4: Identify appropriate actions. Now that you've sorted out the Basic Issues you can address from those you cannot, you should identify, for each resolvable Basic Issue, a specific, concrete action you can take on the next sales call with this individual to reduce or eliminate the Lose perception. *Action* here is really another word for Giving Information. What you're trying to do here is to identify the information you can give on the next sales call that will best address his or her Basic Issues.

Again, your Unique Strengths list should be of benefit. When you've identified appropriate actions/information for each Basic Issue, write them down in your notebook. For example: "Tell Jane Beddoes how this package got her counterpart at Wilson Industries a promotion." We don't pretend that writing yourself messages like this is going to solve either your problem or your customer's instantly. But it will make visible to you those remaining areas of difficulty so that you can pay attention to them next time out.

This action list is not a blueprint, but it can be a valuable pre-call rehearsal tool. So hang on to it. By checking it over before you go in to meet Ms. Beddoes again, you'll be better equipped to give her information that can turn her Lose into a mutual Win.

PART B: UNKNOWN BASIC ISSUES

As we've said, there are usually known and unknown Basic Issues in most buyer/seller relationships. If there's been a commitment problem in your sales calls to a certain customer but you can't pin down why, we encourage you to do the following exercise to prepare for your next sales call on that person.

Step 1: Is there a Basic Issue? First, determine whether or not the problem you've been having with this customer is a Basic Issue problem. Ask yourself whether the selling situation as it now stands fits the typical pattern of sales being blocked by Basic Issues. In that pattern, we've found, three elements are present:

- First, there is a real match—or at least a potential match—between the salesperson's product or service and the customer's solution image. Before you try to seek out unknown Basic Issues, be sure first of all that there really is a fit between what you have and what the customer needs.
- Second, both you and the customer experience a sense of uneasiness. If every time you come out of a meeting with this person, you feel irritated and/or confused, there's a pretty good chance you're picking up on Basic Issue Signals.
- Finally, there's no movement toward commitment. In spite of the good potential match, you cannot get the customer to agree to do anything but schedule one more meeting. So you're doing all of the work.

When one or more of these three elements is present, you can be fairly confident there's a Basic Issue involved.

Step 2: Phrase Basic Issue Questions. The next step is to phrase good Basic Issue Questions that will help you identify which Basic Issue is involved. Since you're not certain what you're looking for, and since you don't want to put words in your customer's mouth, it's important not to ask closed or "leading" questions, but to help him to express his own concerns. Refer to the Basic Issue key words we suggested earlier in the chapter and try to come up with two or three well-phrased questions you can ask next time out to find out why this individual thinks he's losing.

It's hard to give specific phrasing guidelines here because each buyer/seller relationship is different. We know one exuberant young sales rep who, when he senses a customer feels he's losing, throws his cards brashly on the table. "Tim," he'll say, "there's something that's bugging you here, and I can't figure out what. I know you're not happy. What's wrong?" He can get away with that (most of the time) because of his particular warmth and charm, although for many of us such a direct method would be a disaster. You have to create your own style of questioning, depending on your individual relationships. But we can give you some tips.

- We've found that the key word *concern* generally tends to get better results—that is, more reliable information—than almost any other key word. It seems less threatening to most people than the potentially condescending *puzzled* and *upset*. "What are your concerns with this proposal?" is one of the best of all Basic Issue Questions.
- You can sometimes get a reluctant individual to talk more freely if you ask the Basic Issue Question in a positive rather than negative manner. If he's hesitant to tell you why he's concerned, you might ask: "If I could give you

a proposal that would make you entirely comfortable, what would it look like?"

- Asking a customer to identify what's making him uncertain can sometimes help reduce or eliminate the uncertainty. We've said that people don't always consciously understand what their Basic Issues are. Asking "Is there something you're uncertain about here?" can often help both you and the customer to bring his Basic Issue to the surface.

- Always use your own feelings as a guide. You project your own uncertainties and concerns out onto your customers no less than they do onto you. Therefore, if you're uncomfortable with the way you've phrased a question—if you feel uneasy about asking it—rephrase it so that you are comfortable.

- Remember Golden Silence. This technique, which we described in Chapter 11, is important in phrasing and asking any type of question. Since Basic Issue Questions, like Attitude Questions, deal with feelings, it's especially important to *wait* for answers when you lay out these questions.

Step 3: Do you need coaching? Finally, consider the possibility that for this individual at this time, you need to seek coaching from someone else in order to get reliable information. There are essentially three ways to get Basic Issue information. One is to guess, which is worthless. Another is to ask the relevant customer directly, and that's what you've been practicing in this Personal Workshop. A third and often very valuable way is to ask someone who knows your customer well about his or her possible Basic Issues. This is an especially useful method in those cases where the person himself doesn't know—or doesn't want you to know—why he feels he's losing.

Of course you can't ask just anybody. When you're trying to verify information regarding a customer's Basic Issues, we advise you to look for potential "coaches" who trust you and your company personally; are trusted by the customer's organization; and want you, for whatever reason, to make this sale. If you test your potential information sources against these three criteria, you can dramatically increase the probability that the data they give you about this customer is going to be accurate and useful.

Once you've found out from your customer and/or from other sources what his Basic Issues are, the unknown obviously becomes the known. And when each Basic Issue becomes known, you can then go back to the beginning of this Personal Workshop and run through Steps 1 to 4 of Part A again as a way of further clarifying your information.

COMMITMENT SIGNALS

We've said that if you ignore or try to avoid a Basic Issue, you are in effect ignoring the customer's Lose perception—and thus setting yourself up to lose too. Oddly enough, sellers often also ignore their customers' Win perceptions. The results of that are no better. In order to avoid this trap, you need to be attentive to what we call Commitment Signals.

A Commitment Signal is a message from the customer to the salesperson indicating that she is ready to move the buy/sell process forward. She may or may not be ready to sign an order, but she's certainly considering the how and the when of doing so.

Since we've emphasized that Getting Commitment means getting the customer to do something, you might think that salespeople would be continually alert to Commitment Signals. Not so. We've found that although the buyer will invariably tell you when he is ready to buy, many sellers never hear the message and as a result they lose major business.

There's the salesperson who's so busy showing off bells and whistles that she doesn't hear the prospect say "I'll take it." Or the sales rep who ignores his customer's query, "When can we get the training started?" and goes rattling on about the features and benefits. This kind of behavior is what we call "snatching defeat from the jaws of victory." It happens generally because salespeople mistake a Commitment Signal for "just another question" or because they have not thought out clearly in advance what kind of commitment they want on a sales call—and so they miss it when it is offered.

In order to actually get the commitment you want when it's offered, you have to attend to the buyer's signals. Luckily, they're not difficult to identify. Commitment Signals are almost always phrased in the form of a question or statement about *implementation*. Implementation can refer to a huge range of issues—not just the "end business" of getting an order—but in general the signals all have one thing in common: They show that in thinking about your solution, the customer has made a critical move from "whether" to "how."

Some major implementation areas are itemized in the box on page 313. Here are some questions that are typically asked with regard to these areas:

- "How long will it take for delivery?"
- "When can my techs be retrained?"
- "How much lead time will we need to schedule a pilot run?"
- "Will you be able to give us a loaner until ours arrives from the factory?"
- "I'd like to check out three references."

IMPLEMENTATION AREAS

- cost
- timing
- references
- installation
- training
- administration
- conversion
- servicing
- credit
- terms
- financing
- payments
- demonstration
- trial run
- pilot program
- tests
- validation
- spec measurements
- logistics

Behind all these sample questions lies the same basic implication. It's that the customer is ready to give commitment and that he just wants to be told how to go about it.

It should be clear why we call such questions and statements Commitment Signals—and why you have to respond to them when they happen. It all comes back to hearing your customer—to listening to what she has to say, whatever phase of the sales call you are in. The entire information-exchange process—call it a teaching process or a selling process—begins with what's in your customer's mind with her Concept of what she's trying to accomplish.

As our discussion of the three phases has made clear, the only truly effective way of tracking and working with your customer's Concept is to ask much more than you tell and to listen—really listen—to the answers. That's the way you develop positive information now. It's the way you ultimately get commitment. And it's the way, over the long run, that you nurture the Win-Win relationships we all require.

PART VI

ZERO HOUR—
AND BEYOND

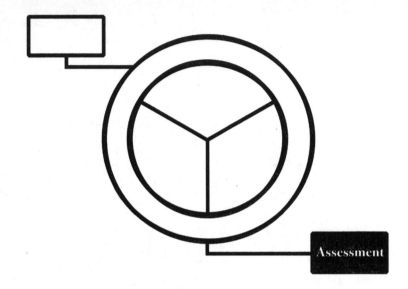

Assessment

CHAPTER 16

PRE-CALL PLANNING AND REHEARSAL

Every professional whose work involves public presentation appreciates the importance of rehearsing. Public speakers, actors, athletes, teachers—the best of them spend time practicing their performances over and over without the audience so that when it's time to go on, the work becomes almost automatic. In many cases, success in these fields very often comes not to the person who puts in the most effort during the performance but to the person who has already put so much into rehearsing that he can manage the performance as if by instinct. Since selling also involves the art of public presentation, the same thing is true here too. But with one important proviso.

We've emphasized throughout this book that good selling is never a song and dance that you "put on" for your customers. Yes, a good sales call is a kind of performance. But it's a performance in which you and the customer are equally significant to the outcome—one in which her lines are as much a part of the script as anything in your presentation. In fact, the whole point of Conceptual Selling is to interact with each of your customers, rather than to "act" to, at, or in spite of them. In effective selling, you are not simply on stage; indeed, success comes from transcending the performer/audience distinction and establishing dialogue.

This doesn't mean that rehearsing is unimportant to the sales professional. It's extremely important. In fact, running through the possible "lines" of a sales call can be a very productive exercise for you to perform just before you are ready to sit down with the client. In this chapter you're going to walk through just such an exercise by pulling together all the tactical planning you've done so far and applying it, in a coordinated fashion, to a last-minute dress rehearsal. The difference between you and an actor or speaker is that you will be rehearsing an anticipated conversation rather than a cut-and-dried, show-and-tell delivery.

The first step is for you to pick the specific sales call you will be rehearsing. Since this chapter will be both a review of the tactical planning principles we've already introduced and a practical application of those principles, we suggest that you select one of the sales calls you've worked with as a model throughout this book. If your own selling situation has changed since you chose those calls and you're now more eager to have solid tactical help for another call, fine: choose the upcoming sales encounter that is, right now, most important to you. Since this is a last-minute dress rehearsal, you can choose an encounter that is going to happen very soon. The process we'll develop in this chapter, in fact, is most effective when applied only a day or two in advance of the sales call.

The Sales Call Guide

Once you've chosen the call, open your notebook flat so that you have a two-page spread before you. If you prefer, use a single sheet of large paper laid out with the long side horizontal. You're going to be constructing a sales tool, the Sales Call Guide, which involves a little more space than the Personal Workshops you've done before. Across the top of the page or pages write the heading "Sales Call Guide." At the top left-hand corner of the Guide, write in the name of the account you'll be calling on, the name of the person you'll be contacting, and a statement of your Single Sales Objective.

Remember that a good Single Sales Objective defines what you want to have happen in the account that isn't happening right now and that it is always specifc: It tells you what you want to be selling, how much of it you want to be selling, and by what date. Remember, too, that to be realistic, a Single Sales Objective has to be something the individual customer you're calling on can agree with.

Now you can construct the Sales Call Guide by following the format we've laid out on page 320. You'll see that the left-hand half of the Guide is divided into four blocks and the right-hand half is divided into three. Make those divisions on your Guide, and fill in the subheadings and questions as we have filled them in on the sample. Now, with your single upcoming sales call in mind, you can rehearse it by pulling together the information you generated in the Personal Workshops and organizing it into one concise tactical tool. We'll walk you through this trial rehearsal by taking each of the sections of the Sales Call Guide in turn.

SALES CALL GUIDE

Account: _____

Prospect/customer: _____

Single Sales Objective: _____

Concept	Action Commitments	Getting Information
• Trying to fix or avoid: • Who helped shape Concept: • Customer's personal Win:	• Best Action: • Minimium Acceptable: • How to be measured:	• Confirmation Questions: • New Information Questions: • Attitude Questions: • Commitment Questions:
		Giving Information
		• Unique Strengths • So what? • Prove it
Valid Business Reason • Valid Business Reason/ purpose of call: • Connection to customer's Concept:	**Credibility** • Evidence of credibility: • How to check or enhance on this call:	**Getting Commitment** • Questions: Best Action/Minimum Acceptable • Possible Basic Issues: • Basic Issue Questions:

Concept. In the top left section, briefly define the Concept that you believe this individual customer has regarding his or her situation as it relates to your Single Sales Objective. Remember that Concept is defined as a solution image in the customer's mind and that it relates to the immediate business situation. So sharpen your understanding of that solution image by writing down answers to the following questions:

- What is this person trying to accomplish, fix, or avoid?
- How did this person arrive at his Concept? Who was involved in helping him shape that mental picture?
- What's in it personally for this individual to take or recommend action on my solution?

Action Commitments. Now move to the top right block of the left side and review the Action Commitments you defined in the Personal Workshops on this concept in Chapters 6 and 14. Copy down here the Best Action Commitment and the Minimum Acceptable Action that you defined there, and then answer the following questions:

- Are both these Action Commitments realistic, given where I am right now in the selling process?
- Are they both actions to be taken by the customer rather than by me or my company?
- Once either one of them is accomplished, will I have advanced in a positive direction toward achieving my Single Sales Objective?
- How will I know that one or the other of these Action Commitments has in fact been accomplished? In other words, will I be able to document them?
- Are these two Action Commitments consistent with practicing Win-Win and building credibility?

You should be able to answer Yes to all of these questions. If you can't, you may have more thinking to do before you're sufficiently prepared to enter this sales call confidently.

Valid Business Reason. Now, with reference to the Personal Workshop in Chapter 7, state the Valid Business Reason that would encourage this customer to agree to meeting with you, and write it down in the lower-left block. Remember that this is the *purpose* of the meeting, and it must be a purpose that makes sense to this individual customer. Then ask:

- Does this Valid Business Reason have a clear connection to this individual's Concept at this time?

- If I stated this Valid Business Reason at the start of the call, would it clarify the purpose of the call and set a mutually agreeable agenda?
- Does it indicate why this call should be a high-priority item for this customer?
- Is it stated concisely enough and clearly enough to be relayed unambiguously by an assistant or left on voice mail?

Again, the clearer your answers to these questions, the more likely it is that you're really ready for this call

Credibility. In this block, assess your credibility with this customer at this time. Reviewing the information you identified in the Personal Workshop in Chapter 8, ask yourself:

- If I have credibility, what will I do on this call to check or enhance it?
- If I don't have credibility, what can I do on this call to establish it? And if the answer to that is "Nothing," does it make sense for me to be making this call at this time? Should I postpone it, or should I make it as a joint call with someone who does have credibility with this individual?

Getting Information. Now move to the right-hand side of the Sales Call Guide and organize the data you have collected about the three basic phases of the sales call. Start at the top with Getting Information. Refer to the Personal Workshop on questioning and to the Question Grid that you constructed in Chapter 10, and write down the following:

- At least one good Confirmation Question: a question that will validate or invalidate information you think you already have. Test this question by asking yourself: "Does this question build a foundation from which I can move forward?"

- At least one good New Information Question: one that will help you to update information, fill in your information gaps, resolve discrepancies, and/or get further information about this person's desired results.
- At least one good Attitude Question: one that will clarify your understanding of this person's individual values and attitudes. Be sure that it is phrased nonthreateningly, so that it will encourage the person to share her feelings.
- At least one good Commitment Question: a question that will tell you where you are in the selling process and what still needs to be done to move you closer to a Win-Win outcome.

Giving Information. Move down to the middle section of the right-hand side, and refer to the Personal Workshop in Chapter 12. Then, referring to your Unique Strengths chart, identify your Unique Strengths in this selling scenario with this particular customer. Be sure to avoid "strengths" that are merely "me too" strengths, and remember that a difference in degree can also be seen as "unique." Then ask:

- How does this Unique Strength relate to this individual's Concept? How will my delivering it help to provide the solution image he has in mind?
- How does it relate to my Single Sales Objective?
- Test the validity of your supposed "uniqueness" by answering the question "So what?" Remember that the answer or answers you give must be relevant to this person right now.
- Prove it. Write down the "proof" that you're unique by

answering the questions we gave in Step 4 of the Personal Workshop on Unique Strengths: "We are the only ones who" and/or "We are different because." Be sure that each answer you give here effectively links your product or service to this particular customer's Concept.

Getting Commitment. Finally, in the lower-right-hand section of the Sales Call Guide, transfer the information you acquired in Part 5 of the book on Getting Commitment.

- First, referring to the Personal Workshop in Chapter 14, write down one good question related to your Best Action Commitment and one related to your Minimum Acceptable Action.
- Next, ask what are the possible Basic Issues that might impede commitment on this upcoming call. Remember that a Basic Issue is the root cause of an objection being raised; it has to do with the prospective buyer's feeling that he or she is going to lose.
- Now, referring to the Personal Workshop in Chapter 15, write down at least one Basic Issue Question designed to uncover and address the customer's Lose perception.

Once you've displayed all the information you have on the Sales Call Guide, you'll have a concise, organized planning tool that focuses on what is actually likely to happen in the call, based on your past experience with this individual. That's a necessary baseline for rehearsal, but it's still only a baseline. It's approximately equivalent to what an actor has when he has learned the lines cold. In order to put those lines into operation, you can still profit from a dry run, and that's exactly what we suggest as the next step in this rehearsal exercise.

NO-RISK REHEARSAL

In our Conceptual Selling programs, participants work in teams to practice the principles we've introduced, with the person who is actually going to make the sales call playing herself and the partner she is working with taking the part of the customer. This kind of exercise, where people are allowed to run through the basics of a call in a low-stress, no-risk environment, enables them to become comfortable with the process more readily than they could if they just jumped into the call feet first. We recommend that you do a similar exercise. Select a friend, fellow salesperson, or family member to play the role of your customer. Take about five or ten minutes to brief that person on the selling situation. The briefing will, of course, vary depending on the particular situation, but you will at least want to fill your rehearsal partner in on the following:

- the role the individual currently plays in the buying organization
- what business you've done with this person in the past, and the Win-Win history of that business
- your Single Sales Objective
- a description of this person's current responsiveness to your proposal—both in terms of the results he wants and in terms of his personal feelings about the sale
- anything else that is relevant to the way the person is likely to respond to you in the sales call

Once you've briefed the person you'll be trying out the call on, take ten or fifteen minutes to go through the dress rehearsal. Encourage your partner to be as resistant and "difficult" as necessary to reflect the real responsiveness level of your customer. He will be able to do so, of course, only if you have briefed him properly beforehand.

We realize that the exercise we're suggesting here may not always turn out as realistically as you would like. Your partner may not be as perceptive or demanding as your real customer will be—and he certainly won't be as personally involved in the possible sales transaction. Rehearsal is only an approximation of what will happen when you sit down face to face with the client. Yet even such an approximation can bring you enormous benefits. The reason is that even in an artificial setting, you are able to lay down a preliminary but still useful map you can follow, with some necessary adjustments, in the call.

Athletes sometimes speak of mentally going over and over a given motion or technique until it becomes second nature so that they don't have to think about it in performance. Rehearsing a sales call with a friend seems to have the same function: It burns a basic path in your thinking that you can start from when you're actually in the call. Now, in order to be as sure as possible even before the call that this path is an appropriate one, we suggest that you perform one more exercise before the call. Check the fluidity and effectiveness of the path you've laid down by getting some feedback on the rehearsal.

Pre-Call Feedback

In our two-day programs our participants get this feedback from a neutral observer—someone who watches the sales call rehearsal and gives constructive criticism afterward. You can use this same format yourself, or you can simply get feedback from talking to your partner about how the practice call went.

In either case, what you should look for are areas where your interaction was effective and areas where it was defective. In focusing on these areas, we have found the following checklist to be helpful. After the dry run is over, ask yourself:

- Did I clearly state the Valid Business Reason at the outset?
- Did I lead off with a good Confirmation Question?
- Did I ask at least one good New Information Question?
- Did I ask at least one good Attitude Question?
- Did I ask at least one good Commitment Question that invited incremental commitment?
- Was the order of my questions logical?
- Were the questions phrased properly—did they use the appropriate key words?
- Did I fill in the client's cognition gaps (and my own) before moving on to suggest divergent alternatives?
- Did the information I gave the client clearly highlight my Unique Strengths?
- Did I practice Golden Silence I and Golden Silence II?
- Did I avoid using dangerous verbal signals?
- Did I use Joint Venture Selling; or, if I used traditional product-oriented selling, was this in response to the client's specific request for product information?
- Did I check my credibility with this client before and/or during the sales call?
- Did I strive to keep the call Win-Win—and did I make sure the customer knew that?

You'll really only be able to answer these questions after you've gone through the actual sales call and have feedback from your real client. But running this preliminary check often proves to be valuable. It's a way of highlighting problem areas in your presentation and, therefore, of being able to correct them before Zero Hour.

If your rehearsal partner, for example, has the impression that you were rushing too quickly toward the close, then the chances are good your real customer might have the same feeling. Or if your partner doesn't recall your asking a Confirmation Question toward the beginning of the call, you can make a note to yourself not to neglect this factor in the real call. Getting this pre-call feedback is like getting last-minute instructions from a drama coach: It gives you the opportunity to preview what will happen in Zero Hour.

THE UNREHEARSABLE CALL

The kind of exercise we've just outlined can be a sound learning technique even for so-called unrehearsable sales calls—the kind of "calls" you might make, for example, if you are selling over a counter or on a floor, where potential customers come to you. If you're a floor salesperson or involved in over-the-counter sales, therefore, we urge you too to try out your tactical skills on a friend or fellow salesperson. By getting a friend to be the "just browsing" customer or the person who isn't sure what she wants, you can construct your own type of maps for dealing with a variety of situations.

The watchword here is the same one that applies in call situations: Always start with the Concept. Remember the story we told in Chapter 2 about the friend who entered a clothing store intending to buy one blazer and ended up carting home half the stock because a salesperson had focused on his Concept. That's the first and most important lesson anybody in selling can learn, whatever the type of transaction.

Second, we urge you to perform the same pre-call feedback on your rehearsal interactions that we have described above. It's true you can't very well check out a Valid Business Reason or Confirmation Question. But the remaining items on the checklist are relevant to your type of selling—they're relevant to any type of selling—and we encourage you to apply them to your situations.

HOW MUCH REHEARSAL?

Ideally, you should plan tactics for every sales call with the same diligence and comprehensiveness that you have put into the Personal Workshops here. Ideally, you should have a Sales Call Guide, with all the questions designed and all the information filled in, for every meeting you walk into. And ideally, you should rehearse every face-to-face interaction as we've asked you to rehearse this one. If you did these things before every call, there's no question the quality of your calls would go up 100 percent.

But you live in the real world, not an ideal one. And you know that if you performed this kind of extensive analytical labor on every sales call you had coming up, you'd never have time to do any actual selling. Because we understand that, we don't advise you to be as extensive in your sales call analysis every time as you have been for your model calls in this book.

What we've laid out in this book is, we believe, the most complete and comprehensive planning format you can possibly apply to your sales calls. On the most important, most urgent, or most complicated calls, you may want to run through the whole format: You may want to use every one of our Personal Workshops, to organize the information you get from them into a new, specific Sales Call Guide, and to spend time rehearsing the call as well. But not all calls will demand the full treatment. As you use the principles of Conceptual Selling over time, it will gradually become clearer to you which calls deserve the full treatment and which ones can be appropriately managed with something less. But the basic guidelines here are simple ones:

- The more potential *revenue* involved in the sale, the more attention you want to pay to how each individual sales call is managed.
- The more *time* you have already invested in the sale in terms of sales calls already made, the more important the planning. We say this not only because more calls mean more investment, but also because as any sale approaches the close, it becomes notoriously prone to inertia, carelessness, and possible erosion.
- The better chance you have with an individual for establishing a long-term Win-Win relationship, the more sense it makes for you to manage every sales call to that person in a highly organized manner.

Thus the last word here, as in most aspects of Conceptual Selling, is that ultimate sales success depends on looking to the future. It depends on managing each individual sales call not only so it's a success in itself, but so it fits into a larger pattern. The amount of rehearsal you should do for an individual sales call, ultimately, is the amount that will best foster a *long-term relationship* with this customer. You start with the individual sales call, but you never forget the big picture.

As a way of helping you to keep that big picture in mind, and to move your sales calls continually forward, we'll turn now to the final element of tactical planning: the assessment of what Zero Hour has brought you, and how to use it in managing the future.

CHAPTER 17

ASSESSING THE CALL

The last element in our tactical planning system is put into place only after the sales call is made. That element is assessment, and even though it follows the "real" business of the sales call, it is not optional. Just as an actor uses the responses of her audience to adjust and fine-tune future performances, and just as an athlete watches game films, the sales professional analyzes the dynamics of each individual sales call in retrospect as a way of sharpening the management of future calls. Post-call assessment, then, is a critical factor in ongoing success.

Performing an assessment after each call is valuable for two basic reasons:

1. Assessment helps you to measure the actual "hard" data of the call—that is, to understand what information has been successfully exchanged and what still needs to be exchanged.

2. Assessment helps you to judge the "soft," interpersonal data of the call—to evaluate how you interacted with the customer and how you should alter your interaction in the future.

It is to help you gain these two tactical benefits—an understanding of the what and an understanding of the how—that we introduce the element of assessment.

To use this element effectively, you need to sit down as soon as possible after the sales call, take out a notebook and pencil, and run through three distinct but interrelated processes. You'll have the opportunity in this chapter to do this with regard to your model sales call. If you haven't yet made that sales call, we suggest that you wait before reading further. After you have made the call, begin your reading again here.

FIRST PROCESS: REVIEW

Typically, when sales professionals leave a sales encounter they have only a vague sense of how things went. We ask field reps all the time to give us a reading on their calls. Unless they've actually nailed down the order or been thrown out, their responses tend to be nonspecific: "I think it went all right." "She seems really interested." Or "It's hard to say what, but something's wrong." The purpose of the review process is to make better sense of these vague feelings. It's to look more closely at specific elements of the sales call in order to understand why you feel "OK" or "pretty good" or "not sure."

Which elements? Well, the basic elements you want to check in the assessment stage are those that we identified in the pre-call feedback list on page 327. We emphasized the importance of getting feedback from your partner in the rehearsal stage and/or from a neutral observer. It's unlikely that you'll be able to get the same kind of feedback from an actual customer or from someone looking over your shoulder in the actual call. But you can get some feedback by asking yourself these same questions. Do that now, and write the answers in your notebook.

These answers should help you get a better handle on the reasons for your comfortable or uncomfortable feelings, and they should help you to modify your tactics for future calls on this and other customers. For example, if in reviewing the situation you realize that you used too many dangerous verbal signals ("Think about it," "Right?" and so on), then that might partially account for the resistance of your potential client. Or if you realize that you failed to check your credibility with this person on this call, that may help to explain why he was reluctant to open up to you.

Whether the answers to your feedback questions are favorable or unfavorable, they will still clarify your understanding—and that is always favorable. In addition to the pre-call feedback questions, there are three other questions you should ask yourself in the review process of assessment. These relate to the three phases of the sales call.

What is the current information level? That is, what information did you actually receive in the sales encounter, and how does that information relate to the information you knew you needed when you went into the call? Remember that in the Getting Information phase of any sales call, you should be concentrating on the information you need to understand the prospective customer's Concept. If you've just come out of a meeting with Mr. Harrigan and you're still uncertain about his Concept, mark that down as an area of missing information. And start drafting good questions for the next call that will get you that information.

In focusing on the information you need in order to understand the client's Concept, we suggest that you turn back to the Question Grid in Chapter 10 and review the six typical information-poor areas. To find out why the sales call went the way it did, ask yourself, with regard to each one of those areas, what information you wanted when you entered the call—and what information you still have to obtain. This kind of review process can tell you that you have less information than you thought you had. It can tell you that you have more (or different) information than you thought you had. And it can underline the effectiveness, or lack of effectiveness, of your communication process.

If in reviewing the last call you discover that you still have the same information gaps you had going in to the call, then you know there's something wrong with the information flow. Knowing that, you can fine-tune your questioning for next time. The point we're making is that good information flow is not static. It's part of a dynamic system of interpersonal exchange that works to full effect only when you remain alert to your current information level, and work continually to raise it.

What's the current level of differentiation? In the Giving Information phase of the sales call, you deliver data to your customers that will enable them to differentiate. In reviewing this second phase of your last call, you want to find out how successful you were in giving that specialized kind of information.

In doing that, you should focus on statements the customer made in the sales call regarding your specific proposal, your competition's possible proposals, and the current status quo. (Remember that one of your chief competitors in any selling situation is the way the client is doing things right now.) If she made comments indicating that you're the "only supplier" with a given capability or that you're "different from the rest of the field" in some significant way, then your level of differentiation is probably high. But if she claimed she could get "the same solution, only cheaper" somewhere else, or if she's "not ready for this type of change yet," then you obviously have more work to do in this area.

There's only one way that a customer will differentiate in your favor. That's if he sees a Unique Strength in your solution to his particular problem. If the review process reveals that you are less clearly differentiated than you want to be, you need to ask yourself some questions. For example:

- *Do I really have a Unique Strength in this situation?* That is, can I really offer a solution that this customer sees as different (and better) to a significant degree than what anyone else is offering? If you're not sure about this, you should consider the possibility that there's not a real match here between your product or service and the customer's Concept—and you should consider holding off on this sale.

- *Have I made my uniqueness and my strength clear?* If you're sure there's a good match but the customer is still balking on price or still "unclear" about your solution, you may not have highlighted your Unique Strength(s) effectively. If review uncovers this possibility, you need to start thinking about tactics for the next call that will clearly relate your product or service to the Concept.

- *Have I been helping or hindering the decision-making process?* One reason customers may be reluctant to acknowledge your Unique Strengths is that they have been rushed too quickly into divergent thinking and have not been given sufficient time for cognition. You can use your assessment of this possibility to set a tactical plan for the next call that focuses on cognition and on the client's personal solution image.

Again, the point here is to begin with what's in the customer's mind. One of the principal advantages of reviewing the differentiation level reached on the previous call is that it can alert you to the possibility that you have been falling into the "seller-driven" trap. Identifying an insufficient level of differentiation gives you the knowledge and the opportunity to move the next call into a more productive, customer-driven mode.

What's the current level of Action Commitment? This is a relatively easy question to answer because it involves hard facts, not impressions. In evaluating Action Commitment, there are two such facts you need to note.

1. When you walked into the call, had your client already performed the Action that she'd promised to perform by that date? That is, had she actually done what was supposed to have been done by the time of the meeting?
2. Before you left the call, did she give you another, incremental level of commitment for the next time? And was that incremental level of commitment equivalent to your Best Action Commitment or at least to your Minimum Acceptable Action?

If on this past call, your client had done what was promised, and if you got your Best Action Commitment besides, great: the selling process is obviously moving in the right direction. But if he had not come through for you, or if he was unwilling to give you a further, incremental commitment, then you may have some rethinking to do. And if on this past call you were unable to get even your Minimum Acceptable Action for the following call, then you're going to have to make a decision. You have to consider the possibility that it may not be worth the effort to do any more fine-tuning for this customer, at least not at this time. But we recommend that you take this drastic step only after performing the second assessment process: sorting.

SECOND PROCESS: SORTING

We've said that when you don't get your Minimum Acceptable Action from a sales call, you should think about not coming back. But because we know how difficult it is for salespeople to walk away from potential business, and because we believe you should always give your customers a reasonable number of opportunities to stay Win-Win with you, we'll add a small rider. The second assessment process, sorting, enables you to perform a last-ditch check on difficult customers to be sure you're not just letting yourself off easy by backing away from their business.

To sort your prospective clients into those with real potential and those without it, recall the Getting Commitment phase of the sales call. Remember that the root cause of every blocked commitment is a Basic Issue—the client's feeling that he will lose by allowing you to continue the selling process. We ask you here to identify Basic Issues that were raised, resolved, and remaining on the previous call. Before doing this, you may want to refer to the Personal Workshop on Basic Issues you did in Chapter 15.

What Basic Issues were raised? Remember that Basic Issues can be either known or unknown. In the Personal Workshop, you identified which Basic Issues for this customer fell into each of those categories, and in the sales call to this person you should have worked to raise and confront those Basic Issues you had not previously been able to identify. Recall now what Basic Issues—what Lose perceptions—were actually discussed in your last meeting with this person. And ask yourself: Could there still be Basic Issues that I have not identified which are contributing to the lack of commitment? If the answer to that is even a provisional Yes, then you may want to give the customer one more shot to try to bring to the surface his personal reasons for withholding commitment.

What Basic Issues were resolved? If you identified and addressed the customer's Basic Issue concerns on the previous call, how were these concerns resolved? Are you sure you didn't simply dismiss his worries as "unimportant" or "irrelevant" to the situation, rather than working with him to demonstrate the potential Win-Win outcome? If you're not certain that you adequately resolved his Lose perception— and if you think one more call might accomplish that—then maybe you shouldn't dismiss this customer just yet.

What Basic Issues could be remaining? Finally, what Basic Issues might still remain in the buy/sell scenario? Did the customer raise concerns you could not resolve? Did you promise resolution in the past that you haven't yet delivered? And is it possible this person harbors worries about doing business with you that you haven't even identified yet? In other words, are there any possible *hidden* issues remaining? If the answer to any of these questions is Yes, then it may be reasonable for the person to be refusing to make an Action Commitment. And it may be reasonable for you to call on him one more time to see whether the Lose perception can still be turned into a Win.

But what if the answer to all these questions is No? What if, no matter what you've done on previous sales calls and no matter what you can imagine doing on future calls, you feel that this person will not budge? What if, in spite of the salesperson's standard-issue attitude of "Hope springs eternal," when you look at the situation honestly you realize your chances are nil? If that's the case, it's probably time to stop investing your energy and resources here.

Face it. There are always going to be sales situations that you cannot make come out Win-Win. Some of these will be situations where, try as you might, a solid match between what you have and what the customer needs simply doesn't exist; in these cases, "hanging in there" is never an acceptable way to sell. In other cases, with the best match in the world, the individual client just won't see it because she's not interested in staying Win-Win with you; in these Lose-Win cases, you always lose less by leaving than you would by toughing it out. In short, when the selling process becomes a battle, you can be pretty sure it's time to quit the field.

Not only should selling not be a battle, but it should be fun. Even though it's very hard work, you should get pleasure from it, or what's the point? So if you're not enjoying your work with a given customer—if you're both feeling dissatisfied most of the time—it may be time to retire gracefully.

But not necessarily forever. Many times, you'll find that a selling process that founders in March runs along smoothly in July because the situation has changed and a clear match between product and need now exists. So sometimes not only is discretion the better part of valor, but discretion can be extended to the future. The best sales professionals we know, when they are forced to sort a no-Win client out of their possible business, still keep one eye on the situation for months or even years down the line. Sometimes waiting for the timing to improve can be the critical difference between butting your head against a wall and building a solid structure together.

THIRD PROCESS: "FEEDFORWARD"

The third and final process of assessment is to put all the information you now have into the next stage of your tactical planning. You've just reviewed and analyzed all the data that went into the outcome of the previous sales call. Unless that was absolutely the final time you are ever going to sit down with that customer, then it is imperative to use the information to make the next call on this person an improvement. In other words, you've gotten the feedback you need to understand how things just went. You now have the chance to "feedforward" so that you don't make the same mistakes again—and so that, in that next call, you are able to build toward greater commitment.

The bare minimum for doing that is to write down the who, what, when, and where of your next meeting regarding this account. But don't stop there. You should also identify, while it's still fresh in your mind, what specific Action Commitments both you and the client have agreed to perform before your next meeting. Win-Win means sharing commitment. So be very clear in your thinking about what specifically you've promised to do—and what the customer has promised in return. Write these commitments down, as one essential feature of a new tactical plan.

It's not too early to begin laying out that plan now. And since mutual commitment is what is going to move the process forward, you should start by specifying commitments. Not just the two you've identified as being "due" by the beginning of the next call. Write down also the parameters of the client's commitment that you will want by the end of that call: the Best Action you can hope for, and the Minimum Acceptable Action you will settle for.

Once you've done that, we suggest you go through all the other pieces of the assessment process we've outlined in this chapter and pick out those tactical lessons that can help you improve your interaction next time. If you were deficient on this previous call in practicing Golden Silence, put that down in your notebook, and rehearse the technique with a friend before you meet this customer again. If you've made three or four calls on this person and you still don't know who can give financial approval for your proposal, draft a good New Information Question to find that out on the next call. If you were so wrapped up in product specs last time that you lost sight of the customer's Concept, make it a priority of your new tactical plan to shift from a unilateral to a Joint Venture method.

We could multiply such examples forever, but you see our point. The purpose of the assessment process is not simply to tell you where you've been; it's to show you how to get where you're going with more clarity and efficiency and with a maximum of cooperation from your clients. Conceptual Selling always looks forward. With the application of "feedforward" after every call, you are able to manage the present and the future. The result is that whether you are in the first stages of a long selling process or twenty minutes from signing a contract, you retain an essential tactical grip on the situation: You always know exactly where you are in each call, and you always know what still needs to be done to move toward a mutually satisfying, Win-Win conclusion.

CHAPTER 18

SELLING BEYOND
THE CLOSE

T he close is not the close.

We said it at the start of the book, and there's no better advice with which to end it. In today's superheated business arena, with salespeople confronting unprecedented pressures from competitors and customers, looking at the order alone is simply not enough. The future belongs to the professional who can sell beyond the close.

The reason is simple. We're in a computer-rich, Web-connected, highly interactive, global environment where whatever you do for a customer, good or bad, will hit the electronic grapevine almost before the ink is dry. In the Old West, where snake oil peddlers were the order of the day, a shifty, Win-Lose operator could stick it to any number of customers and yet escape the consequences: There were all those wide open spaces and no telephones. Nobody can do that today.

Today, electronic communications have made Marshall McLuhan's global village a fact that no business professional can afford to ignore, and evading the consequences of manipulative—or merely thoughtless—selling has become impossible. Burn the buyer, consciously or unconsciously, and within moments, the news of your "victory" will be showing up on email screens a thousand miles from your home. Fail to heed the long-term effects of your selling and you'll soon be paying the price in terms of dissatisfied customers, bad referrals, and lost business. If you don't attend to what happens to your customers *after* the order, sooner or later you will have no business to attend to.

This doesn't mean you have to scoot out in subzero weather when one of your customers has a maintenance problem. That's a service problem that may not be part of your direct responsibility. And it doesn't mean you should follow up on every order by sending out "personalized" Christmas cards or remembering your customer's favorite Scotch. That kind of relationship selling is fast becoming as obsolete as the frontier peddler's spiel. There's nothing wrong with it per se. But by itself it can never ensure solid business.

What selling beyond the close does mean is that every time you go into a selling encounter, you must keep in mind that this call is only one step in an extended scenario and a *long-term* relationship. More than that: Once you pull down the order and the commission, you have to think of that order too as only part of a much longer selling process. Selling beyond the close means constant attention to the care and feeding of that ongoing process.

This has nothing to do with performing face-time tricks and surprisingly little to do with this quarter's revenues or commissions. It has to do with understanding two related ideas:

1. Your long-term success is intimately dependent on your individual customer's success.
2. All good selling, like all good buying, begins with a solution image in the customer's mind.

Linking these two ideas, you can say that good selling must always start by understanding the customer's inner picture of what he or she needs to accomplish in order to succeed. We've called this picture the Concept. Focusing on each individual's Concept is the only reliable way, eventually, to sell to customer "need."

Oddly, many sales professionals still consider this a radical view. Often, when salespeople speak of "need" they mean their own need to sell or their marketing department's need to deliver a certain product mix. Traditionally, selling means convincing a potential buyer—whatever the business requirements or personal feelings involved—that he needs what the salesperson has to offer. So the goal of the traditionally trained salesperson often gets perilously close to that of a drug pusher: *Create* a need that only you can satisfy.

We take the opposite approach. We believe that the customer usually knows at least as well as you, and probably much better than you, the nature of the problems she is facing. But customers don't always know the best way to attack those problems, and that's where you come in. We're saying that if you encourage your customers to explore solutions with you, you have a far better chance of making a quality sale than if you simply push your product and try to hypnotize them into "needing" it.

The downside of this customer-driven philosophy is that sometimes you have to do what no self-respecting salesperson ever wants to do: back away from the sale. Sometimes you have to acknowledge—even when the customer doesn't see this—that there isn't a good match between his Concept and your solution and that the wisest strategy in this case is *not* to push for the close. If this sounds heretical, so be it. Because if you're not willing to walk away from a poor match, you're not really committed to Win-Win selling.

And that means you're not really committed to your customers' success—or, when it comes right down to it, to your *own* success. These are the two inseparable parts of modern sales professionalism. You've got to ensure that your customers feel good about the business relationship and that you feel good about it yourself. Without that mutuality, somebody always loses. And there's certainly nothing professional about that.

The "secret" of Conceptual Selling is just that simple. It makes things easier and more productive for both you and your customers because it's built not on "inspiration" but on selling realities. Conceptual Selling says that every good close must be a step toward the future. It says that you win only when your customers are successful. It says, finally, that success is the predictable result of a logical process—a process where you work with your customers, not against them, to develop solutions both of you can own. To a professional, those are the only solutions worth delivering because they are the only ones that build solid, dynamic business—business that can last beyond the close.

THE QUESTIONING PROCESS REVISITED: CONTINUING THE DIALOGUE WITH OUR CUSTOMERS

We've been teaching Conceptual Selling to sales professionals for nearly twenty years. In that time we've had ample evidence of the fact that excellent selling is driven by Superb Communication—and that the driver of Superb Communication is productive questioning. We've seen this fact especially in our two-day workshops, where our customers have helped us to refine our understanding continually by raising questions that are as inventive as they are challenging.

We end this revised edition of *Conceptual Selling* by sharing our thinking about the best of these queries. The following questions were first raised by participants in our Conceptual Selling workshops. We respond to them here as part of the ongoing dialogue between Miller Heiman Inc. and our most valued asset: our customers.

1. Isn't Conceptual Selling just another name for consultative selling?

There are similarities, to be sure, but they're not the same. Consultative selling, the brainchild of business consultant Mack Hanan, focuses on understanding your customers' corporate issues so that you can provide solutions that affect their bottom line; as Hanan describes it in his book *Consultative Selling,* it's essentially a way of going beyond mere "vending" (the supplying of products) to the establishment of ongoing relationships (the supplying of profit). These are great ideas, and in fact at Miller Heiman we've been teaching them for nearly twenty years in our workshops on Strategic Selling and Large Account Management Process. They are certainly compatible with Conceptual Selling. But they're not the same thing.

We agree that you must address your customers' profit issues. But that's a description of a goal, not a blueprint for getting there. Conceptual Selling shows you *how* to reach that goal by focusing on individual needs that may be related to, but are not identical to, an overall profit picture. The heart of Conceptual Selling is the customer's solution image, and that image is absolutely personal for each individual. In fact, it's those individuals you must "consult" with.

The consultation that Hanan recommends, moreover, may be ideal when you're meeting with a senior manager or other people to whom organizational health is a paramount issue—although even with them, profit is certainly not the only thing you should be talking about. When you're talking to department heads, middle managers, or other nonsenior individuals, on the other hand, discussing profit and loss may not be appropriate. It might even be damaging to your position because it may indicate to them that you're insensitive to their concerns. So "consultative selling" is a useful strategy when you're selling to the top. Conceptual Selling is a tactical method for selling at *all* levels.

2. You say I should understand the customer's Concept first. But how can a customer even have a Concept if I haven't been in there yet with my product or service?

This question suggests a possible misunderstanding of Concept. The Concept is something that develops in your customer's mind. It's his attempt to frame a solution for a problem that may or may not have anything to do with what you're selling. It may incorporate ideas that he has about your products or services or those of your competition; but essentially it relates to what he believes must be accomplished and to his ideas about how that is to happen.

Because Concepts are so individual, this means that even when you're going in with a menu of established products and related solutions, you've got to be highly selective in how you describe them. Marketing departments are great at supplying you with features-and-benefits descriptions. They're not so good at telling you which feature is likely to appeal to which customer—or whether any of the features they've highlighted are actually relevant to *any* customer. That's what you have to find out. You do it by concentrating *first* on individual's solution images and only then moving on to a product sale.

3. I understood my customer's Concept, I related my product to it perfectly, and I still lost out to a competitor. How can I avoid that scenario next time?

We hear you. We understand you. We're not sure we believe it because it's really not possible for you to relate your product "perfectly" to an individual's Concept and still lose the order. When you think this is what happened, look again. Probably what really happened is one of three things. First, you may have confused the customer's Concept with your own concept—or your company's concept—about what a product or service could do. A second possibility is that the competitor who aced you out understood the customer's Concept—and positioned herself relative to it—just a little bit better than you did. Maybe not perfectly, because very little in business can reasonably be described as perfect. But a shade better—enough better to ruin what you had thought was a sure thing.

When we talk about understanding your customer's Concept, we're not talking about a yes-or-no process, a situation where you either "get the Concept" or you don't. There are no guaranteed results, no certainty that if you connect to the Concept, you'll make the sale. Understanding people's Concepts is itself a process, not a product. The more you work at it, the better you get, and the better you get at it, the more business you close because the greater the value you're able to supply to your customers.

A third explanation of this "perfect understanding but no sale" scenario might be that you understood one individual's Concept almost perfectly, but somehow neglected the Concept of *another* key influence. The more complicated the sale, the more likely it is you'll have to understand the solution images of more than one person. So you may have done a terrific job with this one person, but if she was not the dominant "influencer" in this scenario, then someone else's Concept may have overridden hers. Missing that point is a common mistake as you're learning this process. Success comes from covering everybody's Concepts every time.

4. You've said you can help a customer shape a Concept. How?

By helping him to write the specs for the solution he's considering. You can take "specs" here as precisely or informally as you like: The point is that in order to shape a customer's Concept, you need to provide solid input at the customer's cognition stage—the stage where he's still getting a fix on the shape of his problem. This means, logically enough, *getting in there early.*

We mean early in the customer's decision-making process, and sadly, this isn't where the majority of salespeople get involved. Most salespeople work the "far end" of the customer's decision process, that is, the time between the definition of a problem and the choice of a solution. What happens here is that requests for proposals or bids are sent out by the customer, with all the specifications already laid out on paper. As a potential supplier, you are asked to describe how your product meets those specs and offer a price. Your input into the Concept is absolutely zero: The Concept, and a blueprint for a solution, have already been determined. The best you can do is to read those specs very carefully and hope that they match the capabilities your company can offer.

At the "near end" of the customer's decision-making process, though, the situation is very different. If you can connect with a customer at the "We think there's a problem" (or "We think there's an opportunity") stage, you'll have the chance not only to understand the customer better than your competition can, but to have a dialogue in which you explore the emerging problem cooperatively so that your capabilities and your input will be implicit in *any* potential solution. When you do that, your contribution inevitably becomes part of the customer's Concept.

5. What do you do when the customer demands a solution that you know is wrong for her, and you've got to choose between going along or losing the sale to the competition? Is there any way to resolve this no-Win scenario?

In the short term, maybe not. We've all encountered customers who are just plain inflexible, who even before you first meet them have made up their minds about the solution they think they need and will not be swayed by anything you have to say, even though you know what they've chosen will not do the job. If you want a productive relationship with these people over time, you owe it to them and to yourself to at least make the attempt—to show them, without being argumentative, that their choice won't work and that, even though you have the ability to deliver it, you believe a Win-Win approach dictates otherwise. If that doesn't work—and sometimes it just doesn't—you have a choice.

First, you can agree to sell the customer the inappropriate solution; then get ready to rescue her (with another solution) when it fails to deliver. That may appeal to you because it sounds like *two* sales. But it seldom works out that way because unyielding customers have another unattractive quality: selective memory. When the first solution goes bad, bet on this fact: The customer will not remember that you tried to talk her out of it. She'll blame you for the very problem you predicted would occur. And you'll be looking at Buyer's Remorse in spite of your best efforts.

Alternatively, you can decline the business. It's not an option that salespeople are trained to embrace, but sometimes it's the best choice in a bad situation. If you're convinced of the limitations of your customer's "one and only" solution, *let your competition provide that solution.* Let them take the heat when it goes bad. And position yourself as the savior with a new solution.

6. Having a Valid Business Reason implies that you know something about the customer before you go in. How do you do that when you're making a cold call?

You're still making cold calls? The whole point of a Valid Business Reason is to render them unnecessary. And increasingly, good salespeople are getting that message. Whether or not they've been officially trained to sell "conceptually," today's top producers understand that going in to see a customer without having any kind of prior knowledge about him or his business situation—the definition of a cold call—is increasingly likely to leave them out in the cold. The days are long gone when you could pop in on a prospect because you just happened to be in the neighborhood or when you could rely on a charming personality to get you a half-hour appointment. Customers simply don't have time for that kind of thing any more.

Nor, by the way, do most sales organizations. Good salespeople are too expensive and too short on time to risk sending them on "knock in the dark" calls where they will risk annoying the customers and embarrassing themselves. On the majority of sales calls today, homework is done first. Maybe it's actual library or Internet research. Maybe it's direct-mail querying or a telephone contact—telemarketers being among the sole remaining cold callers. But calling blind in the field is a losing proposition. It tells the customer that you don't care enough about his business to do some basic preparation before you take up his time. If you're willing to be that "coldhearted," don't expect a warm response.

7. Do I really need a Valid Business Reason on every call? Can't you make calls just to keep in touch?

If you're making sales calls just to keep in touch, you must have a lot of time on your hands. Most sales professionals are long past the days when they could get all their client calls done by two in the afternoon and then head for the golf course. Selling is a full-time job, with six- or seven-day weeks, and if you want to be truly successful, you've got to spend that time *selling*. That's why we insist: Every sales call you make should move you closer to an order. This means every call must have a well-defined business agenda. It must be clear to the person you're calling on, no less than to you, what value will accrue to her business from her meeting with you, what returns she may reasonably expect to receive for her investment of time. And the way you spell that out is with a Valid Business Reason.

Now, if you're having lunch with an old friend—business associate or not—and the conversation is purely social, that's fine. We're not advising you to drop all your social contacts and to turn everything into money. But when you have this kind of friendly encounter, take it for what it is. Don't refer to it as a sales call. On a sales call, you're there for a reason. The reason is intimately related to business—the business of the person you're calling on. That person accepts the call as a valid use of his time. And he understands that the call should help you explore the possibility of doing business *together*. If these criteria are not met, you're not selling.

8. As important as good questions are, I don't want to overload my customer with too many. Is there an optimum number of questions you should ask on a sales call?

There's no optimum number because each sales call is unique. The appropriate number of questions to ask on a given call is determined by several factors, including the information you need to uncover, whether or not anything has changed since you last met with this customer, and—maybe most important of all—this individual's comfort level with the questions you're asking. A good questioning process creates a flowing dialogue. If your questions aren't doing that, you can ask four or forty—it won't matter.

The extremes to avoid are, on the one hand, jumping into presentation mode before you've asked enough questions to clarify where you stand; and, on the other, insisting that the customer fill in all the blanks on your questions-to-be-asked laundry list before you're ready to tell him anything about your product. Because most salespeople are so product-oriented, this second extreme may seem out of character, but we've seen it happen, and it can be disastrous—just as disastrous in its own way as giving a dog-and-pony show. It tells the customer not that you're interested in expanding your knowledge about his situation, but that you've memorized an official format that must be followed and that he'll have to follow it with you if he wants to proceed. No matter who the customer is, that's the wrong message.

The crucial point is that the customer must be comfortable in answering your questions. If the call starts to feel like an interrogation, or if you're approaching the questioning process as an obligation rather than an opportunity, you're doing something wrong. Moreover, if you sense uneasiness—if the customer seems in any way reluctant to provide you with answers—you should do an on-the-spot check of your credibility with this person and adjust the questioning sequence to increase his comfort level. The only "optimum" number of questions to ask is the number that the customer *wants to answer* on this call.

9. Some sales trainers recommend using "closed" or "tie down" questions to keep the sales call moving where you want it to go. What are your thoughts on this?

"Closed" questions are questions that invite only one answer—Yes—and "tie down" questions are a variation of this type. An example would be "Do you want more security for your family?" and (the tie-down version) "You want more security for your family, *don't you?*" The idea is that if you ask questions like this, the customer will give the only sensible answer, and a series of those "little Yes" answers will get him in the mood for the "big Yes" at the end of the call: "Yes, I want to buy your product."

The philosophy behind this gimmick is both cynical and inane. For one thing, it's a perversion of the notion of commitment because it assumes that a customer who "commits" to a general proposition ("I love my children") is also committing, implicitly, to your very specific spin on that proposition ("I should therefore buy your insurance policy"). It also assumes that customers are dim, almost infinitely malleable, and so unaware of the nuances of such linguistic maneuvers that you can get their signature on a contract before they even know it. Maybe that was true in the old drummer days. It's certainly not true today. So our advice about "tie down" questions is very simple: They insult your customers' intelligence, so don't use them.

10. I've been using closing questions for years. Aren't these the same as Commitment Questions?

Commitment Questions ask your customer to move the sales process forward. So a closing question is certainly a *type* of Commitment Question: It asks the customer to move the process to the contractual or final agreement stage. But you should be wary of equating these two terms because *closing* and *commitment* mean very different things. You can get commitment from a customer far short of closing—indeed, we advise you to get incremental commitment throughout the sales cycle—and you can also "close" a customer *without* getting commitment. Hit-and-run salespeople do this all the time, and it's for this reason we caution you to "sell beyond the close."

In many traditional views of selling, closing is practically a fetish. It's supposed to be the entire point of being a salesperson. It *is* important, of course; in the short term, it's what pays the bills and keeps you in business. But becoming obsessed with closing is also a trap. It can lead you to rush your customers into uncommitted sales, and the long-range effect of that rushing is often Buyer's Remorse.

Think of just two of the more popular closing techniques: the so-called alternative close and the Ben Franklin. In the alternative close, you offer the customer a choice: "Would you like delivery this month, or would next month be better?" This is fine if the customer is already at that level of commitment where he sees delivery as a foregone conclusion; if that's not the case, you're pushing the process. A similar pushing is evident in the "balance sheet" or Ben Franklin close—so named because Franklin was fond of weighing the pros and cons of a situation before he made a decision. Here you ask the customer to tally up the pros and cons of buying your product and (surprise, surprise) the balance sheet comes out in your favor. Again, you risk "closing" the customer before she is ready.

11. What if you wait that four or five seconds using Golden Silence and nothing happens?

First, remember that until you've had some experience using the Golden Silence technique, half a second can seem like four or five seconds, and four or five seconds can seem like half an hour. But if that's not the problem—if you really are waiting the appropriate amount of time and your customer isn't responding—then you should probably test whether the person has understood the question. Ask the customer: "Have I expressed that point clearly enough?" Or "Would it be helpful if I put that question another way?" Then, if the customer requires it, rephrase the original question.

Another technique is to explain *why* you've asked the question. Customers are much more comfortable answering questions if they understand that there's a rationale behind them and that providing you an answer will be in some way to their benefit. Sometimes hesitation is an indirect way of telling you, "I'm not sure I want to answer that" or "I don't want to answer that honestly." So if those four or five seconds are starting to feel like an eternity, you might try this reframing phrase: "The reason that I asked that question, Ted, is this." Or you might probe directly for why the person is not responding. "If you're not comfortable answering that, Ted, that's fine. We can move on to something else." Golden Silence is supposed to improve the conversational flow. In those rare cases where it doesn't accomplish that objective, adjust your approach.

12. Can you use Golden Silence effectively on the telephone?

Sure. It's tricky because you're deprived of the visual cues of body language and facial expression that you can rely on in face-to-face conversation. But it can be done if you remember the basic advantage Golden Silence affords you: the opportunity for expansion and clarification of ideas—yours *and* your customer's. In fact, using the technique here can reduce the clatter of simultaneous talking and interruption that so often inhibits telephone communication. The main difficulty seems to be in trusting your instincts well enough to allow the other person to collect her thoughts when you have no visible assurance that this is what she's doing. After all, when all you hear is silence on the other end of a phone, you might be forgiven for wondering whether the other person is listening, is daydreaming, or has been disconnected.

A friend of ours who routinely uses Golden Silence on the telephone admits that it can seem unnerving to people who aren't used to it. "If I'm quiet for more than a couple of seconds, they think I'm asleep," he says. "But the best way to deal with that problem is to make it a plus. If somebody asks whether I'm still there, I turn it to his advantage. 'Yes. Sorry—you've posed an interesting question, and I'm thinking about it. Give me a couple of moments to consider what you've said.' That usually reassures the person, it gives us both time, and it establishes a more leisurely pace for the rest of the call. After the first two or three times you do this, the other person gets the idea, and I usually find that the pausing becomes reciprocal."

Of course, few people will articulate their thoughts in this way. But they may be thinking something similar, and knowing that can make you less uneasy during phone-to-phone pauses. So can you use the technique on the telephone? Absolutely. Just have faith in the integrity of the conversation, and be willing to wait.

13. Is a Joint Venture approach always preferable to a unilateral presentation? What about when the customer specifically requests a product pitch?

Then give him one. We're not saying that a Joint Venture approach is always right or that a unilateral approach is always wrong. At certain times you do have to move into a pitch-the-product mode, and one of those times is when the customer asks you to do so. But if you're "invited" into this kind of presentation, be careful that you don't let it degenerate into a shotgun features-and-benefits litany: "Here's everything I know about our product in twenty-five minutes." Even when you're selling unilaterally, it should be part of your overall strategy to create a dialogue between you and the people who, for the time being, may be merely your "audience."

In sustaining that strategy, it's a good idea to stop every now and then to test where the pitch is going, to see whether it's fulfilling your needs and those of your customers. Add to your "pitching" repertoire the ability to interrupt yourself every five or ten minutes and ask an open-ended question like, "How is what I'm saying relevant to your concerns?" or "Which of the areas I've touched on would you like me to elaborate?" If all you get at that point is dead silence, you may be talking to an audience that's "awake but away." And it would then be appropriate to reconsider the "keep on pitching" approach.

Remember that your ultimate goal in a sales call is to cooperatively shape an alignment between the customer's Concept and your possible solutions. Pitching your product may well be part of that process. But if the pitch isn't giving the customer information she needs—if it's merely an exercise that her company protocol calls for—then you may be wasting your time and hers by forging ahead with it. Unless the customer is responding to the pitch, you may be in the wrong room.

14. Is Unique Strength another name for "competitive advantage"? And should I compare my company's Unique Strengths to those of the competition?

Not exactly. In economic theory, "competitive advantage" is a point of superiority that one company has over its competitors in a market segment generally: Low labor costs might be a competitive advantage for one company, and cutting-edge design an advantage for another. A Unique Strength is much more specific than that: It's the contribution *one* company's solution can make to *one* customer in *one* area that the customer perceives as better than any competing solution. "Competitive advantage" is global and theoretical; a Unique Strength is local and highly practical. A market leader in computers, for example, might have a competitive advantage in R&D capabilities, but that advantage would translate into a Unique Strength only if a given customer saw it as making a contribution to his business that no other computer company could match. Because every customer is different, there's no such thing as a globally relevant Unique Strength.

Should you highlight your Unique Strengths? Absolutely. But doing this *against* the competition is a risky approach. When you're trying to position yourself with a Unique Strength, you're essentially saying to the customer, "Here's a one-of-a-kind contribution that only we can bring you." If the customer wants to take that contribution to the competition and ask them, "Can you do this?" that's his prerogative. But it's not something that you should initiate. You almost never gain by bringing in the competition, and the chances are good that you'll complicate the scenario by deflecting attention away from your unique solution. In addition, every competitive comparison strategy is a *defensive* strategy. It positions you as a "me too" or "better than" solution. That may temporarily make you feel good, but it won't impress the customer. What a customer wants to hear about is the results *you'll* deliver. You should present those results as unique, not competitive, advantages.

15. *What if your personality is a Basic Issue? In other words, what do you do when the customer just doesn't like you?*

It happens. Not as often as the "personality" school of sales would have you believe, but it does happen. However hard you try to stay Win-Win with a customer and however diligently you try to assess and speak to his Concept, sometimes the chemistry just isn't there, and you find yourself confronting that most humbling of Basic Issues: the fact that you are the reason this customer won't buy.

If this happens to you a lot, you should probably reexamine your personal style to see if you can identify any idiosyncrasies that may, unbeknownst to you, be putting your customers off. One way to do this is to ask another salesperson or your manager to accompany you on a call and then to ask that person to assess your style. If the customer just not liking you is a rare occurrence (as it is for most salespeople), then the best way to confront it is usually to do just that: confront it. Acknowledge that there seems to be a personality conflict or "something that's just not working here," and ask the customer to confirm or disconfirm that. Then offer him a gracious way out of the situation by asking whether he'd be more comfortable talking to a different representative.

That may sound radical, but it's really a logical extension of the Win-Win philosophy. One of the smartest salespeople we know, on those rare occasions when a customer just doesn't like him, resorts to exactly this strategy. He takes the initiative by ending the sales call early and saying something along these lines: "Look, I don't really understand why, Scott, but there just seems to be something not clicking between us. Nobody's fault. It just happens sometimes, and I don't want to waste your time and mine exploring opportunities together if you're not comfortable dealing with me. I do think that my company has a lot to offer you, though, so if you'd like, I'd be happy to arrange for one of my colleagues to meet with you to see if dealing with somebody else would be more productive for you."

This may sound incredibly risky—not to mention vulnerable—but it almost *always* unties the personality tangle. When you say something like this—and *mean* it—the clouds usually part, as the customer understands that you're at least doing your best to satisfy his needs in a difficult situation. Sometimes the customer will take you up on your offer. Sometimes he'll be so struck by your candor that he'll say, "Well, maybe we can still work something out." Either way, you'll have thrown light on a murky area and have reopened at least the possibility of a Win-Win outcome.

Whether you win *this* sale or not, that's something worth working for. And it brings you back to the basic goals of Concept-driven selling: repeat sales, great referrals, and ongoing relationships.

INDEX

365

ABOUT MILLER HEIMAN

MILLER HEIMAN, INC. IS A GLOBAL LEADER IN BUILDING EXCEP-
TIONAL sales organizations. The company's team of world-class sales
consultants helps organizations dramatically improve sales productivity through consistent, field-ready processes, benchmarking tools,
development programs, and process consulting.

Best known for its time-tested *Strategic Selling*® program,
Miller Heiman provides solutions for introducing a consistent
sales process throughout an organization, identifying the strengths
and weaknesses inherent in every sales force, and ensuring the cul-
tural indoctrination of training programs.

With a prestigious client list including KLA-Tencor, BAX Global,
Marriott Corporation, Dow Chemical, PricewaterhouseCoopers,
and Wells Fargo, Miller Heiman understands the issues and challenges facing sales leaders in virtually every major industry, from manufacturing and consumer goods to technology and finance.

PREPARE YOUR ENTIRE ORGANIZATION

The Miller Heiman portfolio of sales training and development services addresses the most critical aspects of the selling cycle. From
getting the right people doing the right things to uncovering new
opportunities with your most established accounts, we prepare
your entire sales organization to succeed.

Our consulting and training is supported worldwide through a
global network of more than two hundred sales consultants in over
twenty-five countries. Each is an independent sales professional
with an average of eighteen years of real-world sales and sales management experience. Prior to working with Miller Heiman, our
sales consultants were sales directors and vice presidents, so they
truly understand your challenges and aspirations.

TRAINING SOLUTIONS

Our training solutions are proven to help establish and grow more productive customer relationships. These practical solutions include:

- *Conceptual Selling®*
- *Strategic Selling®*
- *Large Account Management Process (LAMP®)*
- *Negotiate Success^{SM}*
- *Channel Partner Management^{SM}*
- *Executive Impact^{SM}*

BENCHMARKING TOOLS

Our benchmarking tools can help you quickly evaluate the strengths and weaknesses of your sales organization, analyze personnel data against position requirements, and make sure you have the right people in the right positions. We help you establish benchmarks to reach your sales goals. We bring clarity to what works and what doesn't. These powerful tools include:

- *Predictive Sales Performance^{SM}*
- *StartPoint^{SM}*
- *Conversion, Penetration, Retention (CPR^{SM})*

SALES WORKSHOPS

Throughout the world, we conduct hundreds of convenient and accessible sales workshops where your staff can learn the Miller Heiman sales process and apply it to real sales opportunities in their funnels. They'll learn to uncover why the customer is really buying, to identify a fit, and to develop and execute an action plan that's right for you and your customer.

For further information on LAMP or any of our other service offerings, call Miller Heiman today and we'll find you the right consulting partner who understands you, your company, and your market.

Miller Heiman Corporate Headquarters
10509 Professional Circle, Suite 100
Reno, Nevada 89521
1-877-552-1757
www.millerheiman.com

Miller Heiman International Headquarters
Nelson House, 1 Auckland Park
Milton Keynes, MK1 1BU England
+44 1908.211212
www.millerheiman.co.uk